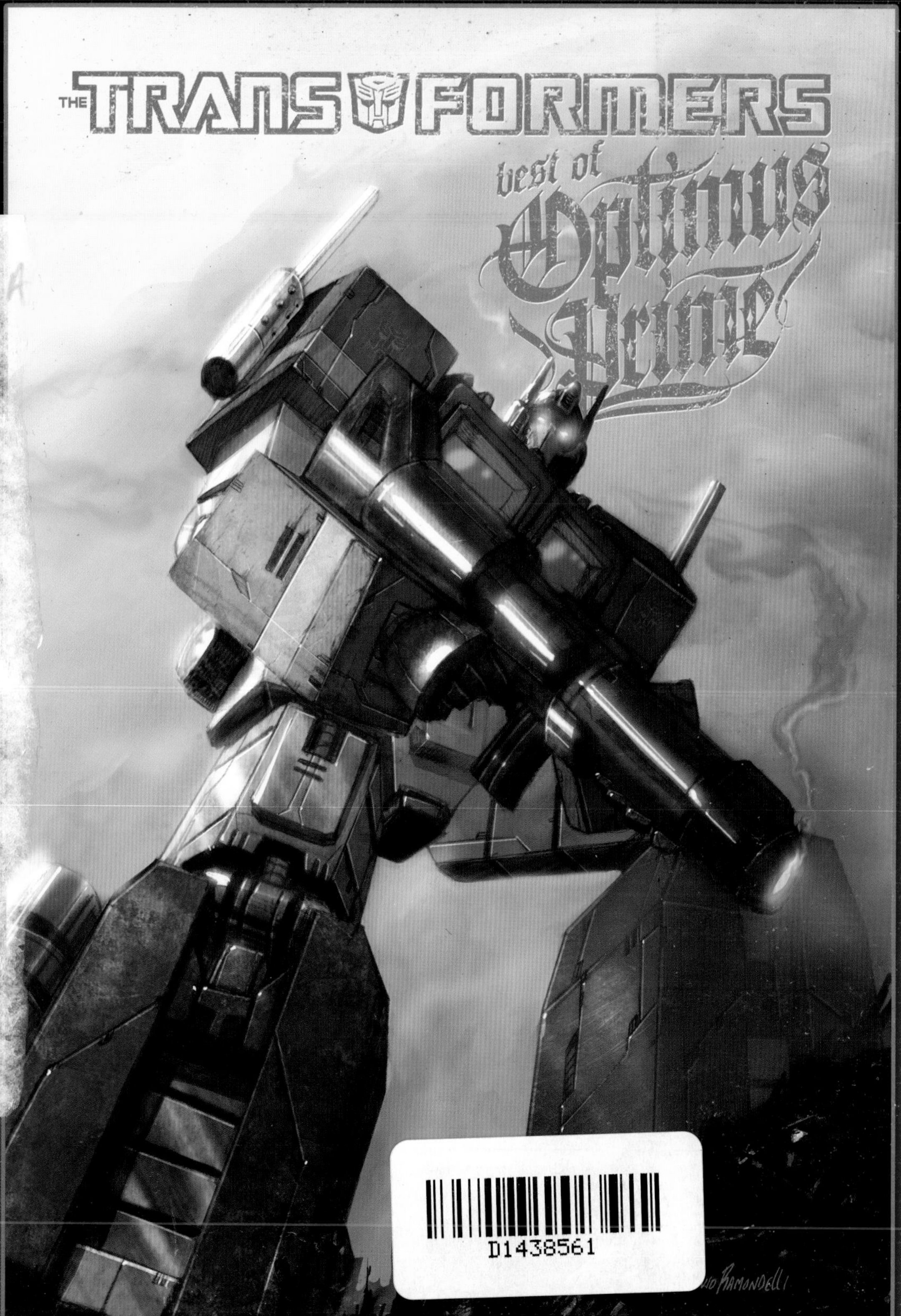
THE TRANSFORMERS
best of Optimus Prime

Cover Art by Livio Ramondelli • Collection Edits by Justin Eisinger
Editorial Assistance provided by Steven Serrano

Collection Design by Chris Mowry • Production Assistance by Shawn Lee

Special thanks to Hasbro's Aaron Archer, Michael Kelly, Amie Lozanski,
Ed Lane, Michael Provost, Val Roca, Erin Hillman, Jos Huxley,
Samantha Lomow, and Michael Verrecchia for their invaluable assistance.

IDW Publis
Operati
Ted Adams, Chief Executive Of
Greg Goldstein, Chief Operating Of
Matthew Ruzicka, CPA, Chief Financial Of
Alan Payne, VP of S
Lorelei Bunjes, Dir. of Digital Serv
AnnaMaria White, Marketing & PR Man
Marci Hubbard, Executive Assis
Alonzo Simon, Shipping Man
Angela Loggins, Staff Accoun
Cherrie Go, Assistant Web Desi

Edito
Chris Ryall, Publisher/Editor-in-C
Scott Dunbier, Editor, Special Pro
Andy Schmidt, Senior E
Bob Schreck, Senior E
Justin Eisinger, E
Kris Oprisko, Editor/Foreign
Denton J. Tipton, E
Tom Waltz, E
Mariah Huehner, Associate E
Carlos Guzman, Editorial Assi

De
Robbie Robbins, EVP/Sr. Graphic A
Neil Uyetake, Art Dir
Chris Mowry, Graphic A
Amauri Osorio, Graphic A
Gilberto Lazcano, Production Assi
Shawn Lee, Production Assi

Licensed By:

ISBN: 978-1-60010-666-8
13 12 11 10   1 2 3 4

Since the first appearance of the Transformers in 1984, there has always been a heroic AUTOBOT helping to battle and hinder the seemingly never-ending onslaught of DECEPTICON treachery. He is the bearer of the AUTOBOT Matrix of Leadership, inheriting the title and wisdom of the PRIMEs. His name is OPTIMUS PRIME.

A commander, a counselor, a father figure, a source of wisdom, and a beacon of hope, OPTIMUS PRIME has defined the true nature of the AUTOBOT plight throughout his many incarnations in the past two and a half decades. From ORION PAX to OPTRONIX, OPTIMUS PRIME's origins have been told and retold many times over but have always led to one inescapable truth: He is the greatest PRIME that has ever lived (and died many times over for that matter). In this book, we hope to show you the best of OPTIMUS PRIME in as many incarnations and story arcs as possible.

Trying to find the very best of OPTIMUS PRIME from every comic series ever done was not an easy task. We know there are many great stories out there that are testaments to PRIME, and we also expect some of you may think there are stories that may have deserved to be in this book over the ones we've selected, but we also know that these six stories help show PRIME at his very best, from the rookie warrior at the dawn of the Great War, to the experienced leader who battles with dark truths.

We hope you enjoy this trip through the history of OPTIMUS PRIME.

'Til all are One.

– Steven Serrano

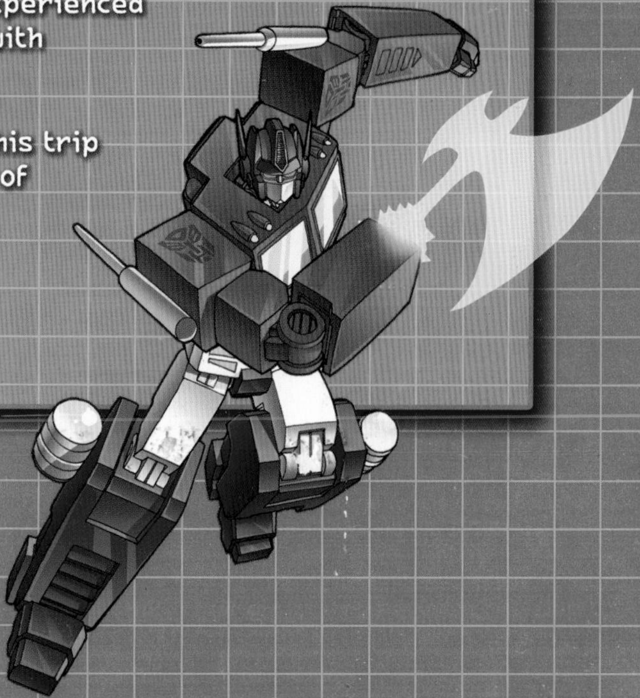

THE TRANSFORMERS
THE BEST OF OPTIMUS PRIME

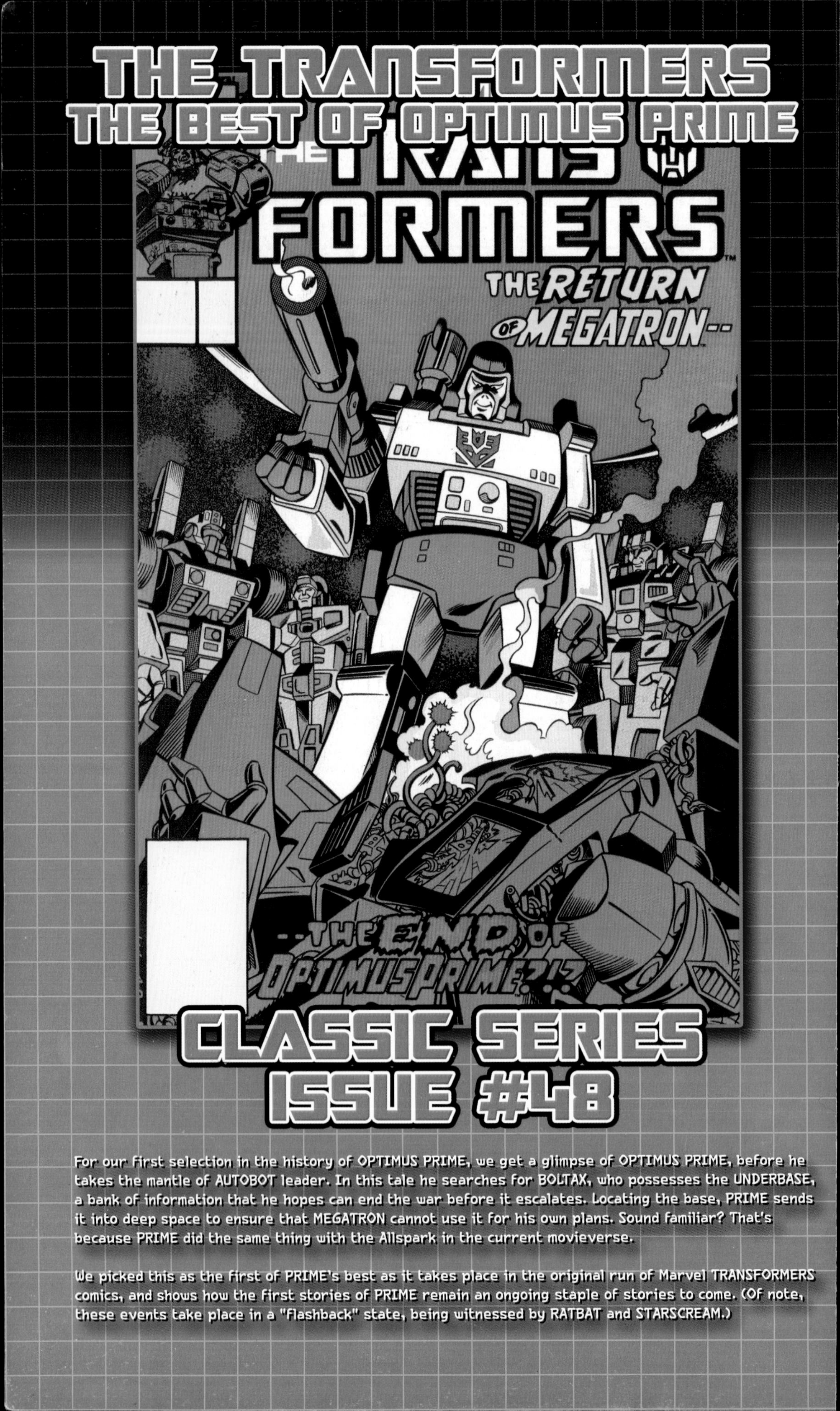
THE TRANSFORMERS
THE RETURN OF MEGATRON--
--THE END OF OPTIMUS PRIME?!?

CLASSIC SERIES ISSUE #48

For our first selection in the history of OPTIMUS PRIME, we get a glimpse of OPTIMUS PRIME, before he takes the mantle of AUTOBOT leader. In this tale he searches for BOLTAX, who possesses the UNDERBASE, a bank of information that he hopes can end the war before it escalates. Locating the base, PRIME sends it into deep space to ensure that MEGATRON cannot use it for his own plans. Sound familiar? That's because PRIME did the same thing with the Allspark in the current movieverse.

We picked this as the first of PRIME's best as it takes place in the original run of Marvel TRANSFORMERS comics, and shows how the first stories of PRIME remain an ongoing staple of stories to come. (Of note, these events take place in a "flashback" state, being witnessed by RATBAT and STARSCREAM.)

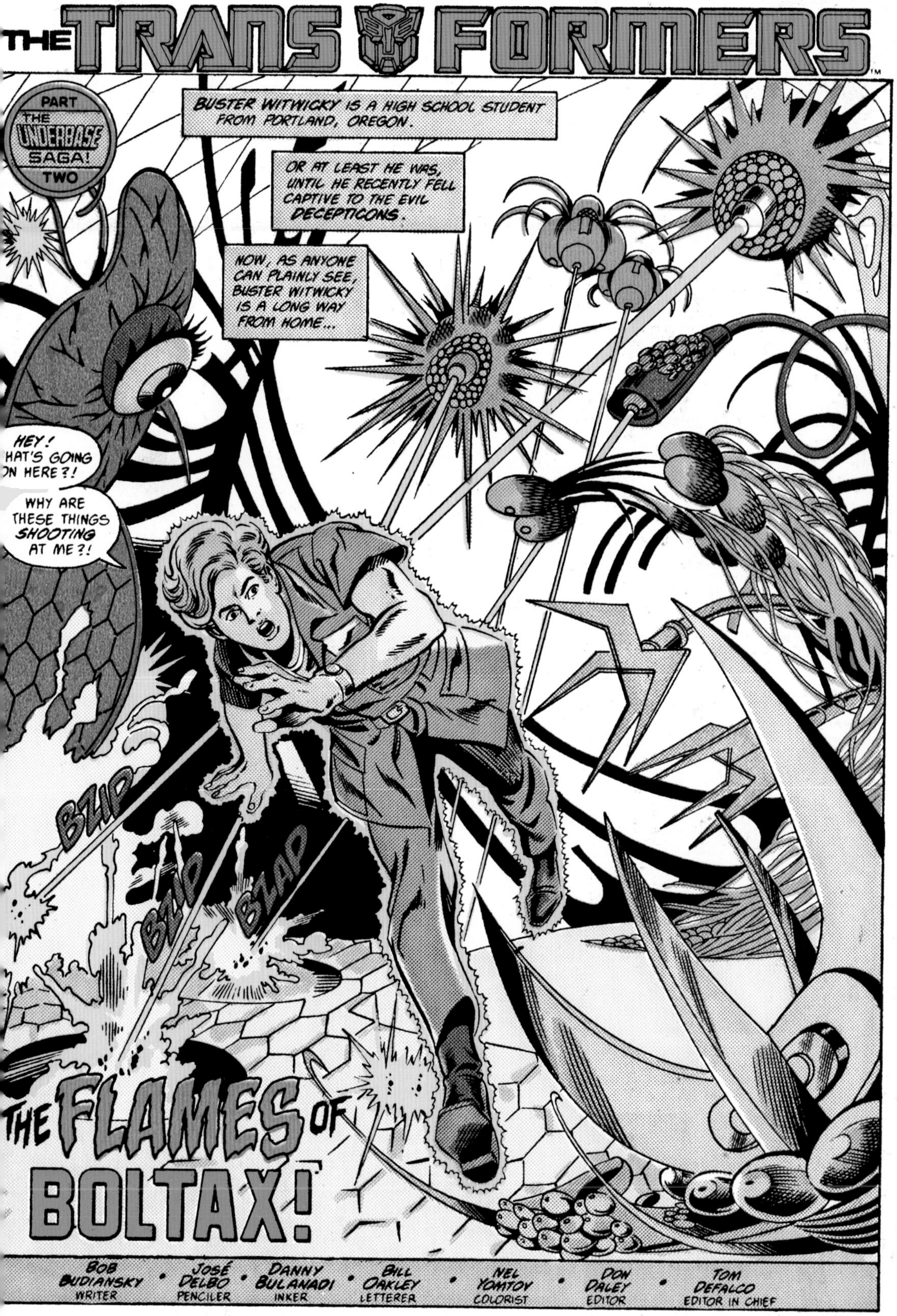
THE TRANSFORMERS
PART TWO
THE UNDERBASE SAGA!
BUSTER WITWICKY IS A HIGH SCHOOL STUDENT FROM PORTLAND, OREGON.
OR AT LEAST HE WAS, UNTIL HE RECENTLY FELL CAPTIVE TO THE EVIL DECEPTICONS.
NOW, AS ANYONE CAN PLAINLY SEE, BUSTER WITWICKY IS A LONG WAY FROM HOME...
HEY! HAT'S GOING ON HERE?!
WHY ARE THESE THINGS SHOOTING AT ME?!
BZIP
BZIP
BZAP
THE FLAMES OF BOLTAX!
BOB BUDIANSKY WRITER • JOSÉ DELBO PENCILER • DANNY BULANADI INKER • BILL OAKLEY LETTERER • NEL YOMTOV COLORIST • DON DALEY EDITOR • TOM DEFALCO EDITOR IN CHIEF

OH, NO! I'M TRAPPED!

AIEE--

BWOOM

--EH?

I DIDN'T FEEL A THING!

I DON'T GET IT-- I SHOULD HAV A HOLE IN MY CHE BIG ENOUGH TO PU MY FIST THROUGH

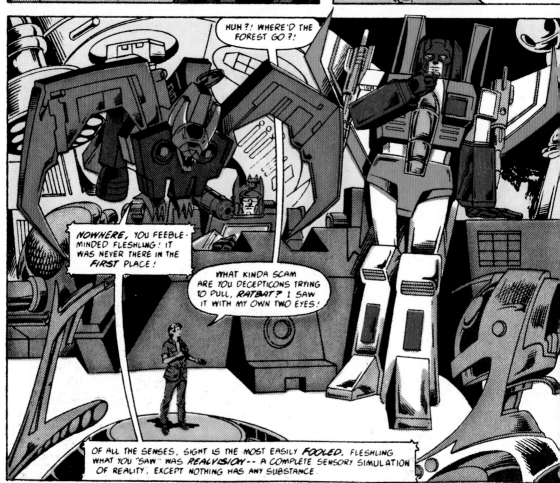

HUH?! WHERE'D THE FOREST GO?!

NOWHERE, YOU FEEBLE-MINDED FLESHLING! IT WAS NEVER THERE IN THE FIRST PLACE!

WHAT KINDA SCAM ARE YOU DECEPTICONS TRYING TO PULL, RATBAT? I SAW IT WITH MY OWN TWO EYES!

OF ALL THE SENSES, SIGHT IS THE MOST EASILY FOOLED, FLESHLING. WHAT YOU "SAW" WAS REALVISION-- A COMPLETE SENSORY SIMULATION OF REALITY, EXCEPT NOTHING HAS ANY SUBSTANCE.

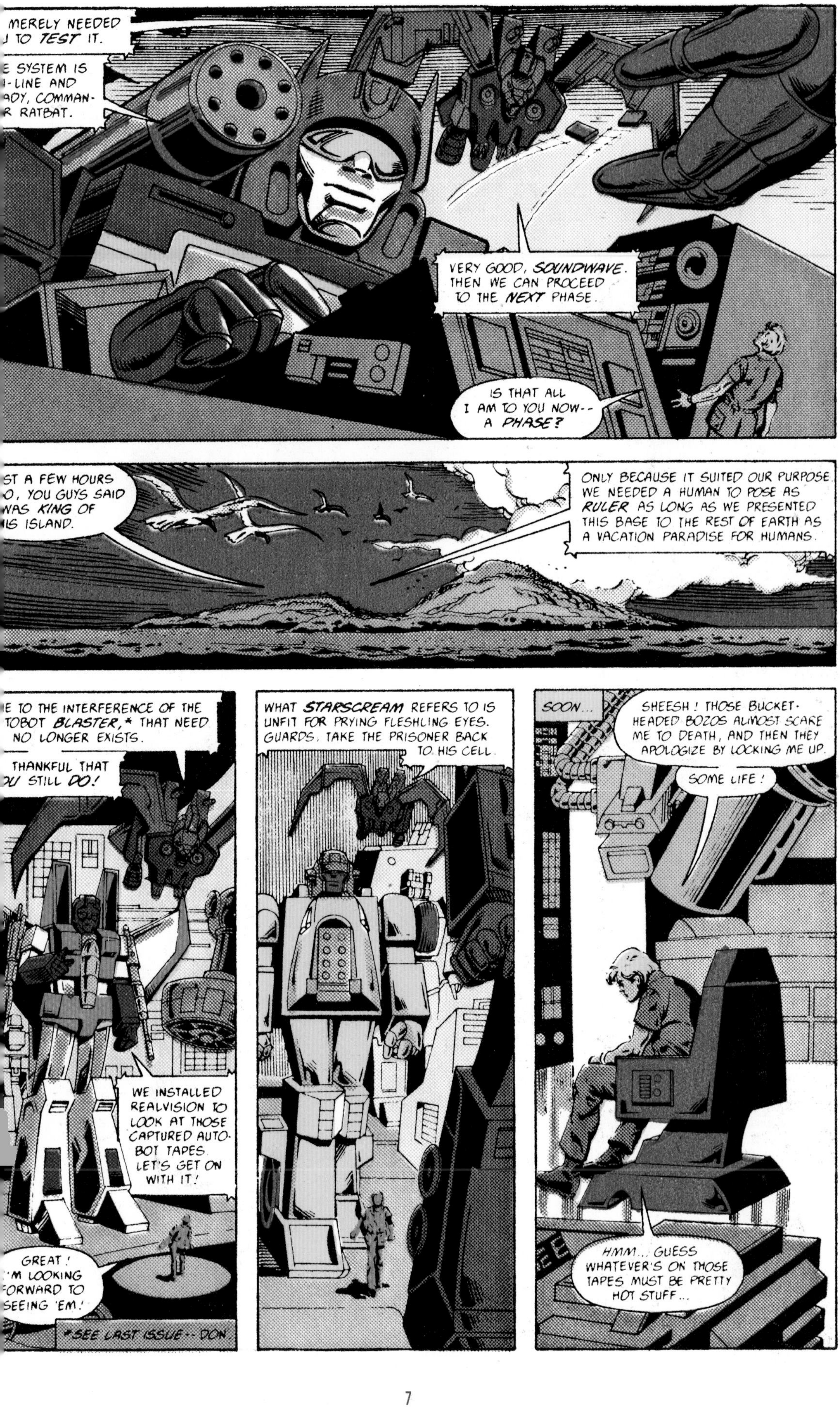

MERELY NEEDED TO TEST IT.
SYSTEM IS -LINE AND ADY, COMMAN- RATBAT.
VERY GOOD, SOUNDWAVE. THEN WE CAN PROCEED TO THE NEXT PHASE.
IS THAT ALL I AM TO YOU NOW-- A PHASE?
A FEW HOURS YOU GUYS SAID WAS KING OF ISLAND.
ONLY BECAUSE IT SUITED OUR PURPOSE. WE NEEDED A HUMAN TO POSE AS RULER AS LONG AS WE PRESENTED THIS BASE TO THE REST OF EARTH AS A VACATION PARADISE FOR HUMANS.
TO THE INTERFERENCE OF THE TOBOT BLASTER,* THAT NEED NO LONGER EXISTS.
THANKFUL THAT STILL DO!
WE INSTALLED REALVISION TO LOOK AT THOSE CAPTURED AUTO-BOT TAPES. LET'S GET ON WITH IT!
GREAT! LOOKING FORWARD TO SEEING 'EM!
*SEE LAST ISSUE--DON
WHAT STARSCREAM REFERS TO IS UNFIT FOR PRYING FLESHLING EYES. GUARDS, TAKE THE PRISONER BACK TO HIS CELL.
SOON...
SHEESH! THOSE BUCKET-HEADED BOZOS ALMOST SCARE ME TO DEATH, AND THEN THEY APOLOGIZE BY LOCKING ME UP.
SOME LIFE!
HMM... GUESS WHATEVER'S ON THOSE TAPES MUST BE PRETTY HOT STUFF...

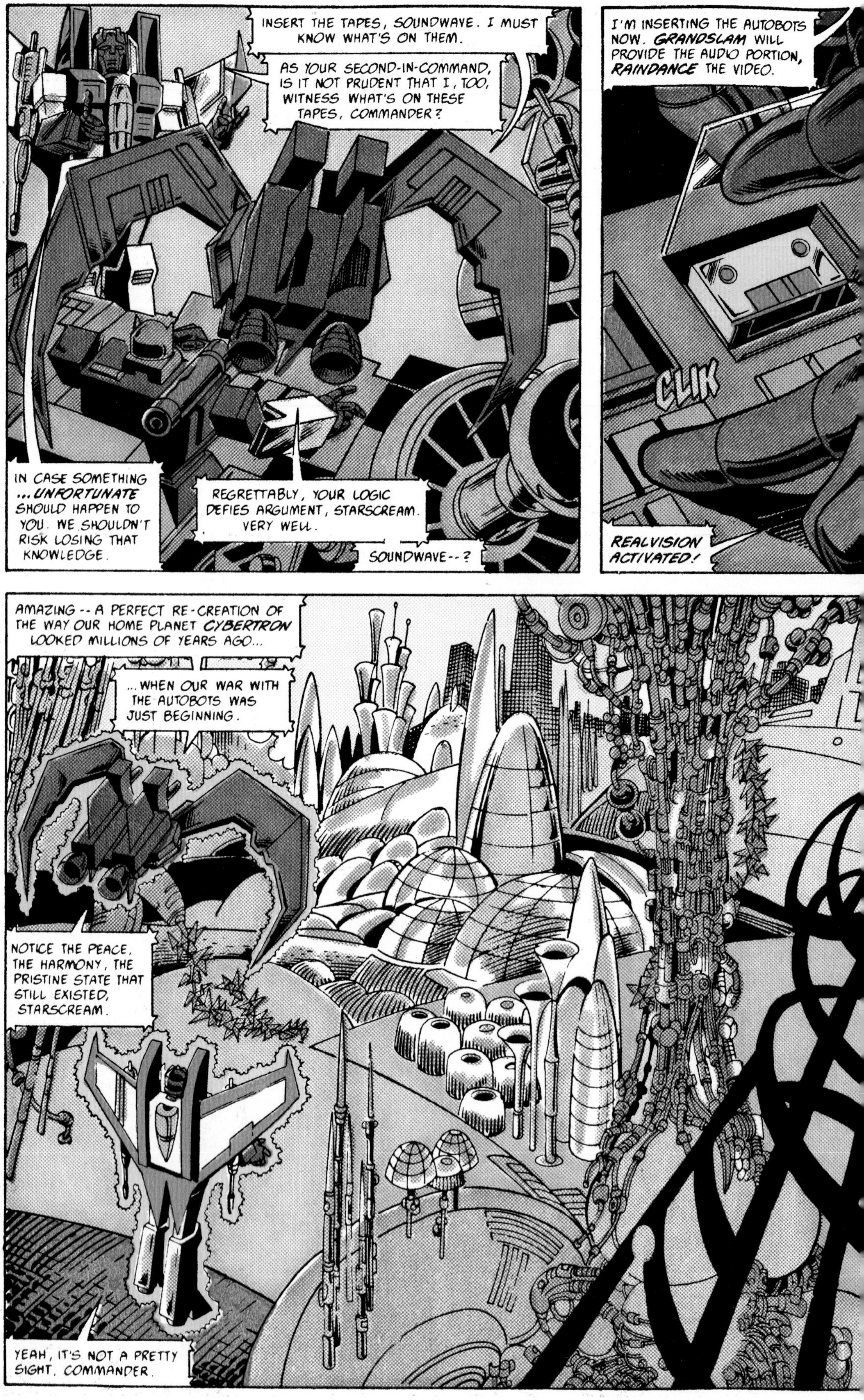
INSERT THE TAPES, SOUNDWAVE. I MUST KNOW WHAT'S ON THEM.
AS YOUR SECOND-IN-COMMAND, IS IT NOT PRUDENT THAT I, TOO, WITNESS WHAT'S ON THESE TAPES, COMMANDER?
IN CASE SOMETHING ...UNFORTUNATE SHOULD HAPPEN TO YOU. WE SHOULDN'T RISK LOSING THAT KNOWLEDGE.
REGRETTABLY, YOUR LOGIC DEFIES ARGUMENT, STARSCREAM. VERY WELL.
SOUNDWAVE--?
I'M INSERTING THE AUTOBOTS NOW. GRANDSLAM WILL PROVIDE THE AUDIO PORTION, RAINDANCE THE VIDEO.
CLIK
REALVISION ACTIVATED!
AMAZING -- A PERFECT RE-CREATION OF THE WAY OUR HOME PLANET CYBERTRON LOOKED MILLIONS OF YEARS AGO...
...WHEN OUR WAR WITH THE AUTOBOTS WAS JUST BEGINNING.
NOTICE THE PEACE, THE HARMONY, THE PRISTINE STATE THAT STILL EXISTED, STARSCREAM.
YEAH, IT'S NOT A PRETTY SIGHT, COMMANDER.

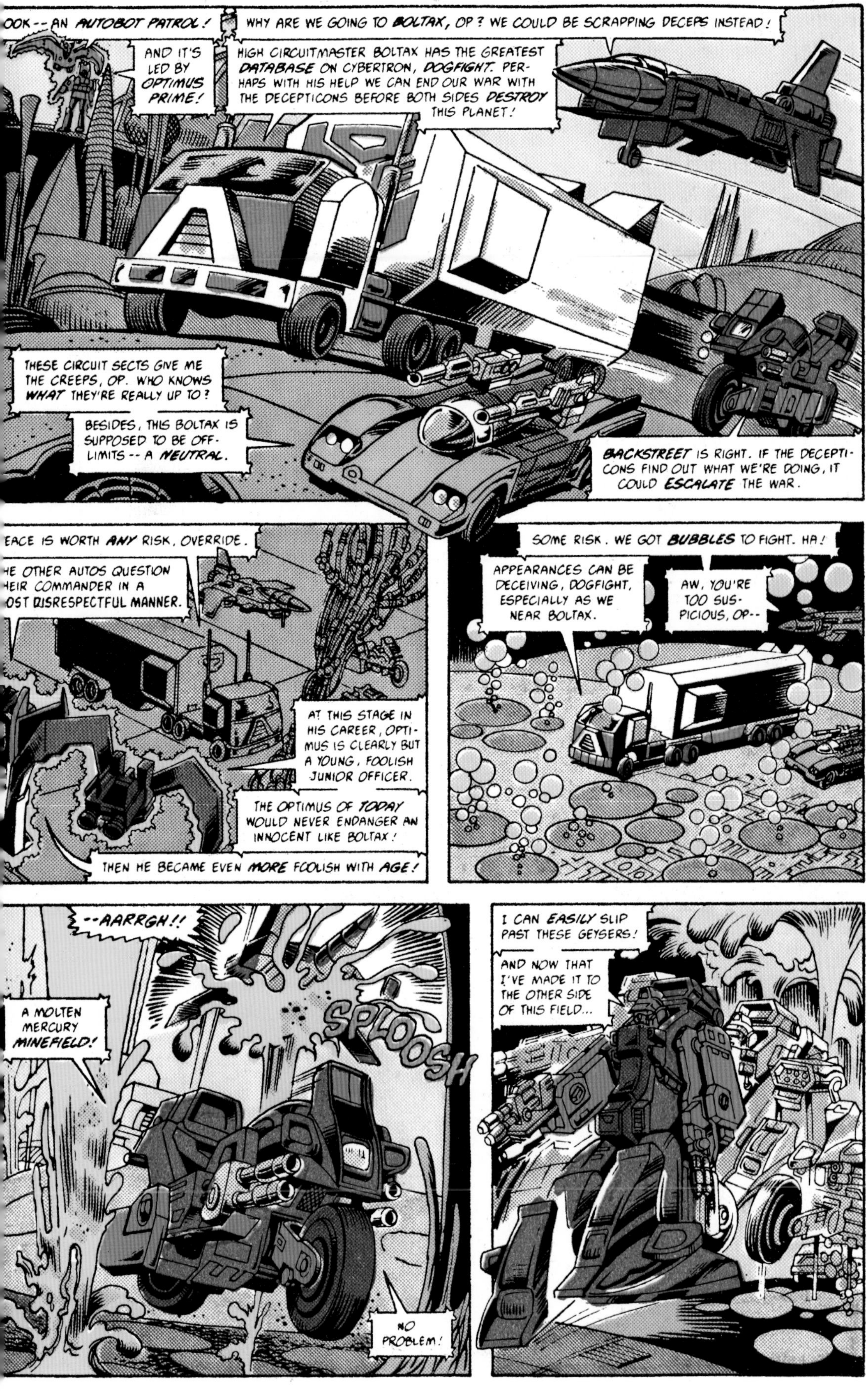
OOK -- AN AUTOBOT PATROL!
AND IT'S LED BY OPTIMUS PRIME!
WHY ARE WE GOING TO BOLTAX, OP? WE COULD BE SCRAPPING DECEPS INSTEAD!
HIGH CIRCUITMASTER BOLTAX HAS THE GREATEST DATABASE ON CYBERTRON, DOGFIGHT. PERHAPS WITH HIS HELP WE CAN END OUR WAR WITH THE DECEPTICONS BEFORE BOTH SIDES DESTROY THIS PLANET!
THESE CIRCUIT SECTS GIVE ME THE CREEPS, OP. WHO KNOWS WHAT THEY'RE REALLY UP TO?
BESIDES, THIS BOLTAX IS SUPPOSED TO BE OFF-LIMITS -- A NEUTRAL.
BACKSTREET IS RIGHT. IF THE DECEPTICONS FIND OUT WHAT WE'RE DOING, IT COULD ESCALATE THE WAR.
EACE IS WORTH ANY RISK, OVERRIDE.
HE OTHER AUTOS QUESTION HEIR COMMANDER IN A OST DISRESPECTFUL MANNER.
AT THIS STAGE IN HIS CAREER, OPTIMUS IS CLEARLY BUT A YOUNG, FOOLISH JUNIOR OFFICER.
THE OPTIMUS OF TODAY WOULD NEVER ENDANGER AN INNOCENT LIKE BOLTAX!
THEN HE BECAME EVEN MORE FOOLISH WITH AGE!
SOME RISK. WE GOT BUBBLES TO FIGHT. HA!
APPEARANCES CAN BE DECEIVING, DOGFIGHT, ESPECIALLY AS WE NEAR BOLTAX.
AW, YOU'RE TOO SUSPICIOUS, OP--
--AARRGH!!
A MOLTEN MERCURY MINEFIELD!
SPLOOSH
NO PROBLEM!
I CAN EASILY SLIP PAST THESE GEYSERS!
AND NOW THAT I'VE MADE IT TO THE OTHER SIDE OF THIS FIELD...

...A BURST FROM MY PARTICLE BEAM CANNONS SHOULD REVEAL THE FEEDER PIPE.

BWAM

THERE. THAT'LL SHUT OFF THE MERCURY FLOW.

BLAST! OVERRIDE *SAVED* THOSE AUTOBOT FOOLS!

OF COURSE. IF HE HADN'T, WE'D NEVER SEE WHAT OPTIMUS PRIME FINDS OUT FROM BOLTAX.

A CABLE JUNGLE!

I DON'T LIKE THE LOOKS OF THIS.

WE HAVE NO CHOICE! THIS IS THE WAY TO BOLTAX.

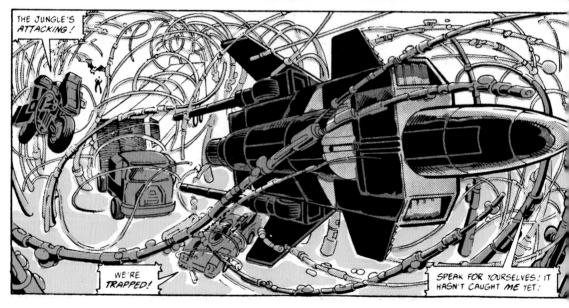

THE JUNGLE'S ATTACKING!

WE'RE *TRAPPED!*

SPEAK FOR YOURSELVES! IT HASN'T CAUGHT *ME* YET!

...ANWHILE...

I'VE GOTTA SEE WHAT'S ON THOSE TAPES.

HMM... THIS VENTILATION DUCT MUST LEAD SOMEWHERE...

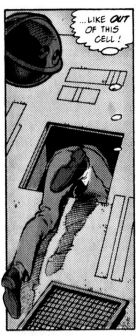

...LIKE *OUT* OF THIS CELL!

THESE WIRES-- WHY ARE THEY MOVING...

...UNLESS I TRIGGERED AN ALARM AND--

--URRK!!

BLAST! DOGFIGHT IS SLICING THROUGH THOSE CABLE-VINES WITH HIS WINGS!

FOLLOW ME, AUTOBOTS! WE'RE ALMOST OUT OF HERE!

WHEW! THAT WAS MORE WORK THAN I EXPECTED! GOTTA REST!

HEY! WHAT'S GOING ON?! THE GROUND'S *COLLAPSING!*

IT'S ANOTHER *TRAP*, DOGFIGHT!

AND I'M... FALLING INTO IT!

I HOPE YOU NOW REALIZE, OPTIMUS...

...THAT *BIGGER* ISN'T NECESSARILY *BETTER!*

WHEN YOU'RE BUILT FOR SPEED LIKE I AM, THESE SHIFTING PLATES LOOK LIKE THEY'RE *STANDING STILL!*

WELL DONE, BACKSTREET.

BY GETTING PAST THIS TRAP, YOU CROSSED THE ELECTRIC EYE BEAMS THAT DEACTIVATE IT.

THEY SURVIVED *AGAIN!* WATCHING SCREWS *RUST* IS MORE ENTERTAINING THAN THIS!

PATIENCE, STARSCREAM.

WAIT-- WHO'S THAT OVER THERE?

I BELIEVE, IF MEMORY SERVES ME CORRECTLY, THAT IS THE MOST FEARE AND RESPECTED DECEPTICON OF ALL TIME

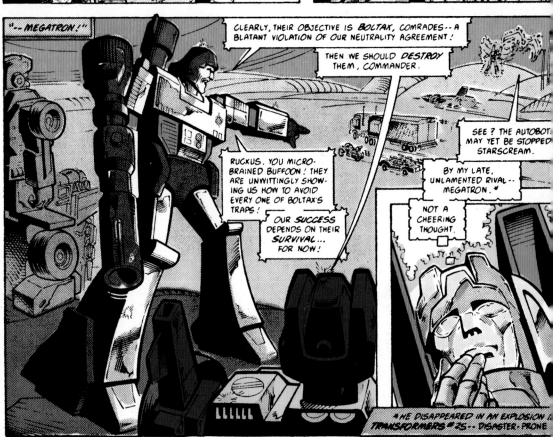

"-- MEGATRON!"

CLEARLY, THEIR OBJECTIVE IS *BOLTAX*, COMRADES-- A BLATANT VIOLATION OF OUR NEUTRALITY AGREEMENT!

THEN WE SHOULD *DESTROY* THEM, COMMANDER.

RUCKUS, YOU MICRO-BRAINED BUFFOON! THEY ARE UNWITTINGLY SHOWING US HOW TO AVOID EVERY ONE OF BOLTAX'S TRAPS!

OUR *SUCCESS* DEPENDS ON THEIR *SURVIVAL*... FOR NOW!

SEE? THE AUTOBOT MAY YET BE STOPPED STARSCREAM.

BY MY LATE, UNLAMENTED RIVAL-- MEGATRON.*

NOT A CHEERING THOUGHT.

*HE DISAPPEARED IN AN EXPLOSION I. TRANSFORMERS #25-- DISASTER-PRONE

12

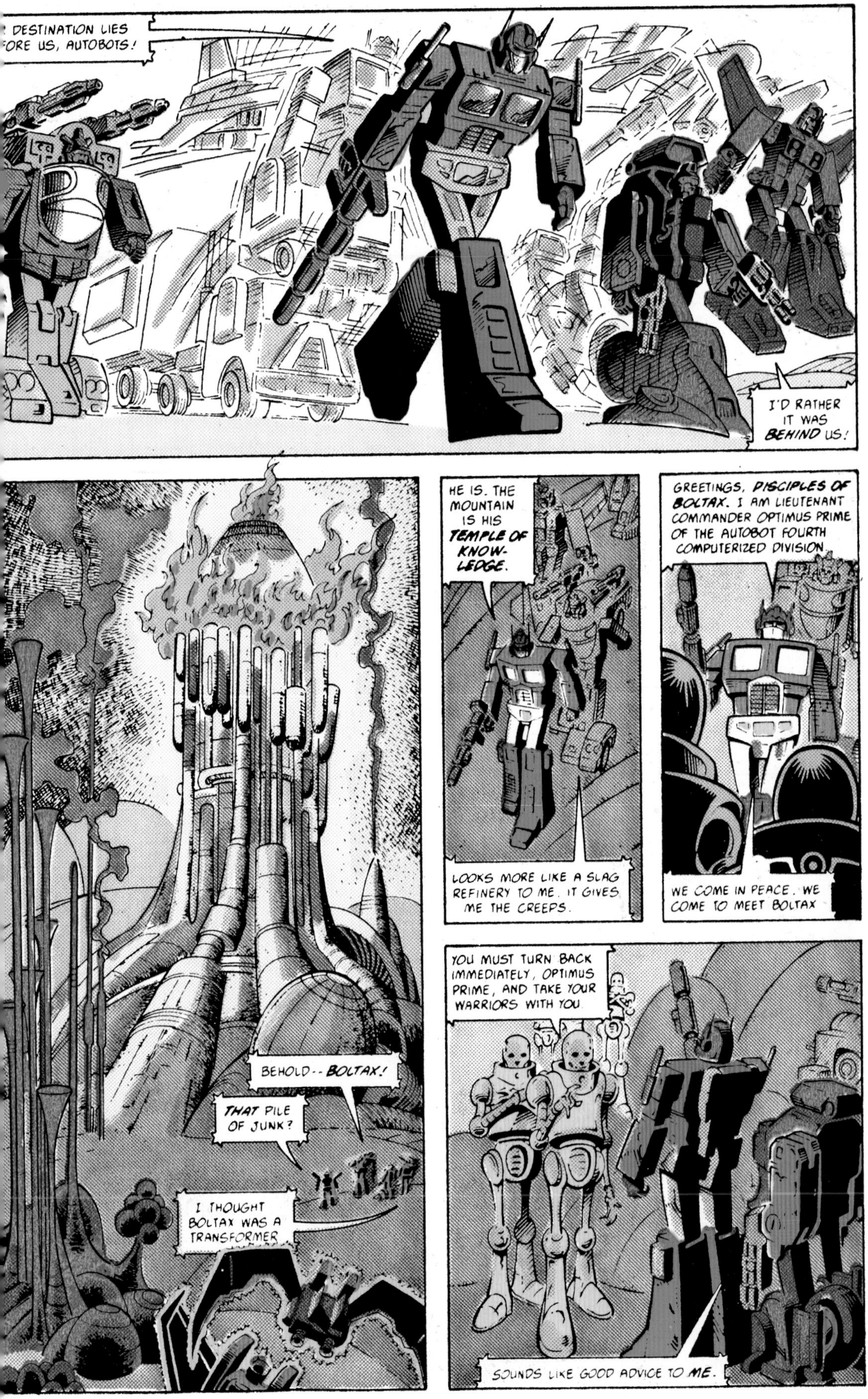

DESTINATION LIES
FORE US, AUTOBOTS!
I'D RATHER IT WAS BEHIND US!
BEHOLD--BOLTAX!
THAT PILE OF JUNK?
I THOUGHT BOLTAX WAS A TRANSFORMER
HE IS. THE MOUNTAIN IS HIS TEMPLE OF KNOW-LEDGE.
LOOKS MORE LIKE A SLAG REFINERY TO ME. IT GIVES ME THE CREEPS.
GREETINGS, DISCIPLES OF BOLTAX. I AM LIEUTENANT COMMANDER OPTIMUS PRIME OF THE AUTOBOT FOURTH COMPUTERIZED DIVISION.
WE COME IN PEACE. WE COME TO MEET BOLTAX
YOU MUST TURN BACK IMMEDIATELY, OPTIMUS PRIME, AND TAKE YOUR WARRIORS WITH YOU
SOUNDS LIKE GOOD ADVICE TO ME.

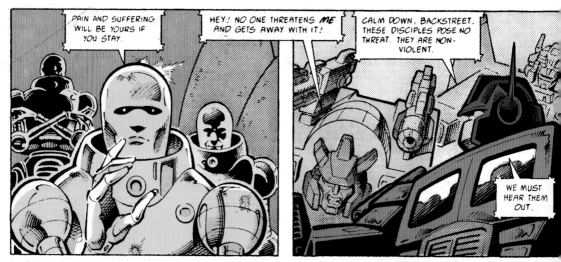

"PAIN AND SUFFERING WILL BE YOURS IF YOU STAY."

"HEY! NO ONE THREATENS *ME* AND GETS AWAY WITH IT!"

"CALM DOWN, BACKSTREET. THESE DISCIPLES POSE NO THREAT. THEY ARE NON-VIOLENT."

"WE MUST HEAR THEM OUT."

"OUR SWORN DEVOTION IS TO KNOWLEDGE AND LEARNING. WAR HAS NO PLACE HERE."

"THOSE WHO PRACTICE IT INVITE *TERMINATION*-- COMPLETE AND UTTER!"

"IF THAT IS THE CASE, I HAVEN'T THE RIGHT TO PUT MY SOLDIERS AT RISK."

"YOU THREE WILL SET UP CAMP OUTSIDE THIS VALLEY AND AWAIT MY RETURN."

"FINE. I HATE GOING WHERE I'M NOT WANTED."

"WHO WANTS TO FIGHT A BUNCH OF SKINNY PIPE CLEANERS, ANYWAY?"

"AND LISTENING TO 'EM IS WOR[SE]"

"GOOD LUCK, COMMANDER."

"YOU ARE SINCERE, OPTIM[US] PRIME... AND WISE IN YO[UR] OWN WAY."

"BUT YOU ARE A *FOOL* [N]TO LEAVE WITH THE OTH[ERS]"

"REGRETTABLY, THE ONLY WAY [TO] *DETER* YOU FROM YOUR QUES[T] [IS] TO ALLOW YOU TO *CONTINUE* O[N]."

"YOU MAY PROCEED."

"OP'S *ALONE.* LET'S JUMP HIM!"

"NOT YET, *CRANKCASE.* OUR CHANCE WILL COME."

"THIS IS GETTING *GOOD.* OP IS [THE] ONLY TRANSFORMER I HATE MORE THAN MEGATRON, AND OP'S ABOU[T] TO GET *CLOBBERED!*"

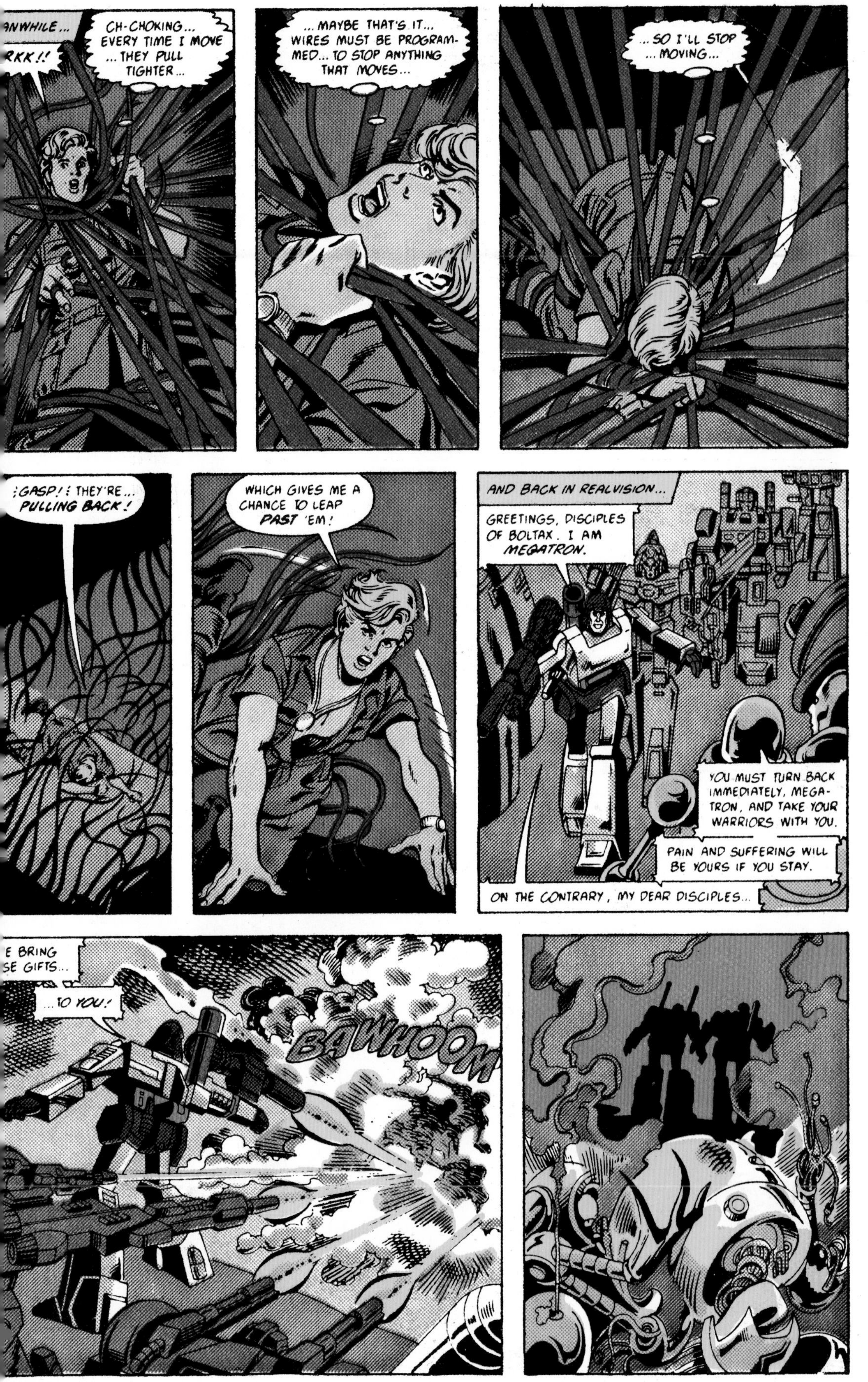

ANWHILE...
RKK!!
CH-CHOKING... EVERY TIME I MOVE ...THEY PULL TIGHTER...
...MAYBE THAT'S IT... WIRES MUST BE PROGRAMMED... TO STOP ANYTHING THAT MOVES...
...SO I'LL STOP ...MOVING...
:GASP!: THEY'RE... PULLING BACK!
WHICH GIVES ME A CHANCE TO LEAP PAST 'EM!
AND BACK IN REALVISION...
GREETINGS, DISCIPLES OF BOLTAX. I AM MEGATRON.
YOU MUST TURN BACK IMMEDIATELY, MEGATRON, AND TAKE YOUR WARRIORS WITH YOU.
PAIN AND SUFFERING WILL BE YOURS IF YOU STAY.
ON THE CONTRARY, MY DEAR DISCIPLES...
E BRING SE GIFTS...
...TO YOU!
BAWHOOM

NEARBY...

THE MOUNTAIN'S ENTRANCE.

IT OPENS...

BY THE *PR... MATRIX* ITSELF—

WELCOME, OPTIMUS PRIME. I HAVE BEEN EXPECTING YOU.

THANK YOU FOR GRANTING ME THIS AUDIENCE, HIGH CIRCUITMASTER BOLTAX.

I COME TO ASK--

I KNOW WHAT YOU WANT. IT IS NOT MINE TO GIVE.

GRAB BOLTAX AND *WRING* THE INFORMATION OUT OF HIM, YOU MISWIRED MORON'!

THAT IS NOT OPTIMUS'S STYLE.

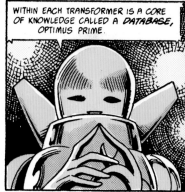

WITHIN EACH TRANSFORMER IS A CORE OF KNOWLEDGE CALLED A *DATABASE*, OPTIMUS PRIME.

THROUGH THAT PORTAL IS SOMETHING MUC... MORE *FUNDAMENTAL*-- A COLLECTION ... KNOWLEDGE THAT UNDERLIES ALL DATABAS... MUCH GREATER AND BROADER IN SCOPE THAN ANYTHING IN THE UNIVERSE.

WE CALL IT THE *UNDERBASE*.

WHAT YOU SEEK CONTAINED WITH...

YOU MAY ENTER.

THE REALVISION SHOULD BE RIGHT BEHIND THAT SCREEN--

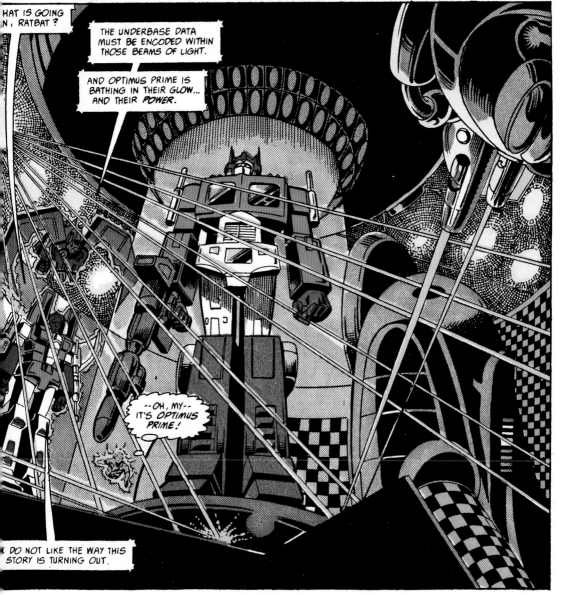

HAT IS GOING N, RATBAT?

THE UNDERBASE DATA MUST BE ENCODED WITHIN THOSE BEAMS OF LIGHT.

AND OPTIMUS PRIME IS BATHING IN THEIR GLOW... AND THEIR *POWER*.

--OH, MY-- IT'S *OPTIMUS PRIME!*

DO NOT LIKE THE WAY THIS STORY IS TURNING OUT.

AH... I SEE A PLOT TWIST ARRIVING OUTSIDE THE UNDERBASE CHAMBER!

STEP ASIDE, BOLTAX!

PLEASE... YOU MUST TURN BACK. I CANNOT ALLOW YOU TO PASS.

I DIDN'T COME TO ASK FOR YOUR PERMISSION!

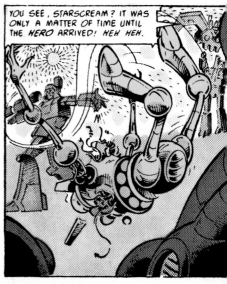

YOU SEE, STARSCREAM? IT WAS ONLY A MATTER OF TIME UNTIL THE HERO ARRIVED! HEH HEH.

OH, NO-- MEGATRON AND HIS BOYS FINISHED OFF BOLTAX AND NOW THEY'RE GOING AFTER OPTIMUS!

I'VE GOT TO WARN--

--ULP! I ALMOST FORGOT-- THIS WHOLE THING IS AN ILLUSION. THERE'S NOTHING I CAN DO... BUT WATCH.

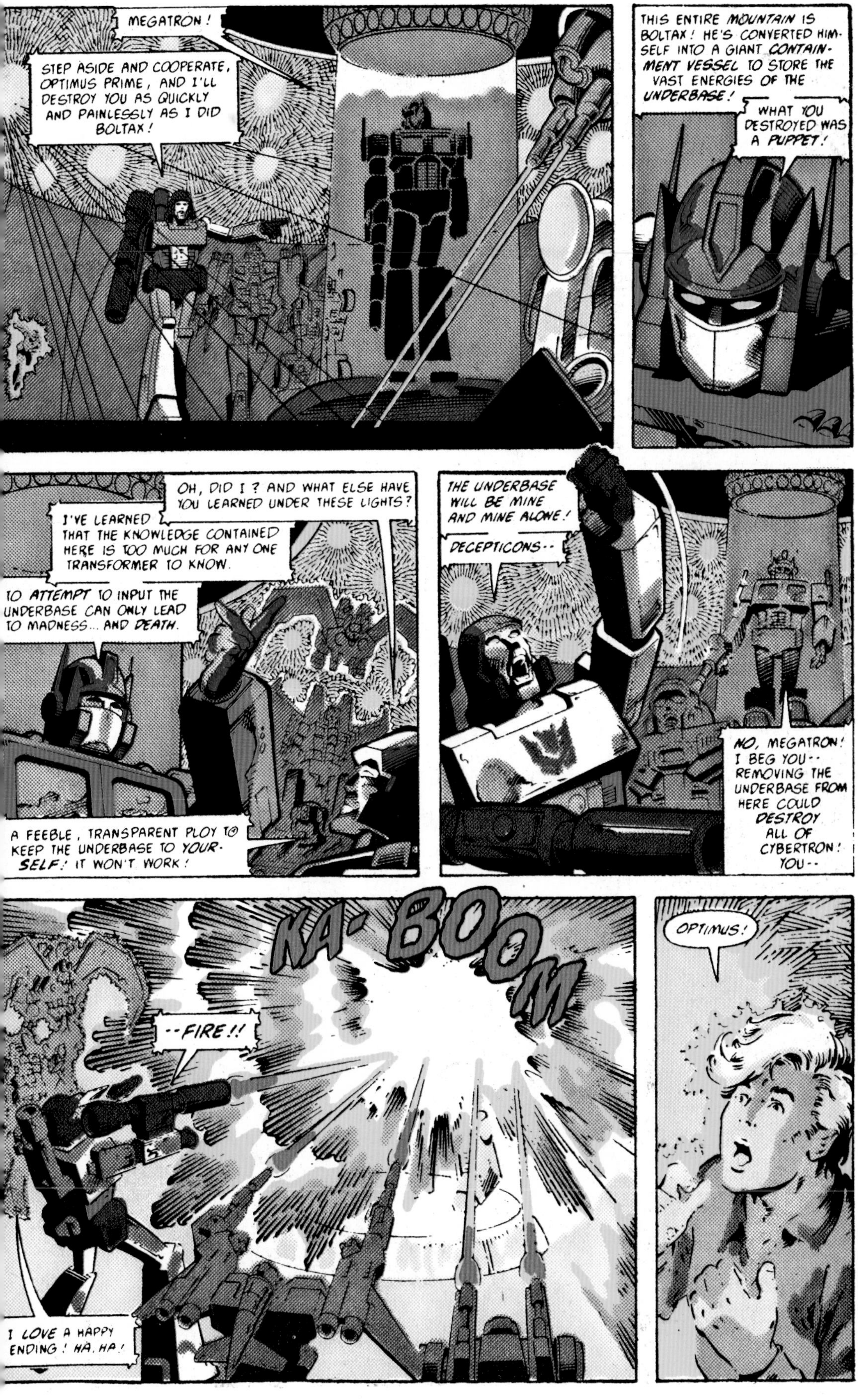
MEGATRON!
STEP ASIDE AND COOPERATE, OPTIMUS PRIME, AND I'LL DESTROY YOU AS QUICKLY AND PAINLESSLY AS I DID BOLTAX!
THIS ENTIRE MOUNTAIN IS BOLTAX! HE'S CONVERTED HIMSELF INTO A GIANT CONTAINMENT VESSEL TO STORE THE VAST ENERGIES OF THE UNDERBASE!
WHAT YOU DESTROYED WAS A PUPPET!
OH, DID I? AND WHAT ELSE HAVE YOU LEARNED UNDER THESE LIGHTS?
I'VE LEARNED THAT THE KNOWLEDGE CONTAINED HERE IS TOO MUCH FOR ANY ONE TRANSFORMER TO KNOW.
TO ATTEMPT TO INPUT THE UNDERBASE CAN ONLY LEAD TO MADNESS... AND DEATH.
A FEEBLE, TRANSPARENT PLOY TO KEEP THE UNDERBASE TO YOURSELF! IT WON'T WORK!
THE UNDERBASE WILL BE MINE AND MINE ALONE!
DECEPTICONS--
NO, MEGATRON! I BEG YOU-- REMOVING THE UNDERBASE FROM HERE COULD DESTROY ALL OF CYBERTRON! YOU--
KA-BOOM
--FIRE!!
I LOVE A HAPPY ENDING! HA, HA!
OPTIMUS!

WITH ULTIMATE *KNOWLEDGE* COMES ULTIMATE *POWER*, DECEPTICONS -- AND THAT KNOWLEDGE IS MINE FOR THE TAKING!

THE AUTOBOTS OF CYBERTRON ARE AS GOOD AS *TERMINATED!*

LOOK! OPTIMUS PRIME STILL FUNCTIONS!

MEGATRON, YOU IDIOT! *SHUT UP* AND TURN AROUND!

BUT OF COURSE, STARSCREAM WORDS GO UNHEARD...

...AND OPTIMUS PRIME STAGGERS UNSEEN TO THE OUTER CHAMBER.

BOLTAX IS AN IRREPLACEABLE TREASURE -- I CAN'T DESTROY IT. BUT IF I DON'T... IT WILL BE LOST TO MEGATRON, ANYWAY.

DOING NOTHING WOULD BE *WORSE* THAN DESTROYING IT.

THIS CONSOLE... MUST CONTROL THE MOUNTAIN'S OPERATION.

IF MY GUESS IS RIGHT... THE FLAMES ESCAPING THE MOUNTAIN'S OUTER VENTS...

...ARE THE EXCESS ENERGY OF THE UNDERBASE BURNING OFF.

THIS SHOULD CLOSE...

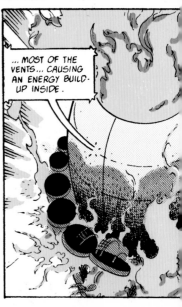

...MOST OF THE VENTS... CAUSING AN ENERGY BUILD-UP INSIDE.

MEGATRON-- WHAT'S HAPPENING?!

THE CHAMBER SEEMS TO BE *OVERLOADING*-- REACHING A *CRITICAL MASS!* BUT HOW?!

OPTIMUS PRIME -- HE'S GON

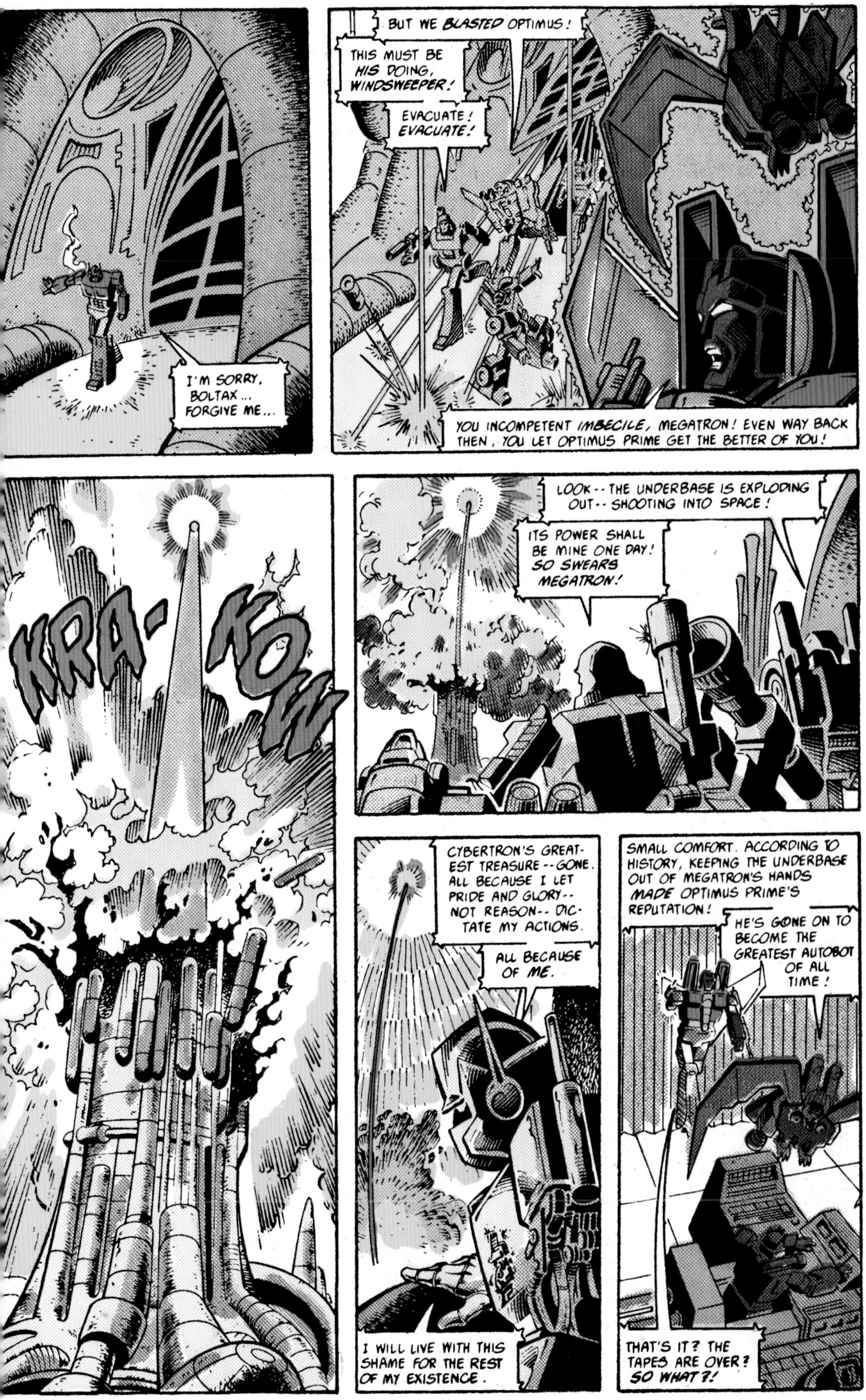
I'M SORRY, BOLTAX... FORGIVE ME...
BUT WE BLASTED OPTIMUS!
THIS MUST BE HIS DOING, WINDSWEEPER!
EVACUATE! EVACUATE!
YOU INCOMPETENT IMBECILE, MEGATRON! EVEN WAY BACK THEN, YOU LET OPTIMUS PRIME GET THE BETTER OF YOU!
KRA-KOW
LOOK -- THE UNDERBASE IS EXPLODING OUT -- SHOOTING INTO SPACE!
ITS POWER SHALL BE MINE ONE DAY! SO SWEARS MEGATRON!
CYBERTRON'S GREATEST TREASURE -- GONE. ALL BECAUSE I LET PRIDE AND GLORY -- NOT REASON -- DICTATE MY ACTIONS.
ALL BECAUSE OF ME.
I WILL LIVE WITH THIS SHAME FOR THE REST OF MY EXISTENCE.
SMALL COMFORT. ACCORDING TO HISTORY, KEEPING THE UNDERBASE OUT OF MEGATRON'S HANDS MADE OPTIMUS PRIME'S REPUTATION!
HE'S GONE ON TO BECOME THE GREATEST AUTOBOT OF ALL TIME!
THAT'S IT? THE TAPES ARE OVER? SO WHAT?!

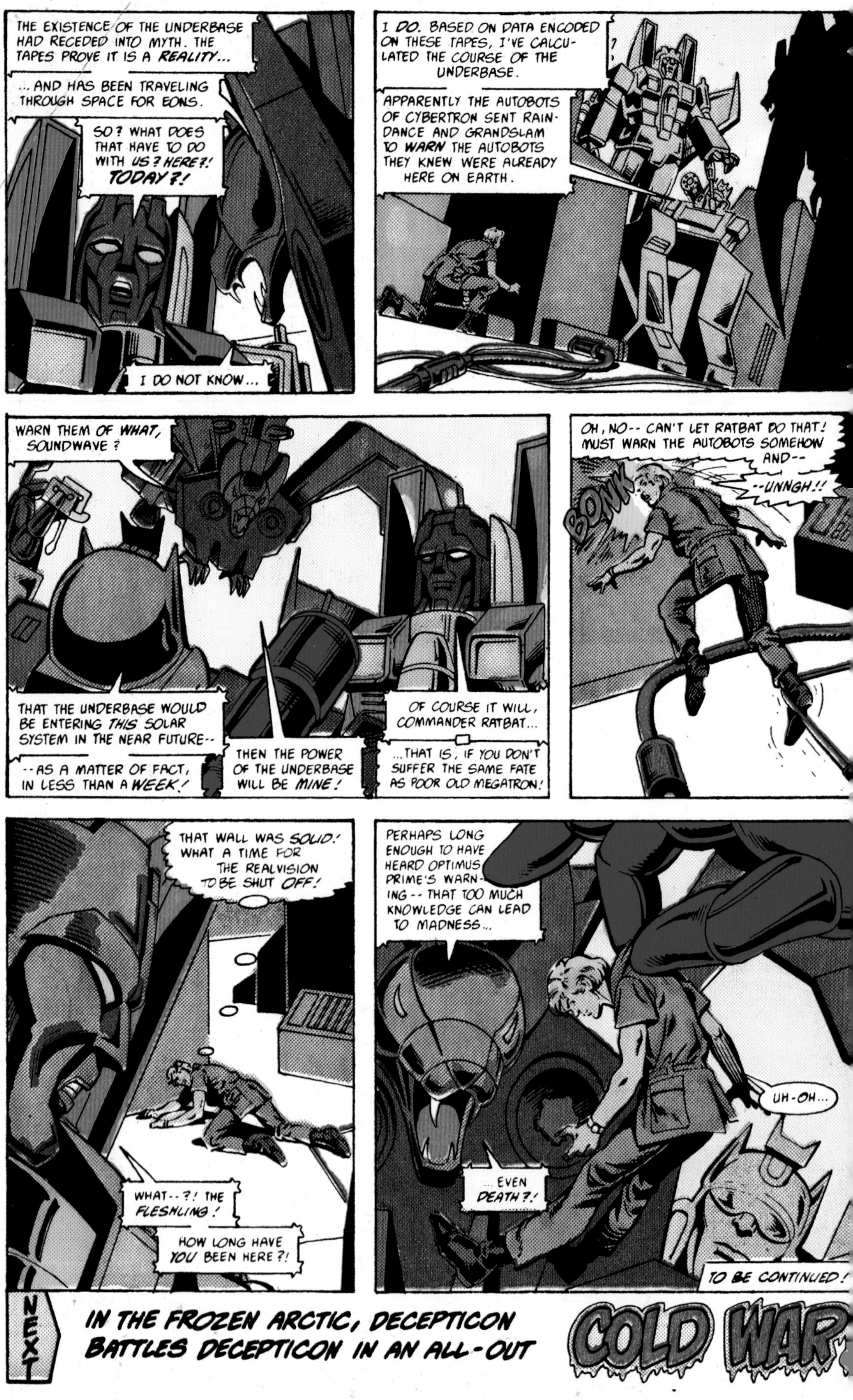
THE EXISTENCE OF THE UNDERBASE HAD RECEDED INTO MYTH. THE TAPES PROVE IT IS A REALITY...
...AND HAS BEEN TRAVELING THROUGH SPACE FOR EONS.
SO? WHAT DOES THAT HAVE TO DO WITH US? HERE?! TODAY?!
I DO NOT KNOW...
I DO. BASED ON DATA ENCODED ON THESE TAPES, I'VE CALCULATED THE COURSE OF THE UNDERBASE.
APPARENTLY THE AUTOBOTS OF CYBERTRON SENT RAINDANCE AND GRANDSLAM TO WARN THE AUTOBOTS THEY KNEW WERE ALREADY HERE ON EARTH.
WARN THEM OF WHAT, SOUNDWAVE?
THAT THE UNDERBASE WOULD BE ENTERING THIS SOLAR SYSTEM IN THE NEAR FUTURE--
--AS A MATTER OF FACT, IN LESS THAN A WEEK!
THEN THE POWER OF THE UNDERBASE WILL BE MINE!
OF COURSE IT WILL, COMMANDER RATBAT...
...THAT IS, IF YOU DON'T SUFFER THE SAME FATE AS POOR OLD MEGATRON!
OH, NO-- CAN'T LET RATBAT DO THAT! MUST WARN THE AUTOBOTS SOMEHOW AND--
BONK
--UNNGH!!
THAT WALL WAS SOLID! WHAT A TIME FOR THE REALVISION TO BE SHUT OFF!
WHAT--?! THE FLESHLING!
HOW LONG HAVE YOU BEEN HERE?!
PERHAPS LONG ENOUGH TO HAVE HEARD OPTIMUS PRIME'S WARNING -- THAT TOO MUCH KNOWLEDGE CAN LEAD TO MADNESS...
UH-OH...
...EVEN DEATH?!
TO BE CONTINUED!
NEXT
IN THE FROZEN ARCTIC, DECEPTICON BATTLES DECEPTICON IN AN ALL-OUT
COLD WAR!

THE TRANSFORMERS
THE BEST OF OPTIMUS PRIME

THE TRANS FORMERS

HEROIC AUTOBOT

Annual

1985 UK ANNUAL

For our second selection, we take you across the pond with an issue from the TRANSFORMERS Marvel UK series. While still being based within the Marvel TRANSFORMERS universe, Marvel UK often differed from the U.S. run as evidenced here by a different story of PRIME's rise to leadership. Retroactively, much of the Marvel UK story arcs have been negated, but it still remains that the purpose for OPTIMUS PRIME's rise to leadership was due to his unique battlefield knowledge within a working class AUTOBOT regime.

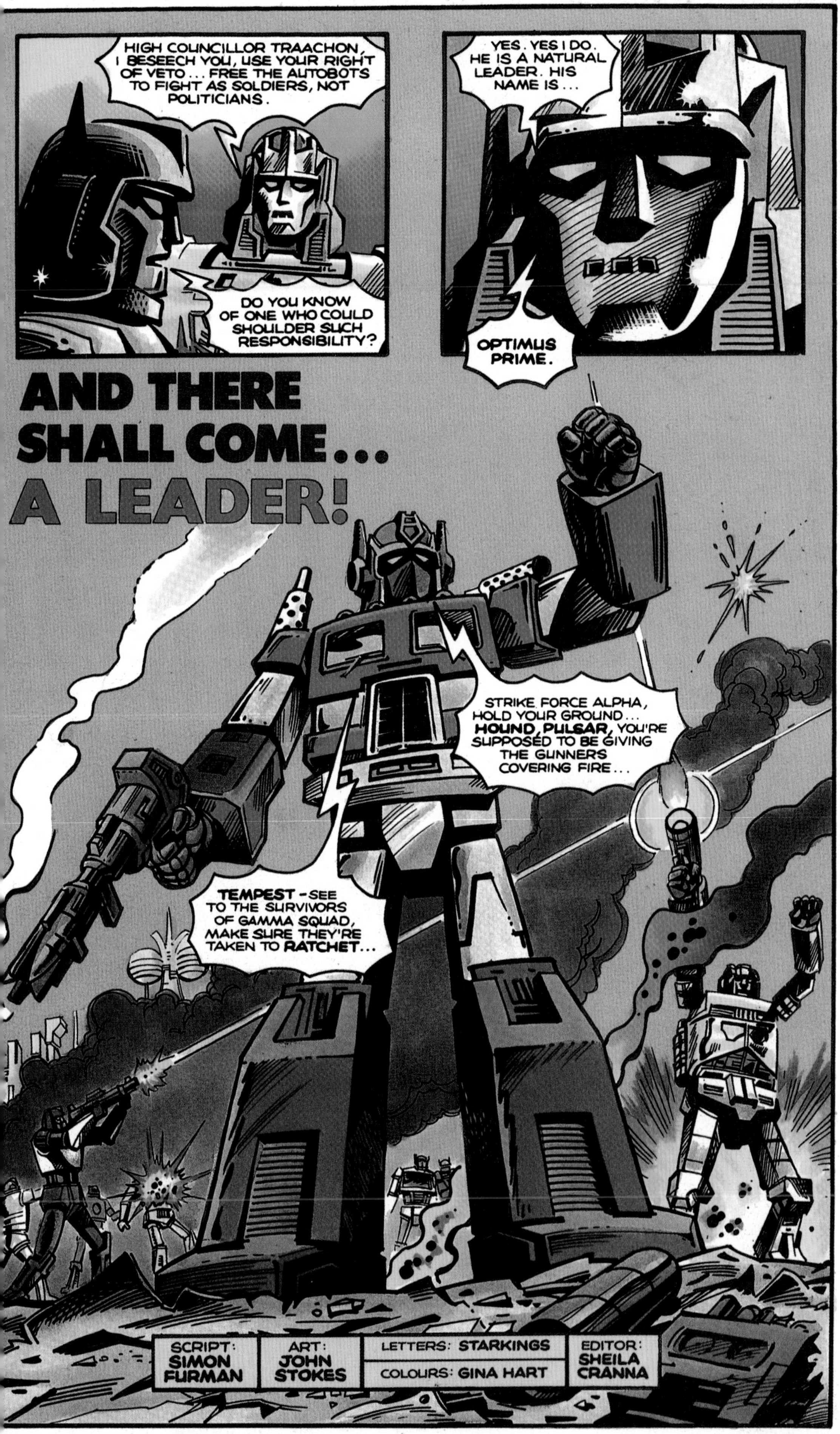
HIGH COUNCILLOR TRAACHON, I BESEECH YOU, USE YOUR RIGHT OF VETO... FREE THE AUTOBOTS TO FIGHT AS SOLDIERS, NOT POLITICIANS.
DO YOU KNOW OF ONE WHO COULD SHOULDER SUCH RESPONSIBILITY?
YES. YES I DO. HE IS A NATURAL LEADER. HIS NAME IS...
OPTIMUS PRIME.
AND THERE SHALL COME... A LEADER!
STRIKE FORCE ALPHA, HOLD YOUR GROUND... HOUND, PULSAR, YOU'RE SUPPOSED TO BE GIVING THE GUNNERS COVERING FIRE...
TEMPEST - SEE TO THE SURVIVORS OF GAMMA SQUAD, MAKE SURE THEY'RE TAKEN TO RATCHET...
SCRIPT: SIMON FURMAN
ART: JOHN STOKES
LETTERS: STARKINGS
COLOURS: GINA HART
EDITOR: SHEILA CRANNA

TALES OF CYBERTRON

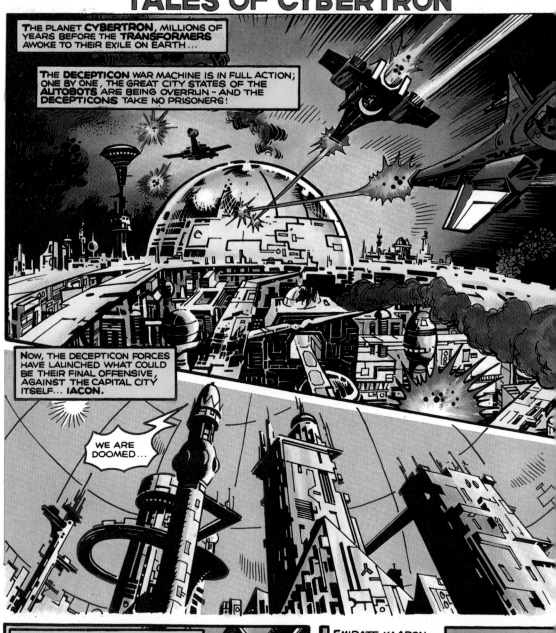

THE PLANET **CYBERTRON**, MILLIONS OF YEARS BEFORE THE **TRANSFORMERS** AWOKE TO THEIR EXILE ON EARTH...

THE **DECEPTICON** WAR MACHINE IS IN FULL ACTION; ONE BY ONE, THE GREAT CITY STATES OF THE **AUTOBOTS** ARE BEING OVERRUN - AND THE **DECEPTICONS** TAKE NO PRISONERS!

NOW, THE DECEPTICON FORCES HAVE LAUNCHED WHAT COULD BE THEIR FINAL OFFENSIVE, AGAINST THE CAPITAL CITY ITSELF... **IACON**.

WE ARE DOOMED...

AND WITHIN THE HEAVILY PROTECTED CELESTIAL TEMPLE, THE COUNCIL OF AUTOBOT ELDERS IS IN SESSION... FOR WHAT MAY BE THE LAST TIME!

THE DECEPTICONS HAVE BREACHED ALL BUT OUR FINAL DEFENCES, OUR TROOPS ARE IN DISARRAY - WE ARE DEFEATED!

NEVER!

EMIRATE XAARON...

OUR FORCES ARE IN DISARRAY BECAUSE FOOLS LIKE YOU, TOMAANDI, INSIST ON COUNCIL CONTROL.

WE MUST LET THEM OFF OUR LEASH... ENTRUST CONTROL TO AN INDIVIDUAL... A **WARRIOR**!

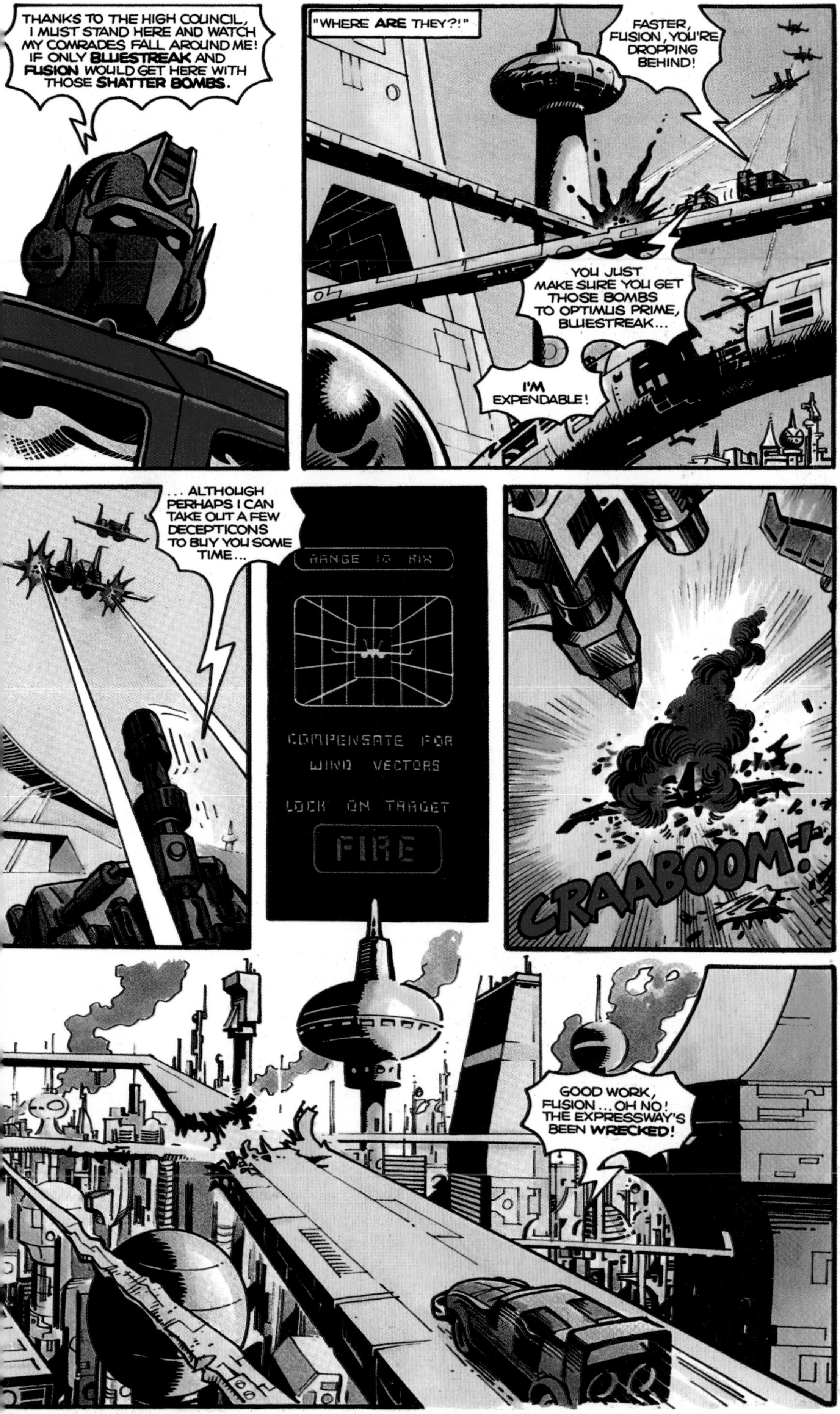
THANKS TO THE HIGH COUNCIL, I MUST STAND HERE AND WATCH MY COMRADES FALL AROUND ME! IF ONLY **BLUESTREAK** AND **FUSION** WOULD GET HERE WITH THOSE **SHATTER BOMBS**.
"WHERE **ARE** THEY?!"
FASTER, FUSION, YOU'RE DROPPING BEHIND!
YOU JUST MAKE SURE YOU GET THOSE BOMBS TO OPTIMUS PRIME, BLUESTREAK...
I'M EXPENDABLE!
... ALTHOUGH PERHAPS I CAN TAKE OUT A FEW DECEPTICONS TO BUY YOU SOME TIME...
RANGE 10 MIX
COMPENSATE FOR WIND VECTORS
LOCK ON TARGET
FIRE
CRAABOOM!
GOOD WORK, FUSION... OH NO! THE EXPRESSWAY'S BEEN **WRECKED**!

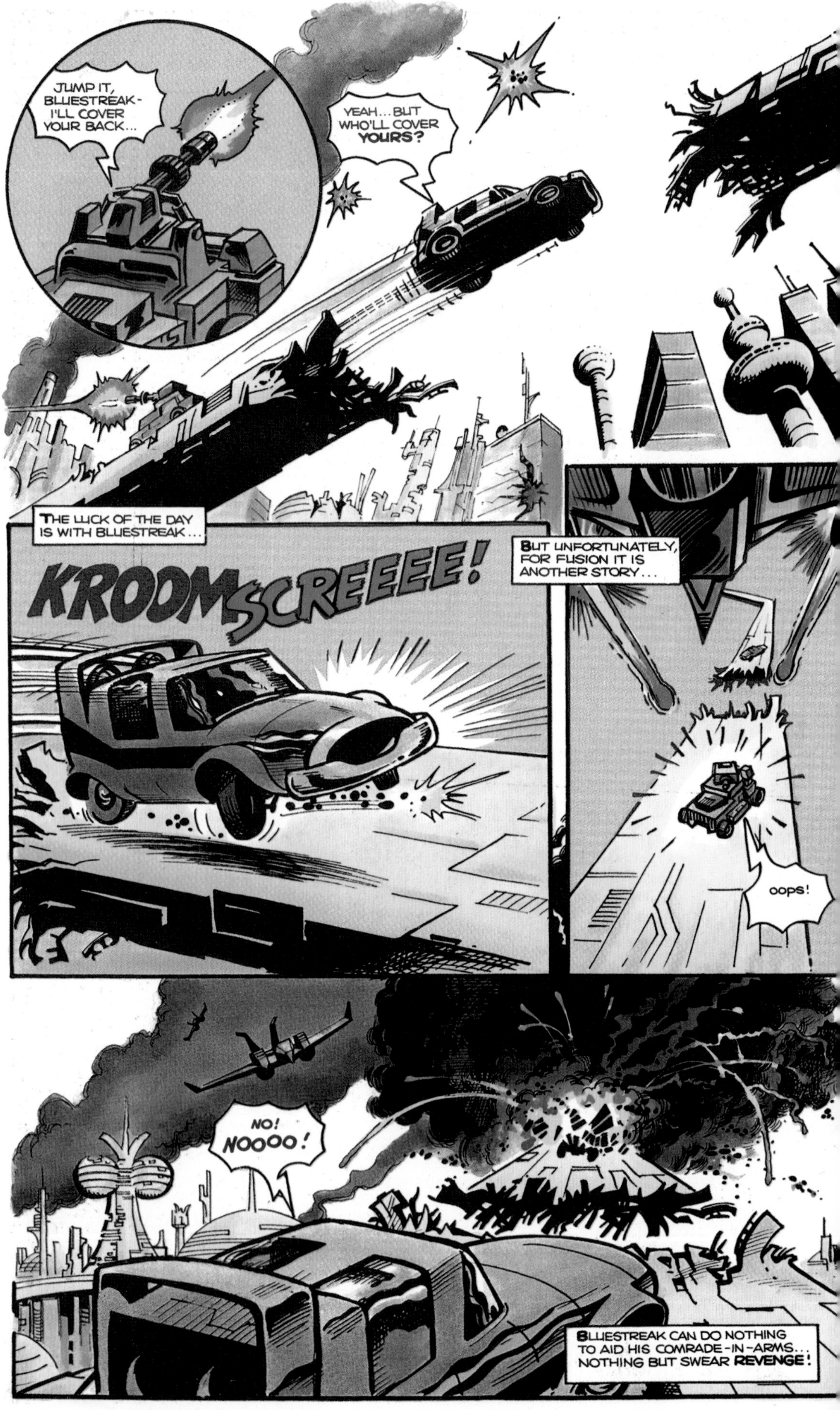
JUMP IT, BLUESTREAK- I'LL COVER YOUR BACK...
YEAH... BUT WHO'LL COVER YOURS?
THE LUCK OF THE DAY IS WITH BLUESTREAK...
KROOM SCREEEEE!
BUT UNFORTUNATELY, FOR FUSION IT IS ANOTHER STORY...
OOPS!
NO! NOOOO!
BLUESTREAK CAN DO NOTHING TO AID HIS COMRADE-IN-ARMS... NOTHING BUT SWEAR REVENGE!

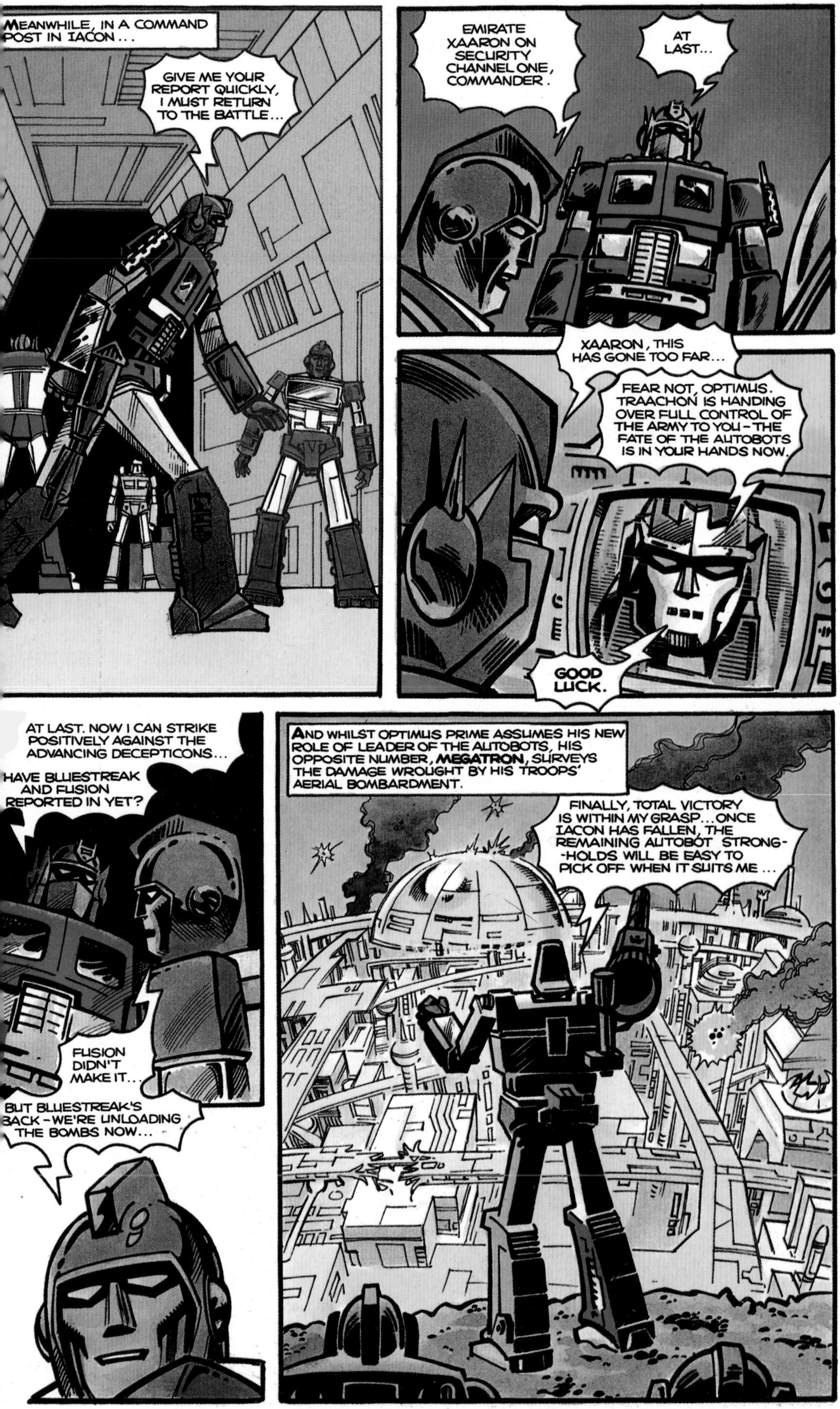
MEANWHILE, IN A COMMAND POST IN IACON...
GIVE ME YOUR REPORT QUICKLY, I MUST RETURN TO THE BATTLE...
EMIRATE XAARON ON SECURITY CHANNEL ONE, COMMANDER.
AT LAST...
XAARON, THIS HAS GONE TOO FAR...
FEAR NOT, OPTIMUS. TRAACHON IS HANDING OVER FULL CONTROL OF THE ARMY TO YOU - THE FATE OF THE AUTOBOTS IS IN YOUR HANDS NOW.
GOOD LUCK.
AT LAST. NOW I CAN STRIKE POSITIVELY AGAINST THE ADVANCING DECEPTICONS...
HAVE BLUESTREAK AND FUSION REPORTED IN YET?
FUSION DIDN'T MAKE IT...
BUT BLUESTREAK'S BACK - WE'RE UNLOADING THE BOMBS NOW...
AND WHILST OPTIMUS PRIME ASSUMES HIS NEW ROLE OF LEADER OF THE AUTOBOTS, HIS OPPOSITE NUMBER, MEGATRON, SURVEYS THE DAMAGE WROUGHT BY HIS TROOPS' AERIAL BOMBARDMENT.
FINALLY, TOTAL VICTORY IS WITHIN MY GRASP...ONCE IACON HAS FALLEN, THE REMAINING AUTOBOT STRONG-HOLDS WILL BE EASY TO PICK OFF WHEN IT SUITS ME...

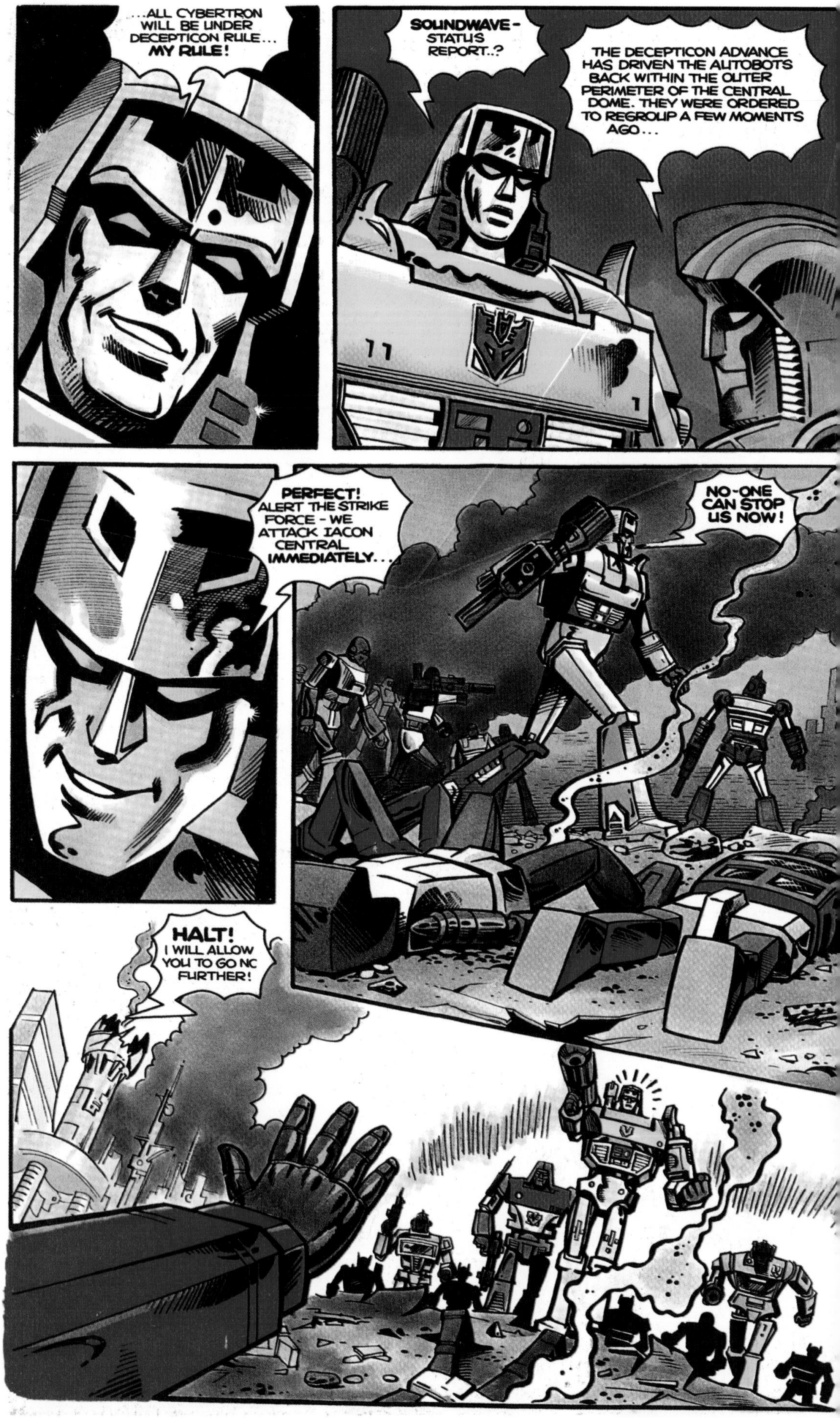
...ALL CYBERTRON WILL BE UNDER DECEPTICON RULE... MY RULE!
SOUNDWAVE - STATUS REPORT..?
THE DECEPTICON ADVANCE HAS DRIVEN THE AUTOBOTS BACK WITHIN THE OUTER PERIMETER OF THE CENTRAL DOME. THEY WERE ORDERED TO REGROUP A FEW MOMENTS AGO...
PERFECT! ALERT THE STRIKE FORCE - WE ATTACK IACON CENTRAL IMMEDIATELY...
NO-ONE CAN STOP US NOW!
HALT! I WILL ALLOW YOU TO GO NC FURTHER!

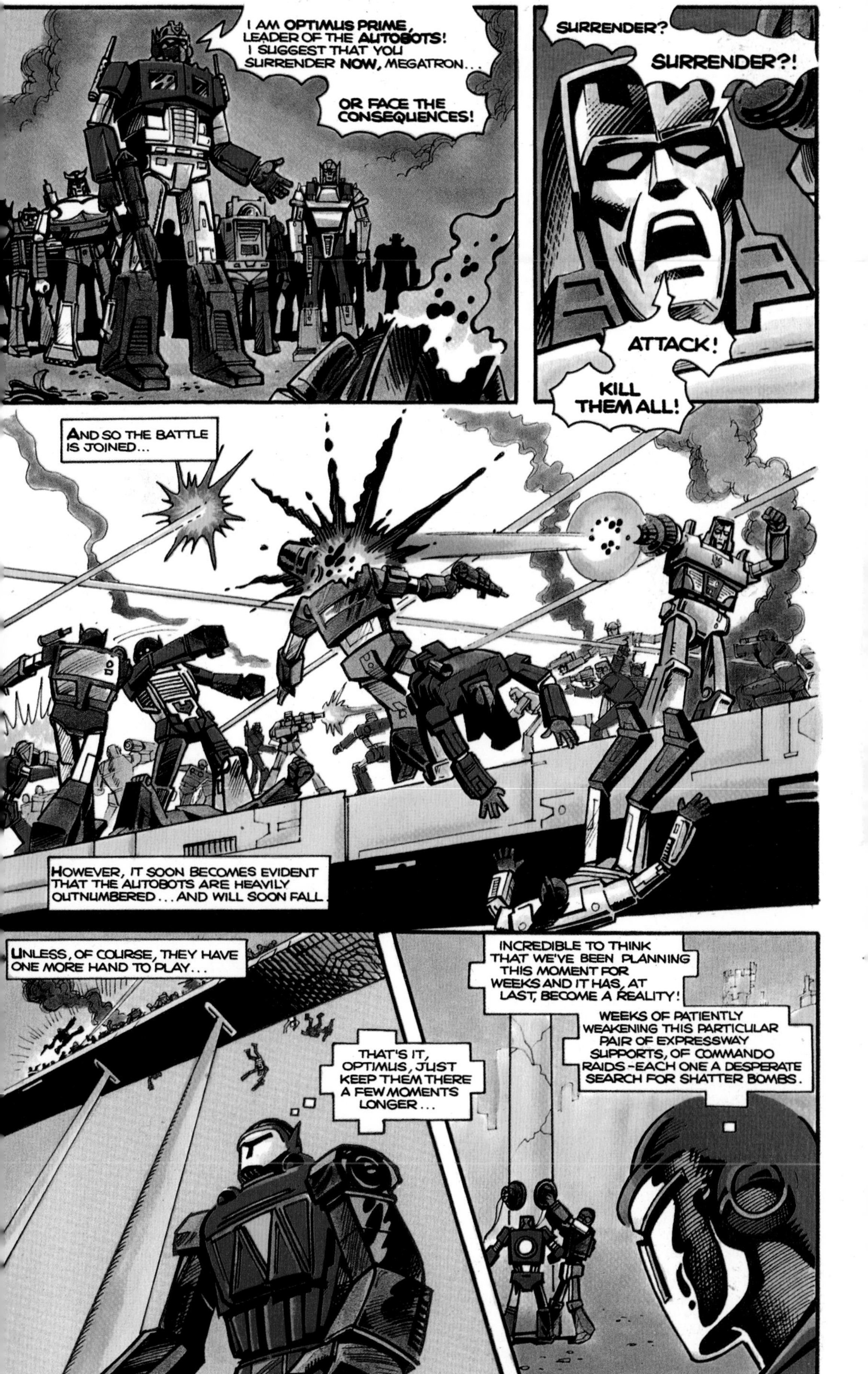
I AM OPTIMUS PRIME, LEADER OF THE AUTOBOTS! I SUGGEST THAT YOU SURRENDER NOW, MEGATRON...
OR FACE THE CONSEQUENCES!
SURRENDER?
SURRENDER?!
ATTACK!
KILL THEM ALL!
AND SO THE BATTLE IS JOINED...
HOWEVER, IT SOON BECOMES EVIDENT THAT THE AUTOBOTS ARE HEAVILY OUTNUMBERED... AND WILL SOON FALL.
UNLESS, OF COURSE, THEY HAVE ONE MORE HAND TO PLAY...
THAT'S IT, OPTIMUS, JUST KEEP THEM THERE A FEW MOMENTS LONGER...
INCREDIBLE TO THINK THAT WE'VE BEEN PLANNING THIS MOMENT FOR WEEKS AND IT HAS, AT LAST, BECOME A REALITY!
WEEKS OF PATIENTLY WEAKENING THIS PARTICULAR PAIR OF EXPRESSWAY SUPPORTS, OF COMMANDO RAIDS--EACH ONE A DESPERATE SEARCH FOR SHATTER BOMBS.

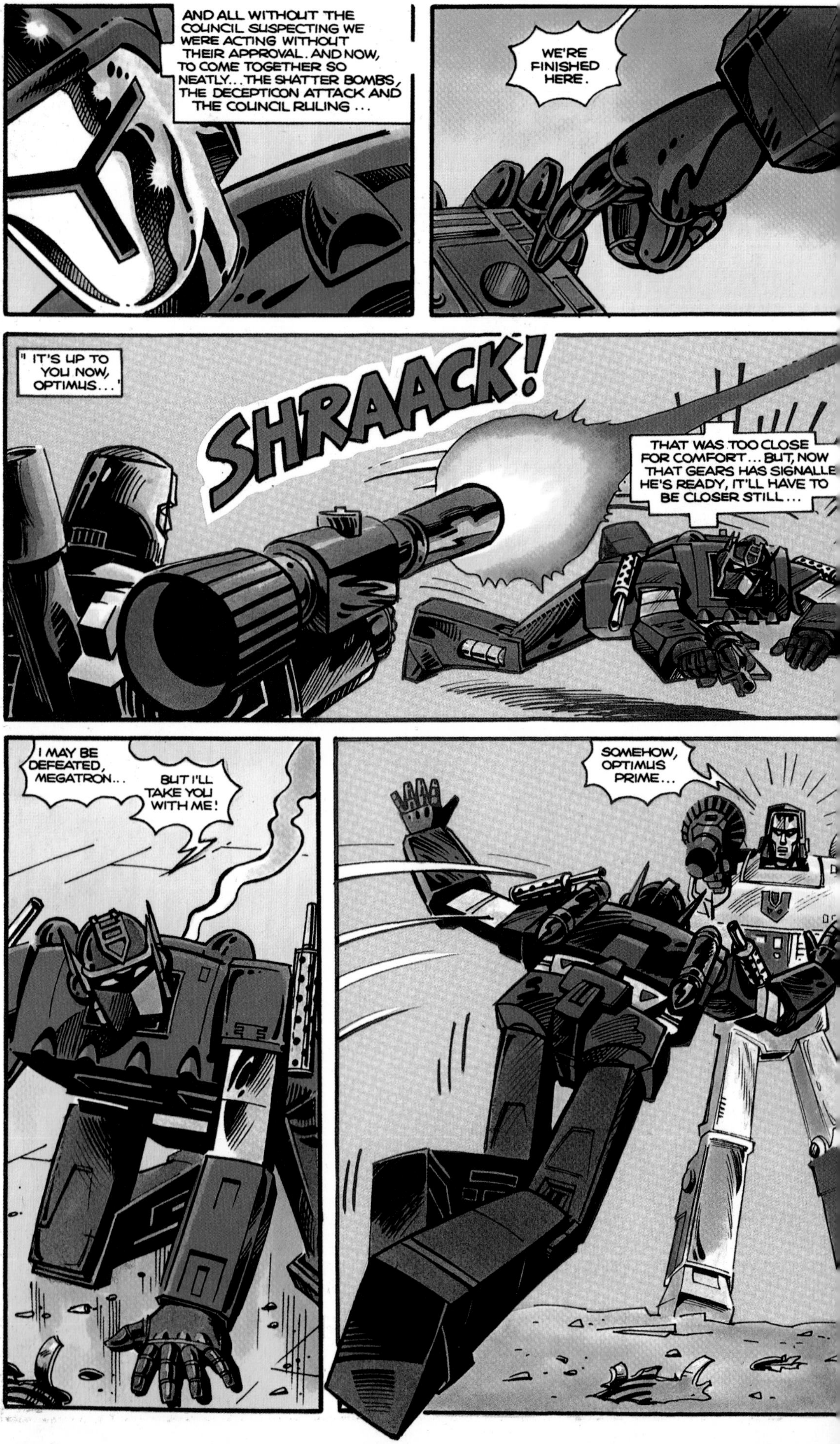
AND ALL WITHOUT THE COUNCIL SUSPECTING WE WERE ACTING WITHOUT THEIR APPROVAL. AND NOW, TO COME TOGETHER SO NEATLY... THE SHATTER BOMBS, THE DECEPTICON ATTACK AND THE COUNCIL RULING ...
WE'RE FINISHED HERE.
"IT'S UP TO YOU NOW, OPTIMUS..."
SHRAACK!
THAT WAS TOO CLOSE FOR COMFORT... BUT, NOW THAT GEARS HAS SIGNALLE HE'S READY, IT'LL HAVE TO BE CLOSER STILL...
I MAY BE DEFEATED, MEGATRON...
BUT I'LL TAKE YOU WITH ME!
SOMEHOW, OPTIMUS PRIME...

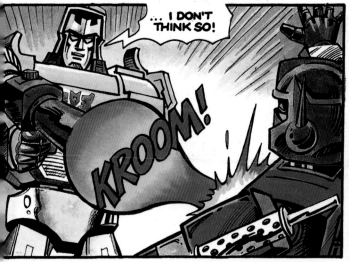

... I DON'T THINK SO!

KROOM!

UNNGH..! FLEE, AUTOBOTS! CARRY ON THE STRUGGLE FOR ME.

OBEYING THEIR LEADER'S LAST COMMAND, THE AUTOBOTS STAGE A SOMEWHAT PANICKED RETREAT...

HA! I MUST THANK YOU, OPTIMUS PRIME, SEEING YOUR TROOPS FLEE IN ABJECT FEAR HAS ALMOST COMPLETED MY VICTORY...

ONLY ONE TASK REMAINS...

YOU'RE SO RIGHT...

KAABOOOM!

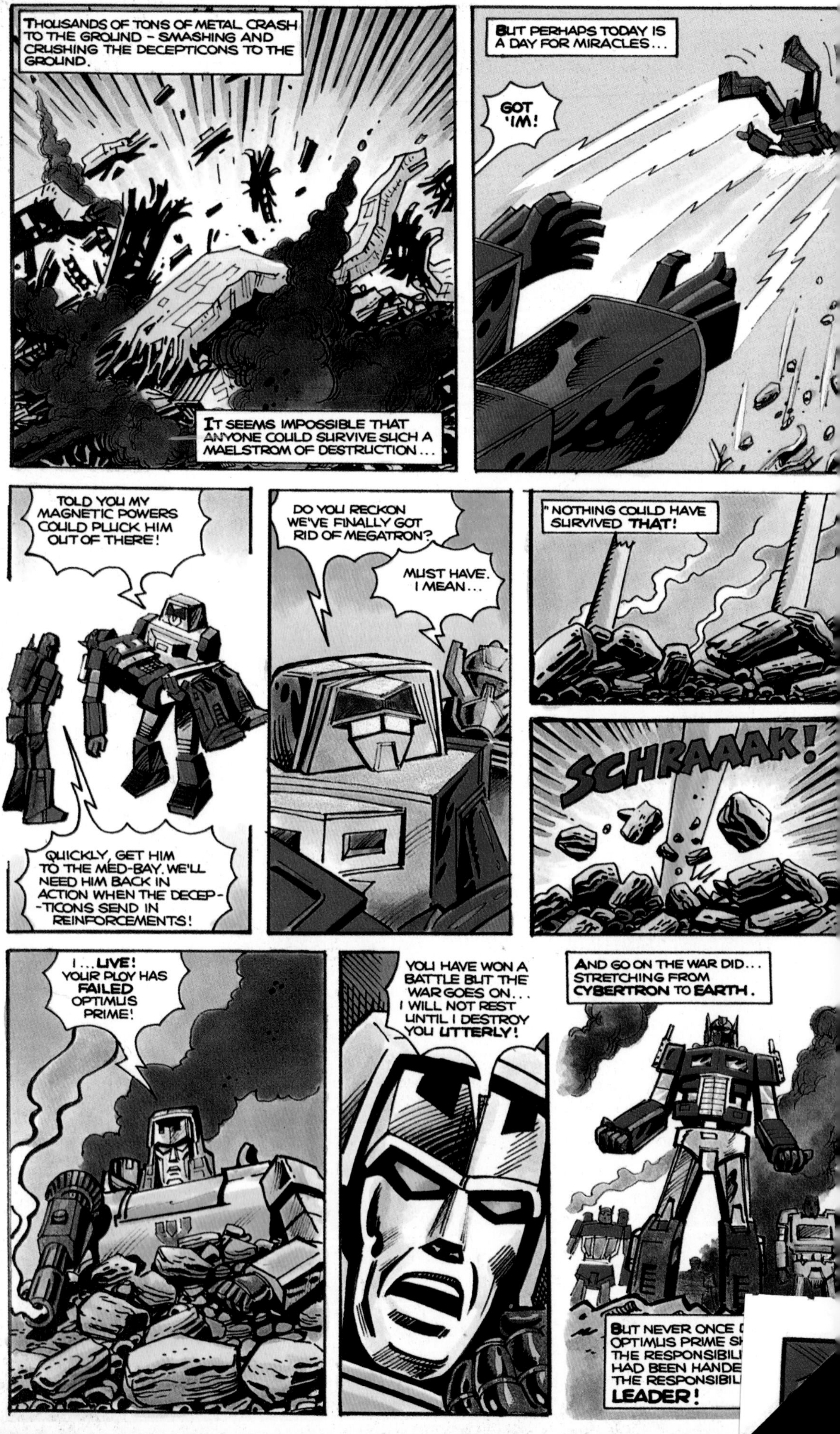
THOUSANDS OF TONS OF METAL CRASH TO THE GROUND - SMASHING AND CRUSHING THE DECEPTICONS TO THE GROUND.
IT SEEMS IMPOSSIBLE THAT ANYONE COULD SURVIVE SUCH A MAELSTROM OF DESTRUCTION...
BUT PERHAPS TODAY IS A DAY FOR MIRACLES...
GOT 'IM!
TOLD YOU MY MAGNETIC POWERS COULD PLUCK HIM OUT OF THERE!
QUICKLY, GET HIM TO THE MED-BAY. WE'LL NEED HIM BACK IN ACTION WHEN THE DECEP-TICONS SEND IN REINFORCEMENTS!
DO YOU RECKON WE'VE FINALLY GOT RID OF MEGATRON?
MUST HAVE. I MEAN...
"NOTHING COULD HAVE SURVIVED THAT!
SCHRAAAK!
I... LIVE! YOUR PLOY HAS FAILED OPTIMUS PRIME!
YOU HAVE WON A BATTLE BUT THE WAR GOES ON... I WILL NOT REST UNTIL I DESTROY YOU UTTERLY!
AND GO ON THE WAR DID... STRETCHING FROM CYBERTRON TO EARTH.
BUT NEVER ONCE D
OPTIMUS PRIME SH
THE RESPONSIBILI
HAD BEEN HANDE
THE RESPONSIBILI
LEADER!

THE TRANSFORMERS
THE BEST OF OPTIMUS PRIME

THE ANIMATED MOVIE
ADAPTATION #1

While both of the previous selections fit within the Generation One era, this next issue is a direct adaptation of the Generation One cartoon, taking place in the first TRANSFORMERS MOVIE, which hit theatres in 1986. OPTIMUS PRIME made his way to Earth and makes the ultimate sacrifice to save his fellow AUTBOTS, breaking the hearts of fans across North America while cementing his stature of greatest AUTOBOT leader of all time.

PRIME's deaths would become somewhat of a necessity in almost every incarnation, even spilling over into the movieverse, but this death affected fans so much that Hasbro would later bring the AUTOBOT leader back to life.

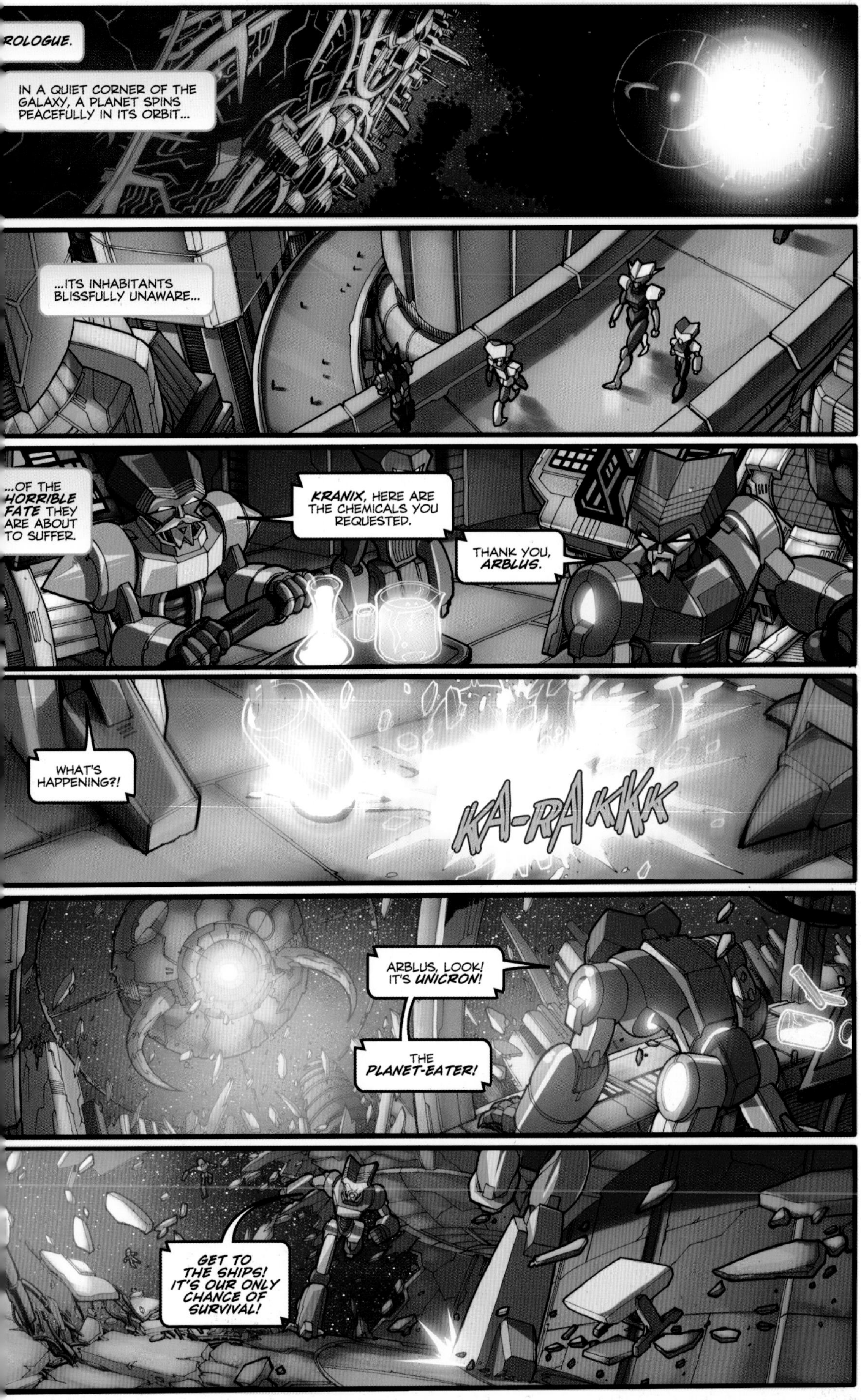

ROLOGUE.
IN A QUIET CORNER OF THE GALAXY, A PLANET SPINS PEACEFULLY IN ITS ORBIT...
...ITS INHABITANTS BLISSFULLY UNAWARE...
...OF THE HORRIBLE FATE THEY ARE ABOUT TO SUFFER.
KRANIX, HERE ARE THE CHEMICALS YOU REQUESTED.
THANK YOU, ARBLUS.
WHAT'S HAPPENING?!
KA-RAKKK
ARBLUS, LOOK! IT'S UNICRON!
THE PLANET-EATER!
GET TO THE SHIPS! IT'S OUR ONLY CHANCE OF SURVIVAL!

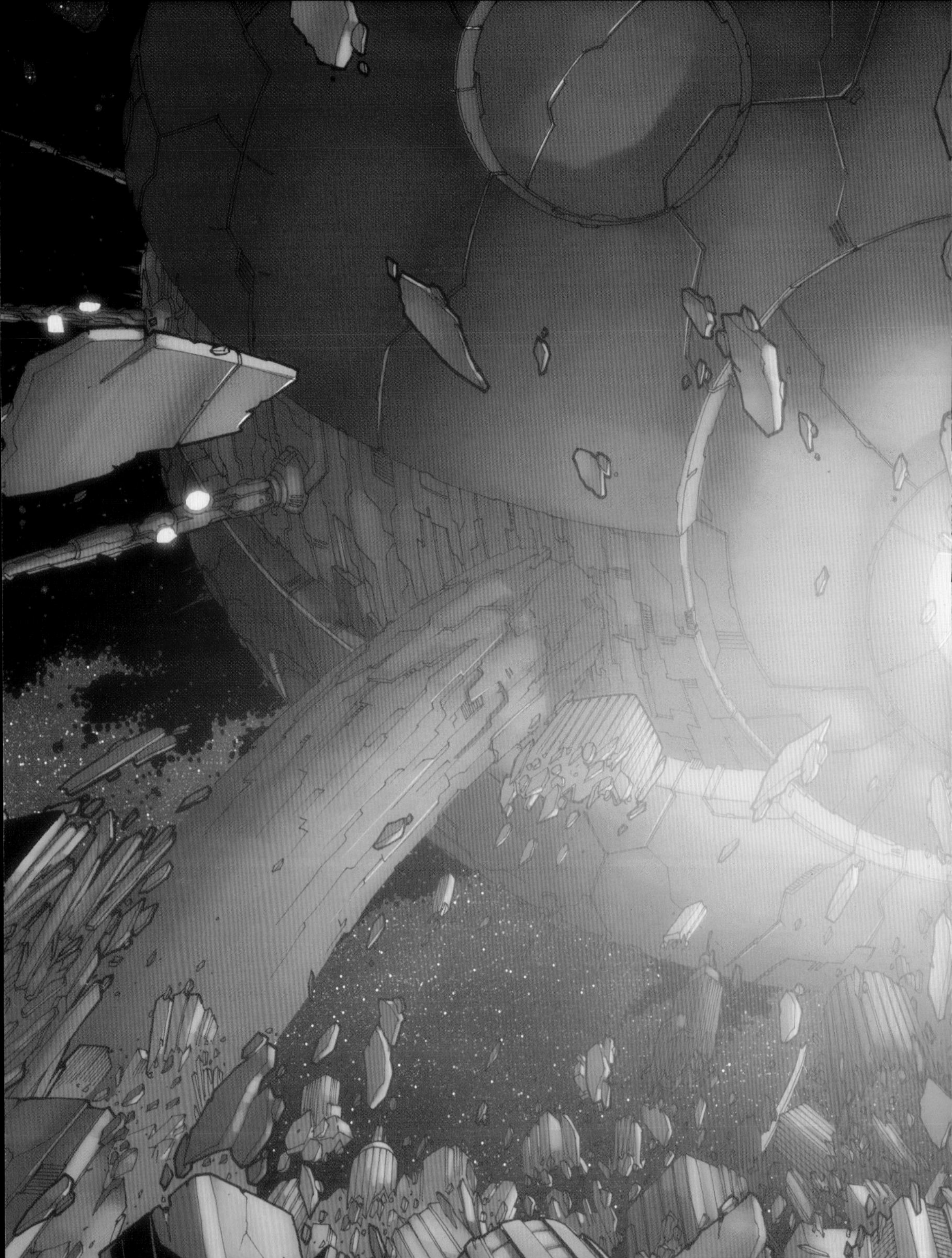

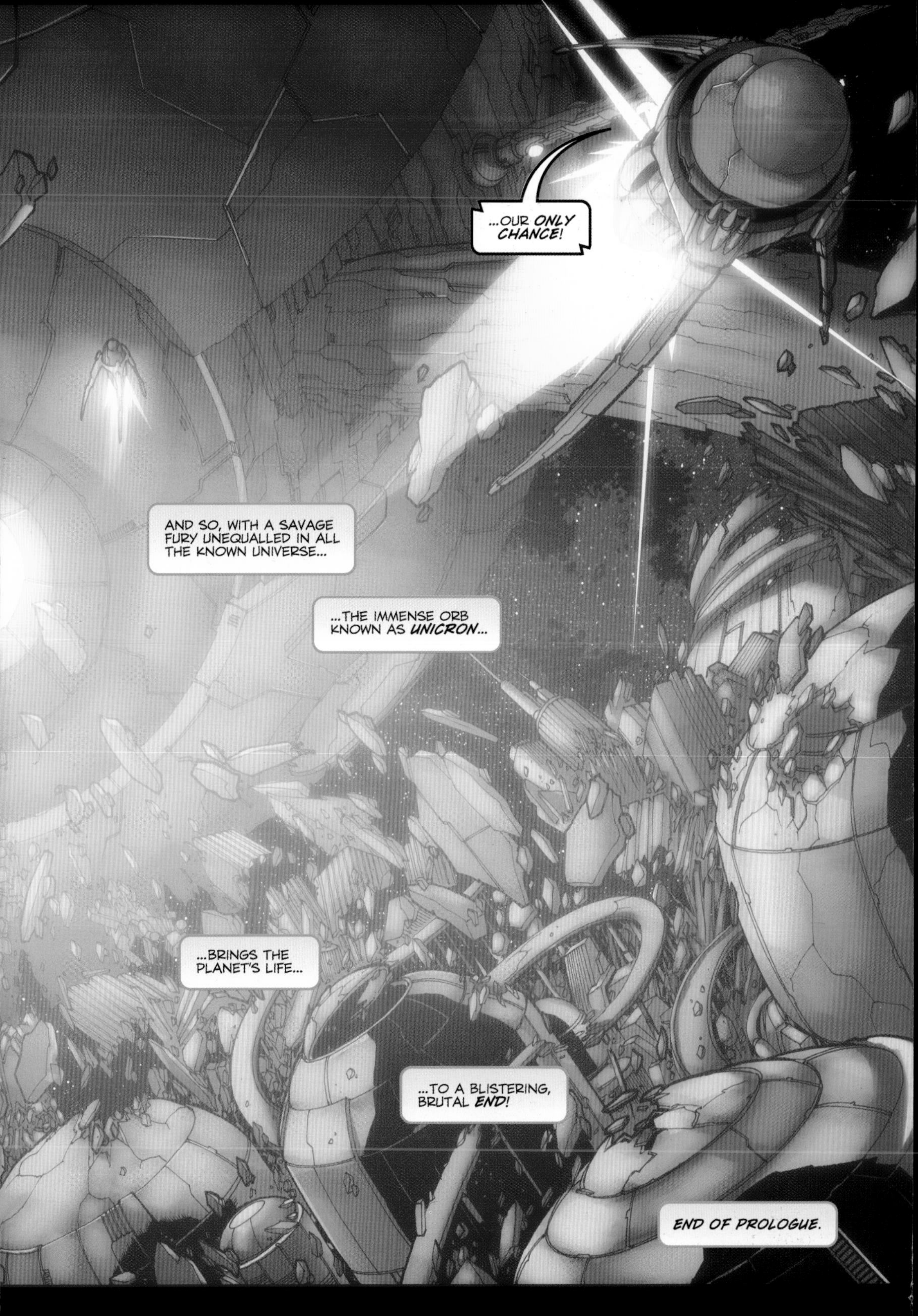
...OUR ONLY CHANCE!
AND SO, WITH A SAVAGE FURY UNEQUALLED IN ALL THE KNOWN UNIVERSE...
...THE IMMENSE ORB KNOWN AS UNICRON...
...BRINGS THE PLANET'S LIFE...
...TO A BLISTERING, BRUTAL END!
END OF PROLOGUE.

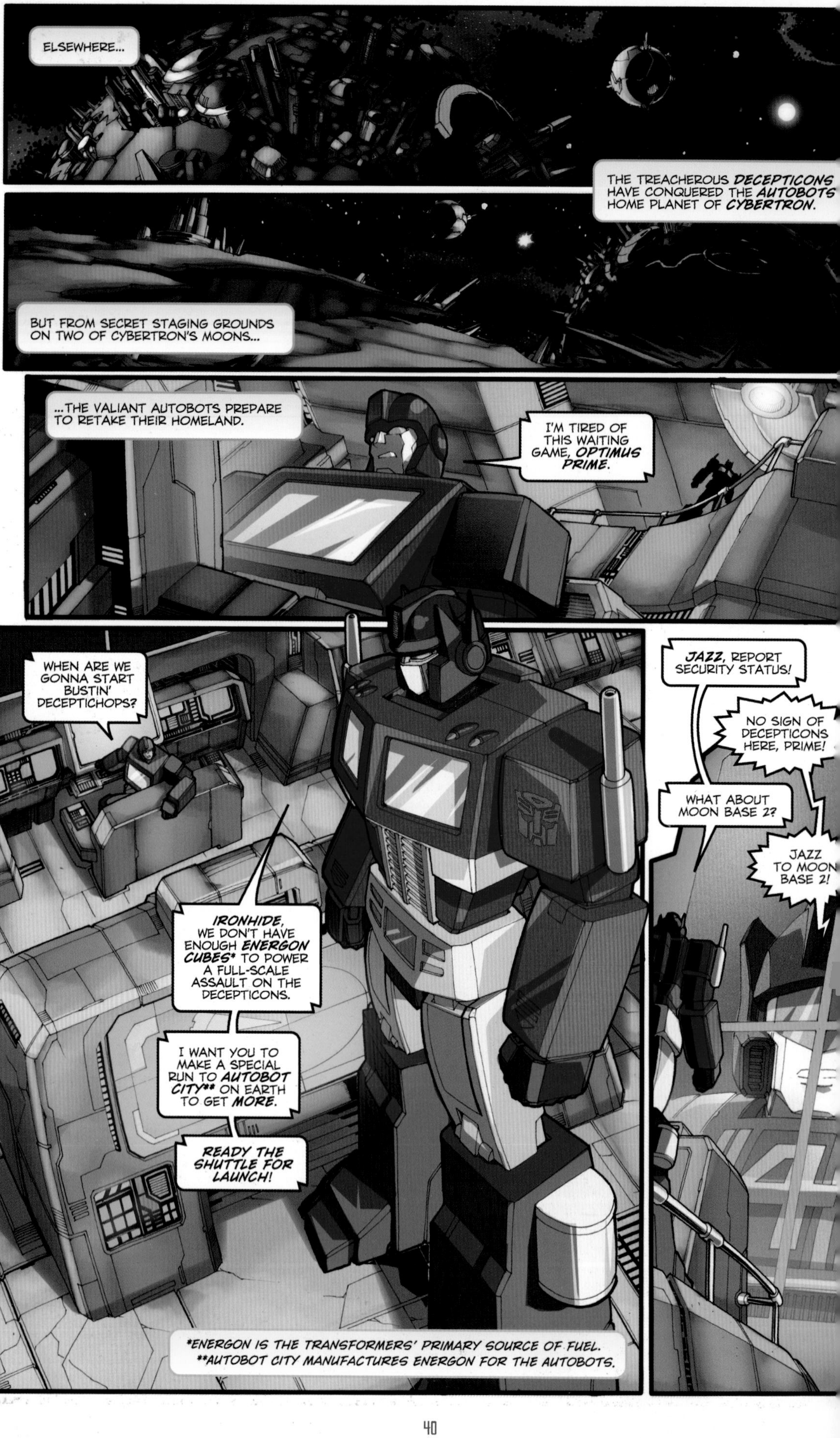
ELSEWHERE...
THE TREACHEROUS DECEPTICONS HAVE CONQUERED THE AUTOBOTS HOME PLANET OF CYBERTRON.
BUT FROM SECRET STAGING GROUNDS ON TWO OF CYBERTRON'S MOONS...
...THE VALIANT AUTOBOTS PREPARE TO RETAKE THEIR HOMELAND.
I'M TIRED OF THIS WAITING GAME, OPTIMUS PRIME.
WHEN ARE WE GONNA START BUSTIN' DECEPTICHOPS?
IRONHIDE, WE DON'T HAVE ENOUGH ENERGON CUBES* TO POWER A FULL-SCALE ASSAULT ON THE DECEPTICONS.
I WANT YOU TO MAKE A SPECIAL RUN TO AUTOBOT CITY** ON EARTH TO GET MORE.
READY THE SHUTTLE FOR LAUNCH!
*ENERGON IS THE TRANSFORMERS' PRIMARY SOURCE OF FUEL.
**AUTOBOT CITY MANUFACTURES ENERGON FOR THE AUTOBOTS.
JAZZ, REPORT SECURITY STATUS!
NO SIGN OF DECEPTICONS HERE, PRIME!
WHAT ABOUT MOON BASE 2?
JAZZ TO MOON BASE 2!

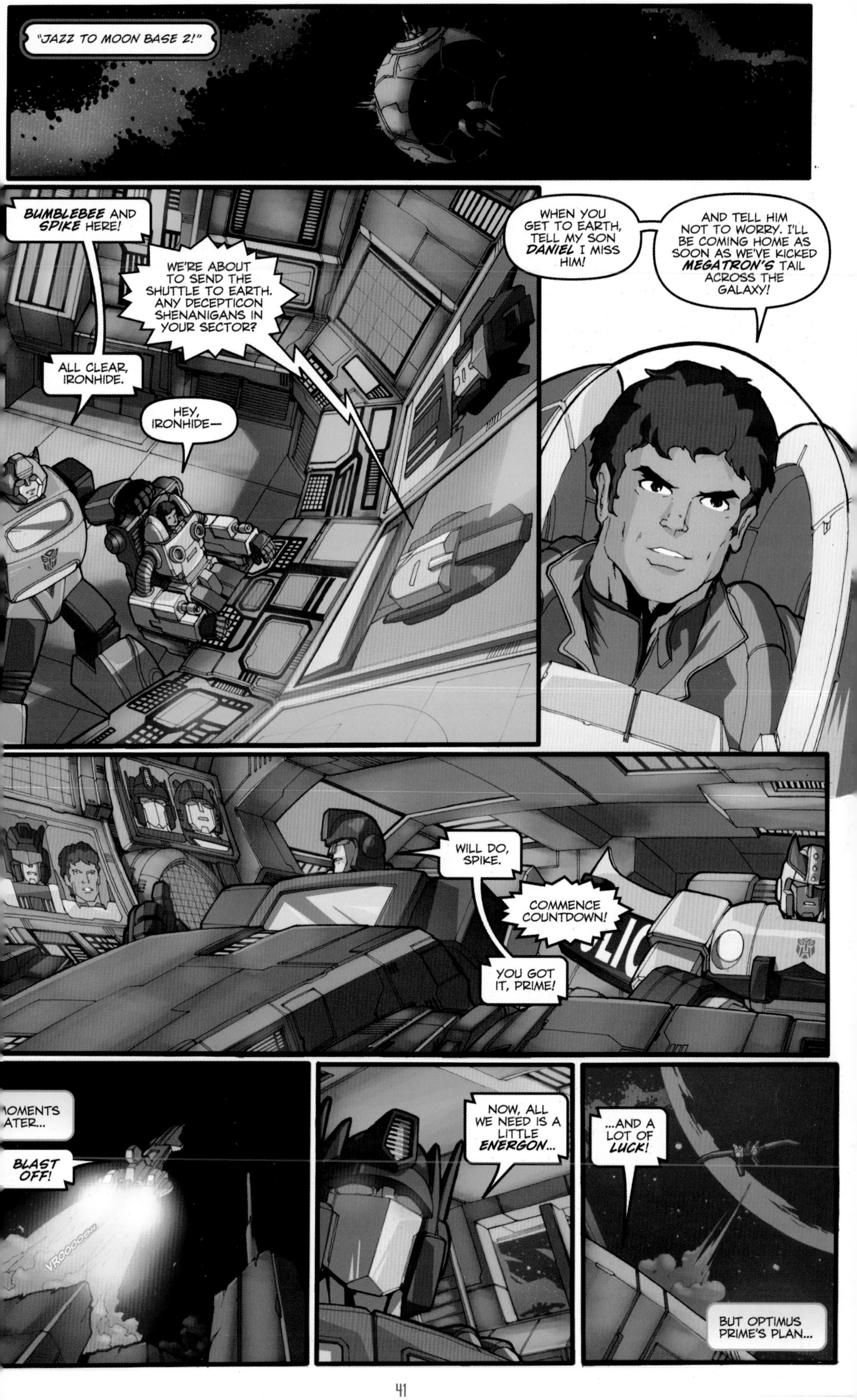
"JAZZ TO MOON BASE 2!"
BUMBLEBEE AND SPIKE HERE!
WE'RE ABOUT TO SEND THE SHUTTLE TO EARTH. ANY DECEPTICON SHENANIGANS IN YOUR SECTOR?
ALL CLEAR, IRONHIDE.
HEY, IRONHIDE—
WHEN YOU GET TO EARTH, TELL MY SON DANIEL I MISS HIM!
AND TELL HIM NOT TO WORRY. I'LL BE COMING HOME AS SOON AS WE'VE KICKED MEGATRON'S TAIL ACROSS THE GALAXY!
WILL DO, SPIKE.
COMMENCE COUNTDOWN!
YOU GOT IT, PRIME!
MOMENTS LATER...
BLAST OFF!
VROOOOOSH
NOW, ALL WE NEED IS A LITTLE ENERGON...
...AND A LOT OF LUCK!
BUT OPTIMUS PRIME'S PLAN...

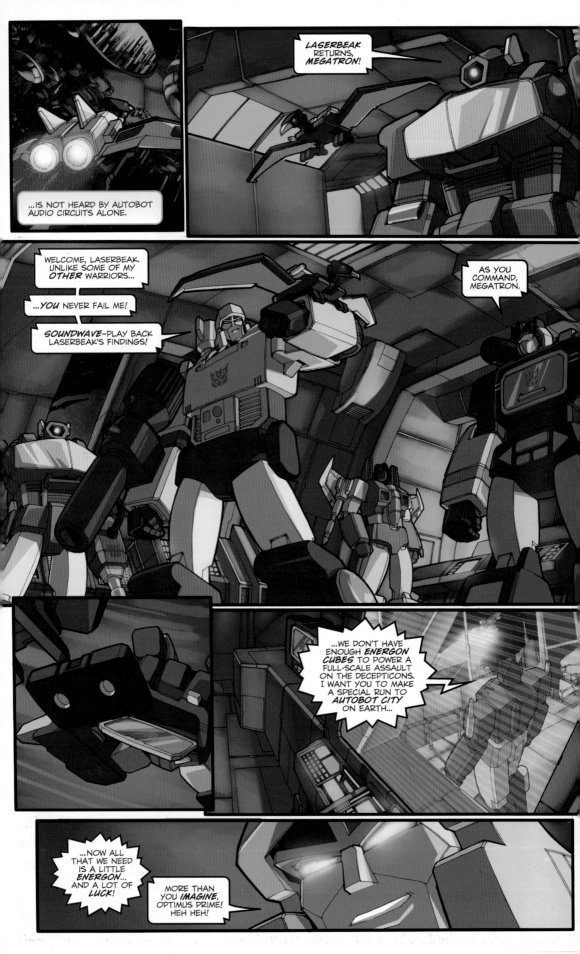

...IS NOT HEARD BY AUTOBOT AUDIO CIRCUITS ALONE.

LASERBEAK RETURNS, MEGATRON!

WELCOME, LASERBEAK. UNLIKE SOME OF MY *OTHER* WARRIORS...

...*YOU* NEVER FAIL ME!

SOUNDWAVE–PLAY BACK LASERBEAK'S FINDINGS!

AS YOU COMMAND, MEGATRON.

...WE DON'T HAVE ENOUGH *ENERGON CUBES* TO POWER A FULL-SCALE ASSAULT ON THE DECEPTICONS. I WANT YOU TO MAKE A SPECIAL RUN TO *AUTOBOT CITY* ON EARTH...

...NOW ALL THAT WE NEED IS A LITTLE *ENERGON*... AND A LOT OF *LUCK!*

MORE THAN YOU *IMAGINE*, OPTIMUS PRIME! HEH HEH!

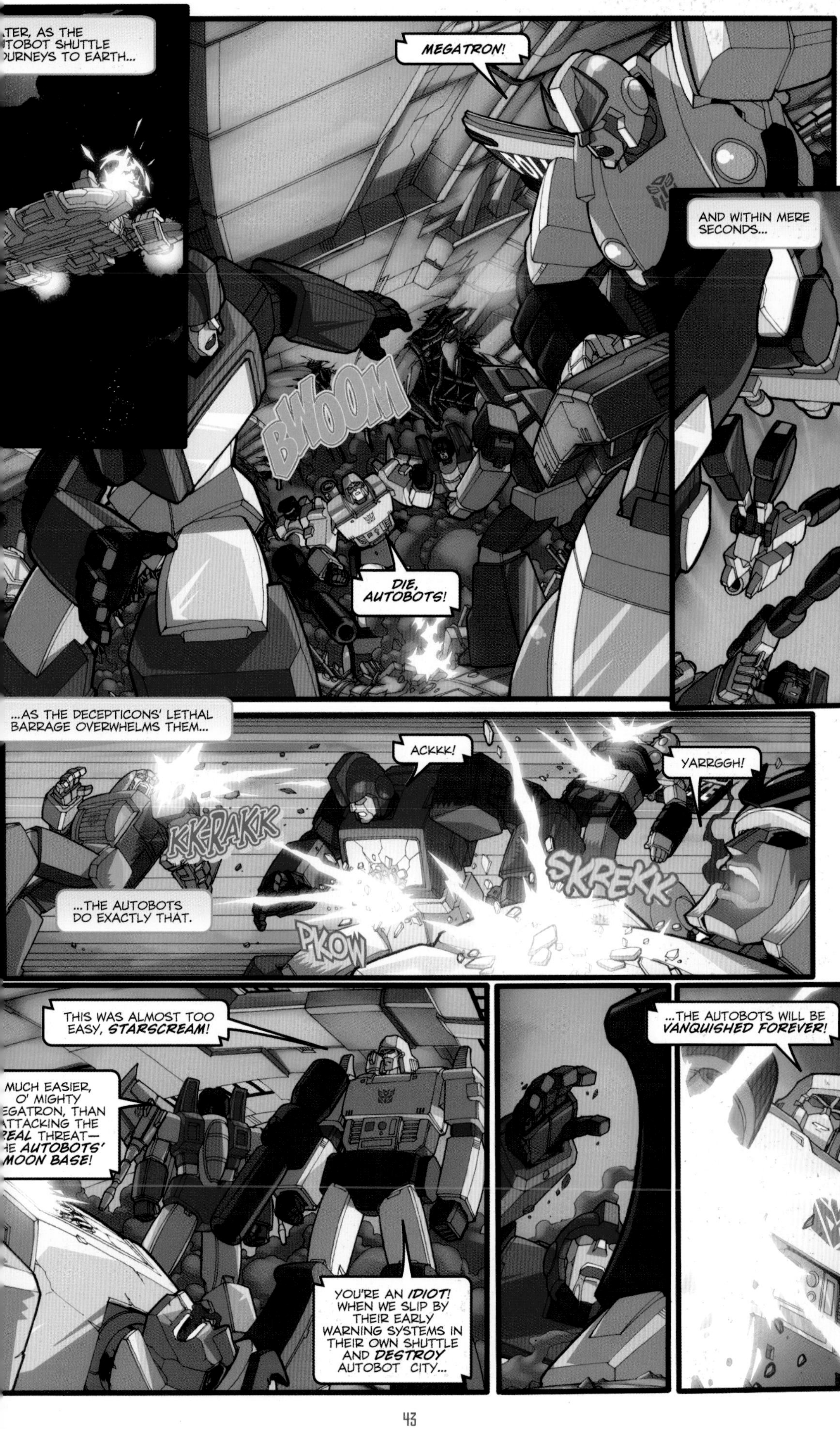

ATER, AS THE UTOBOT SHUTTLE URNEYS TO EARTH...
MEGATRON!
BWOOM
DIE, AUTOBOTS!
AND WITHIN MERE SECONDS...
...AS THE DECEPTICONS' LETHAL BARRAGE OVERWHELMS THEM...
ACKKK!
YARRGGH!
KKRAKK
SKREKK
...THE AUTOBOTS DO EXACTLY THAT.
PKOW
THIS WAS ALMOST TOO EASY, STARSCREAM!
MUCH EASIER, O' MIGHTY EGATRON, THAN ATTACKING THE REAL THREAT— HE AUTOBOTS' MOON BASE!
YOU'RE AN IDIOT! WHEN WE SLIP BY THEIR EARLY WARNING SYSTEMS IN THEIR OWN SHUTTLE AND DESTROY AUTOBOT CITY...
...THE AUTOBOTS WILL BE VANQUISHED FOREVER!

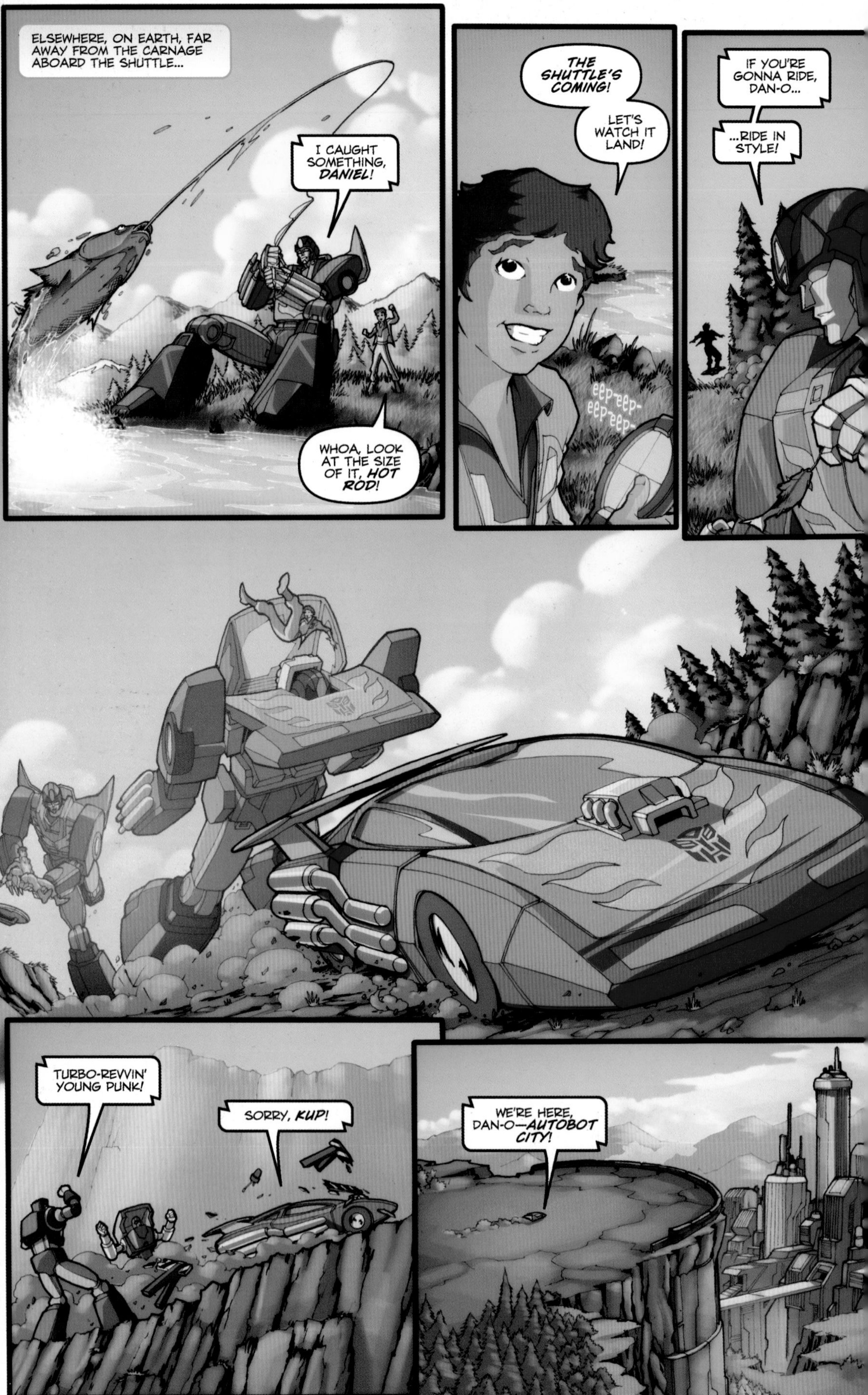
ELSEWHERE, ON EARTH, FAR AWAY FROM THE CARNAGE ABOARD THE SHUTTLE...
I CAUGHT SOMETHING, DANIEL!
WHOA, LOOK AT THE SIZE OF IT, HOT ROD!
THE SHUTTLE'S COMING!
LET'S WATCH IT LAND!
eep-eep-eep-eep-
IF YOU'RE GONNA RIDE, DAN-O...
...RIDE IN STYLE!
TURBO-REVVIN' YOUNG PUNK!
SORRY, KUP!
WE'RE HERE, DAN-O—AUTOBOT CITY!

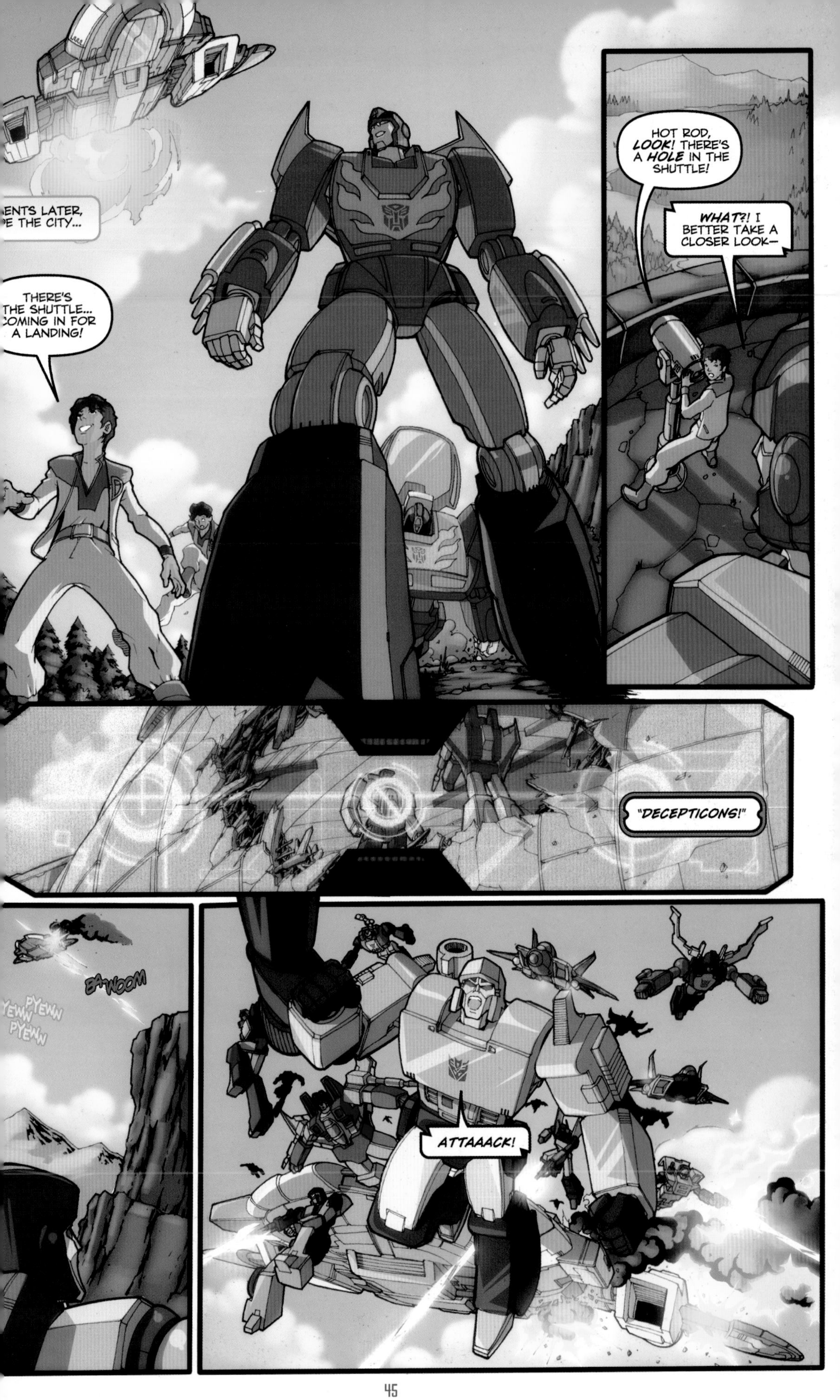

ENTS LATER,
E THE CITY...
THERE'S THE SHUTTLE... COMING IN FOR A LANDING!
HOT ROD, LOOK! THERE'S A HOLE IN THE SHUTTLE!
WHAT?! I BETTER TAKE A CLOSER LOOK—
"DECEPTICONS!"
BA-WOOM
PYEWN
YEWN
PYEWN
ATTAAACK!

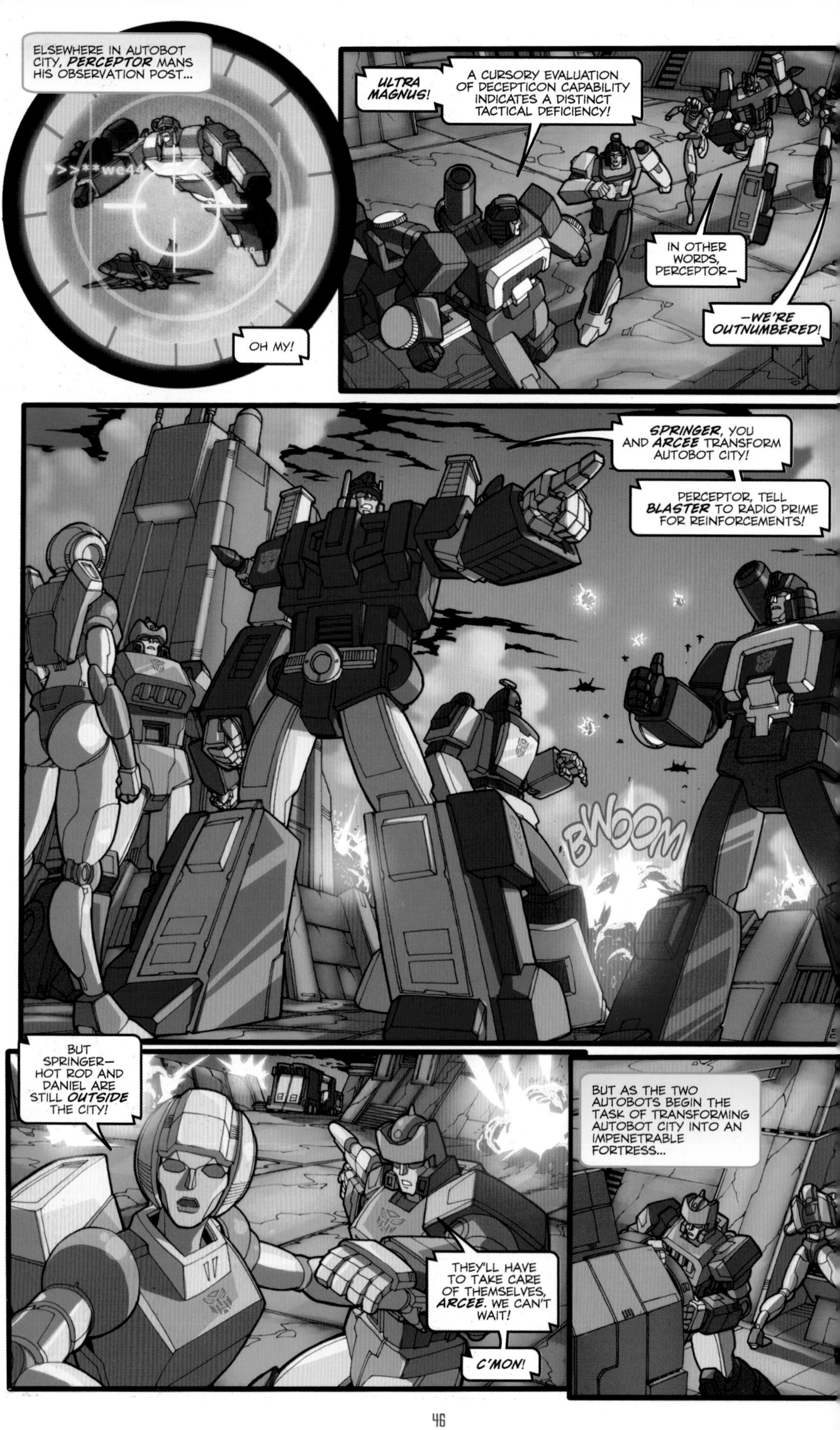
ELSEWHERE IN AUTOBOT CITY, PERCEPTOR MANS HIS OBSERVATION POST...
OH MY!
ULTRA MAGNUS!
A CURSORY EVALUATION OF DECEPTICON CAPABILITY INDICATES A DISTINCT TACTICAL DEFICIENCY!
IN OTHER WORDS, PERCEPTOR—
—WE'RE OUTNUMBERED!
SPRINGER, YOU AND ARCEE TRANSFORM AUTOBOT CITY!
PERCEPTOR, TELL BLASTER TO RADIO PRIME FOR REINFORCEMENTS!
BWOOM
BUT SPRINGER— HOT ROD AND DANIEL ARE STILL OUTSIDE THE CITY!
THEY'LL HAVE TO TAKE CARE OF THEMSELVES, ARCEE. WE CAN'T WAIT!
C'MON!
BUT AS THE TWO AUTOBOTS BEGIN THE TASK OF TRANSFORMING AUTOBOT CITY INTO AN IMPENETRABLE FORTRESS...

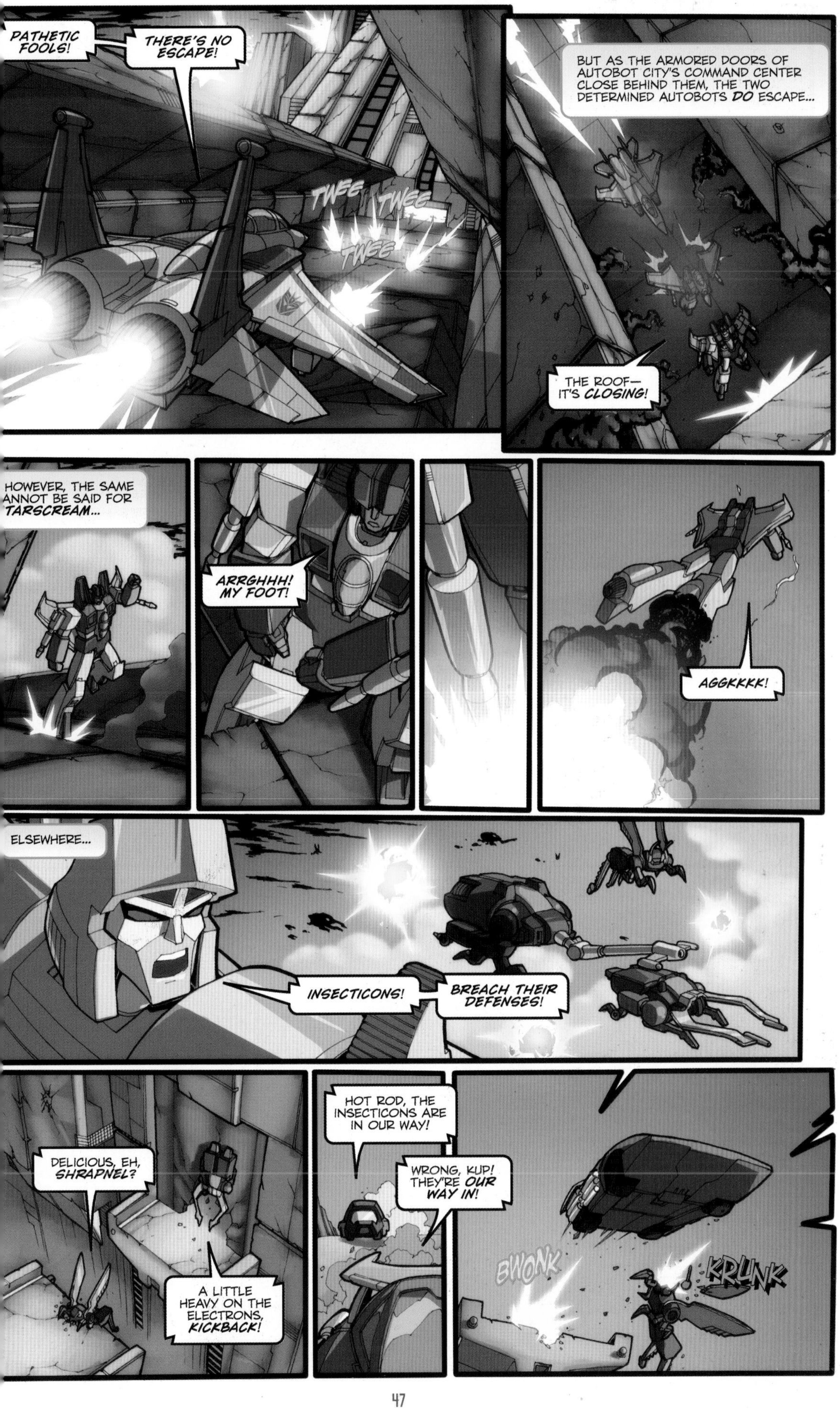
PATHETIC FOOLS!
THERE'S NO ESCAPE!
TWEE TWEE TWEE
BUT AS THE ARMORED DOORS OF AUTOBOT CITY'S COMMAND CENTER CLOSE BEHIND THEM, THE TWO DETERMINED AUTOBOTS DO ESCAPE...
THE ROOF— IT'S CLOSING!
HOWEVER, THE SAME ANNOT BE SAID FOR TARSCREAM...
ARRGHHH! MY FOOT!
AGGKKKK!
ELSEWHERE...
INSECTICONS!
BREACH THEIR DEFENSES!
DELICIOUS, EH, SHRAPNEL?
A LITTLE HEAVY ON THE ELECTRONS, KICKBACK!
HOT ROD, THE INSECTICONS ARE IN OUR WAY!
WRONG, KUP! THEY'RE OUR WAY IN!
BWONK
KRUNK

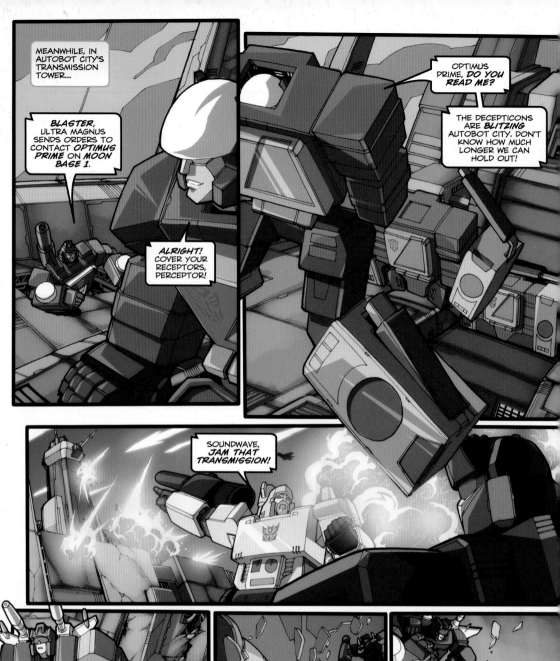

MEANWHILE, IN AUTOBOT CITY'S TRANSMISSION TOWER...

BLASTER, ULTRA MAGNUS SENDS ORDERS TO CONTACT *OPTIMUS PRIME* ON MOON BASE 1.

ALRIGHT! COVER YOUR RECEPTORS, PERCEPTOR!

OPTIMUS PRIME, *DO YOU READ ME?*

THE DECEPTICONS ARE *BLITZING* AUTOBOT CITY. DON'T KNOW HOW MUCH LONGER WE CAN HOLD OUT!

SOUNDWAVE, *JAM THAT TRANSMISSION!*

RUMBLE, FRENZY, RAVAGE, RATBAT—EJECT!

BEGIN *OPERATION INTERFERENCE!*

KA ZRAKKK

FIRST WE CRACK THE *SHELL*—

—THEN WE CRACK THE *NUTS* INSIDE!

NO WAY, TWO CAN PLAY!

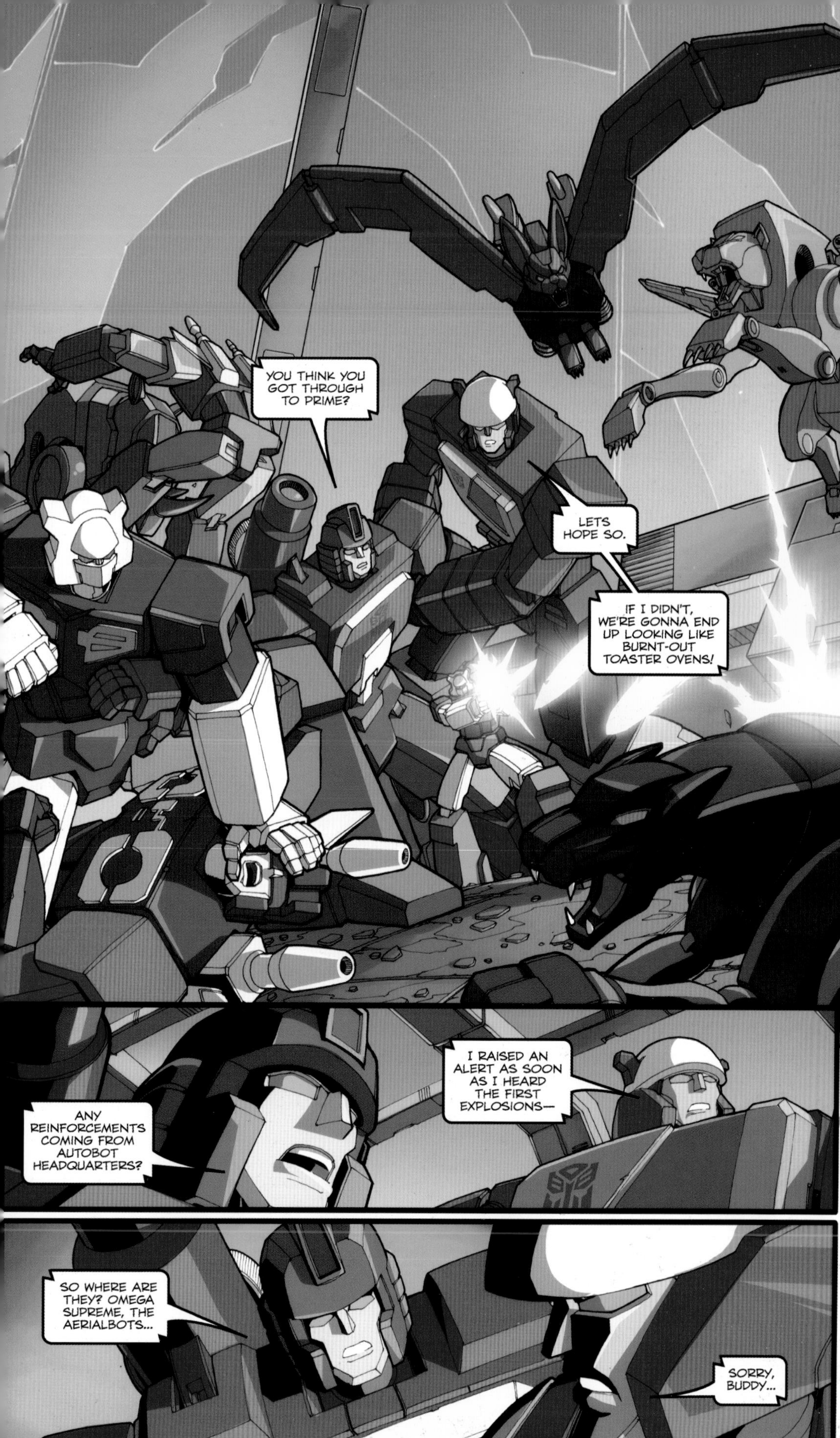
YOU THINK YOU GOT THROUGH TO PRIME?
LETS HOPE SO.
IF I DIDN'T, WE'RE GONNA END UP LOOKING LIKE BURNT-OUT TOASTER OVENS!
ANY REINFORCEMENTS COMING FROM AUTOBOT HEADQUARTERS?
I RAISED AN ALERT AS SOON AS I HEARD THE FIRST EXPLOSIONS--
SO WHERE ARE THEY? OMEGA SUPREME, THE AERIALBOTS...
SORRY, BUDDY...

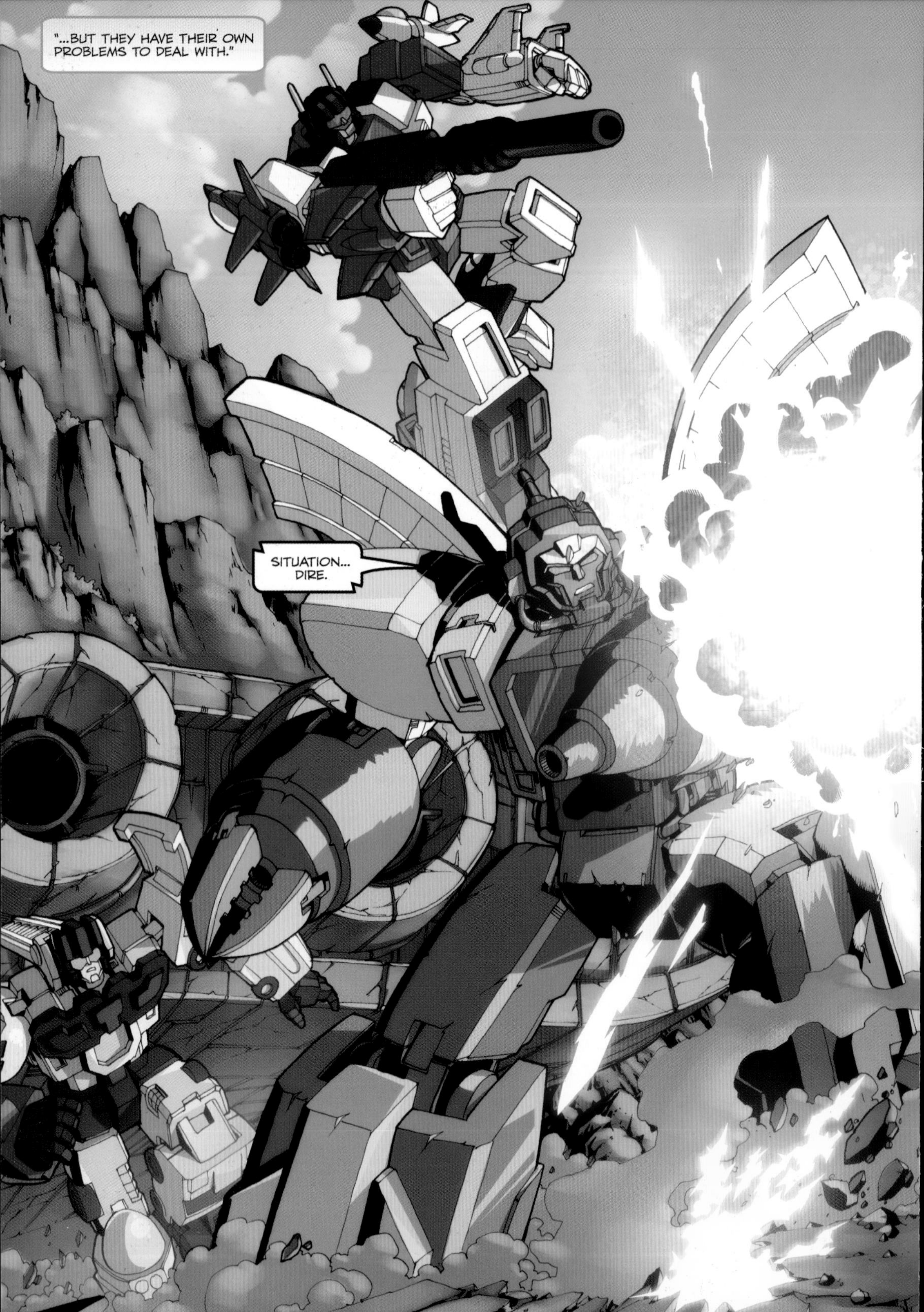
"...BUT THEY HAVE THEIR OWN PROBLEMS TO DEAL WITH."
SITUATION... DIRE.

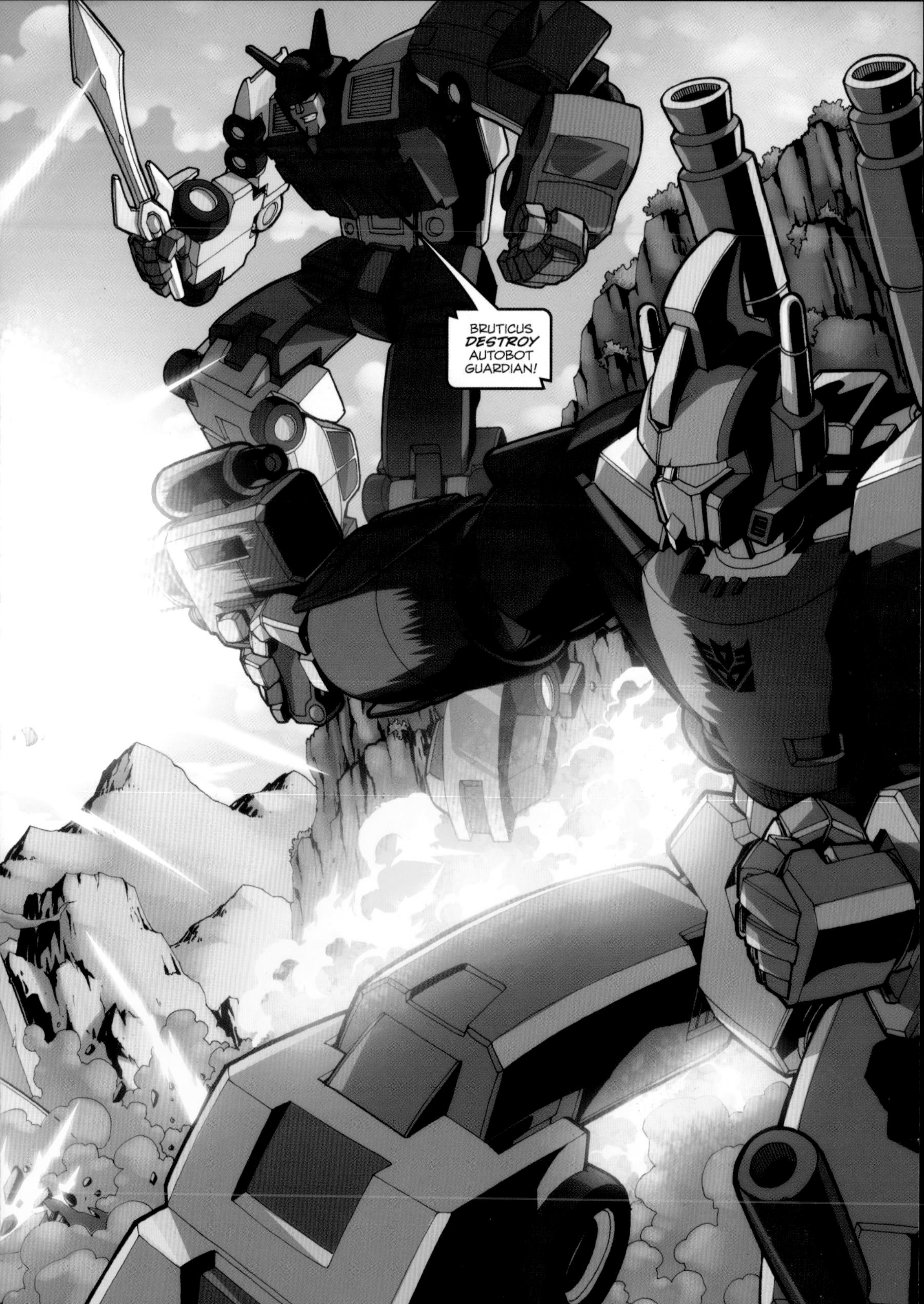
BRUTICUS DESTROY AUTOBOT GUARDIAN!

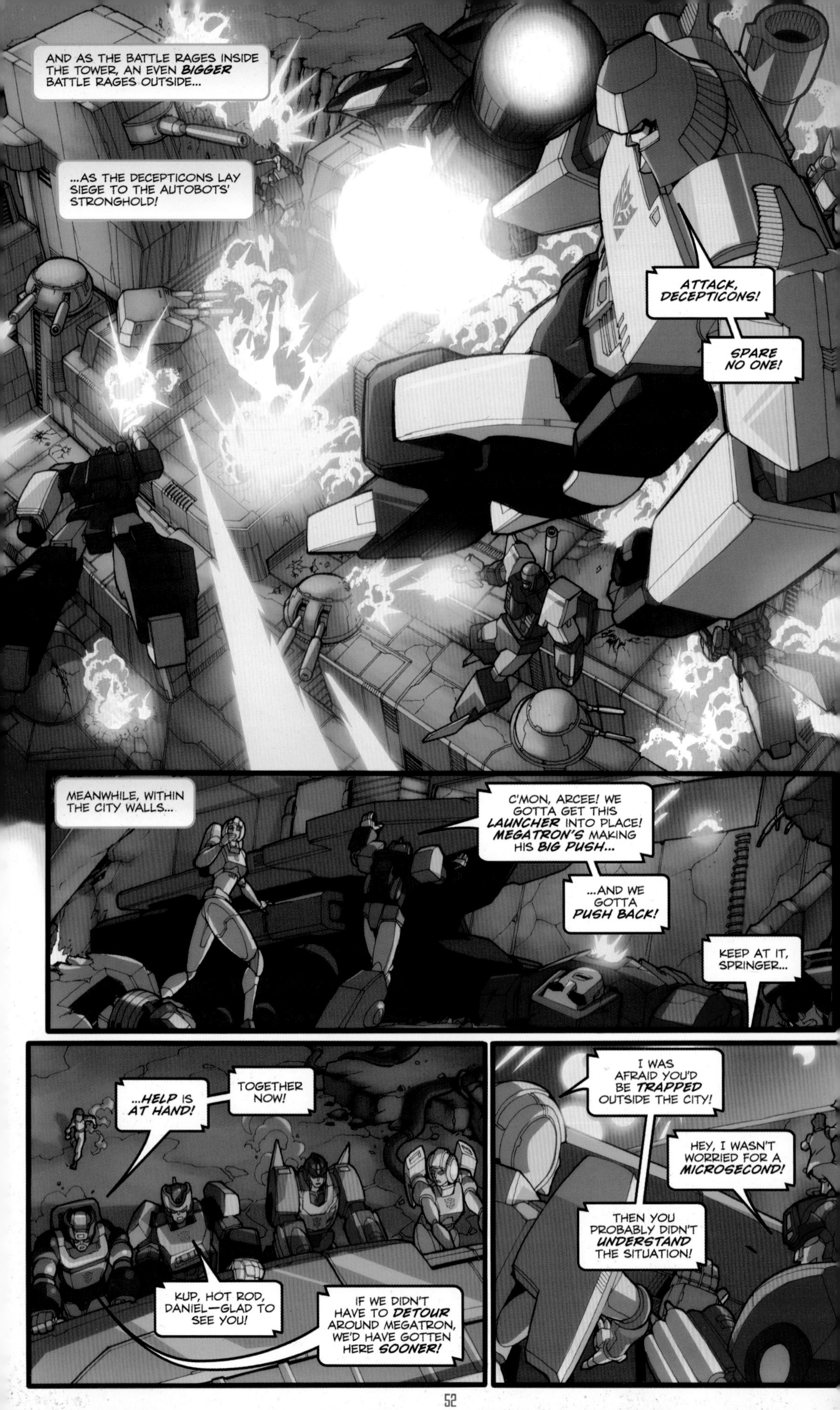

AND AS THE BATTLE RAGES INSIDE THE TOWER, AN EVEN BIGGER BATTLE RAGES OUTSIDE...
...AS THE DECEPTICONS LAY SIEGE TO THE AUTOBOTS' STRONGHOLD!
ATTACK, DECEPTICONS!
SPARE NO ONE!
MEANWHILE, WITHIN THE CITY WALLS...
C'MON, ARCEE! WE GOTTA GET THIS LAUNCHER INTO PLACE! MEGATRON'S MAKING HIS BIG PUSH...
...AND WE GOTTA PUSH BACK!
KEEP AT IT, SPRINGER...
...HELP IS AT HAND!
TOGETHER NOW!
KUP, HOT ROD, DANIEL—GLAD TO SEE YOU!
IF WE DIDN'T HAVE TO DETOUR AROUND MEGATRON, WE'D HAVE GOTTEN HERE SOONER!
I WAS AFRAID YOU'D BE TRAPPED OUTSIDE THE CITY!
HEY, I WASN'T WORRIED FOR A MICROSECOND!
THEN YOU PROBABLY DIDN'T UNDERSTAND THE SITUATION!

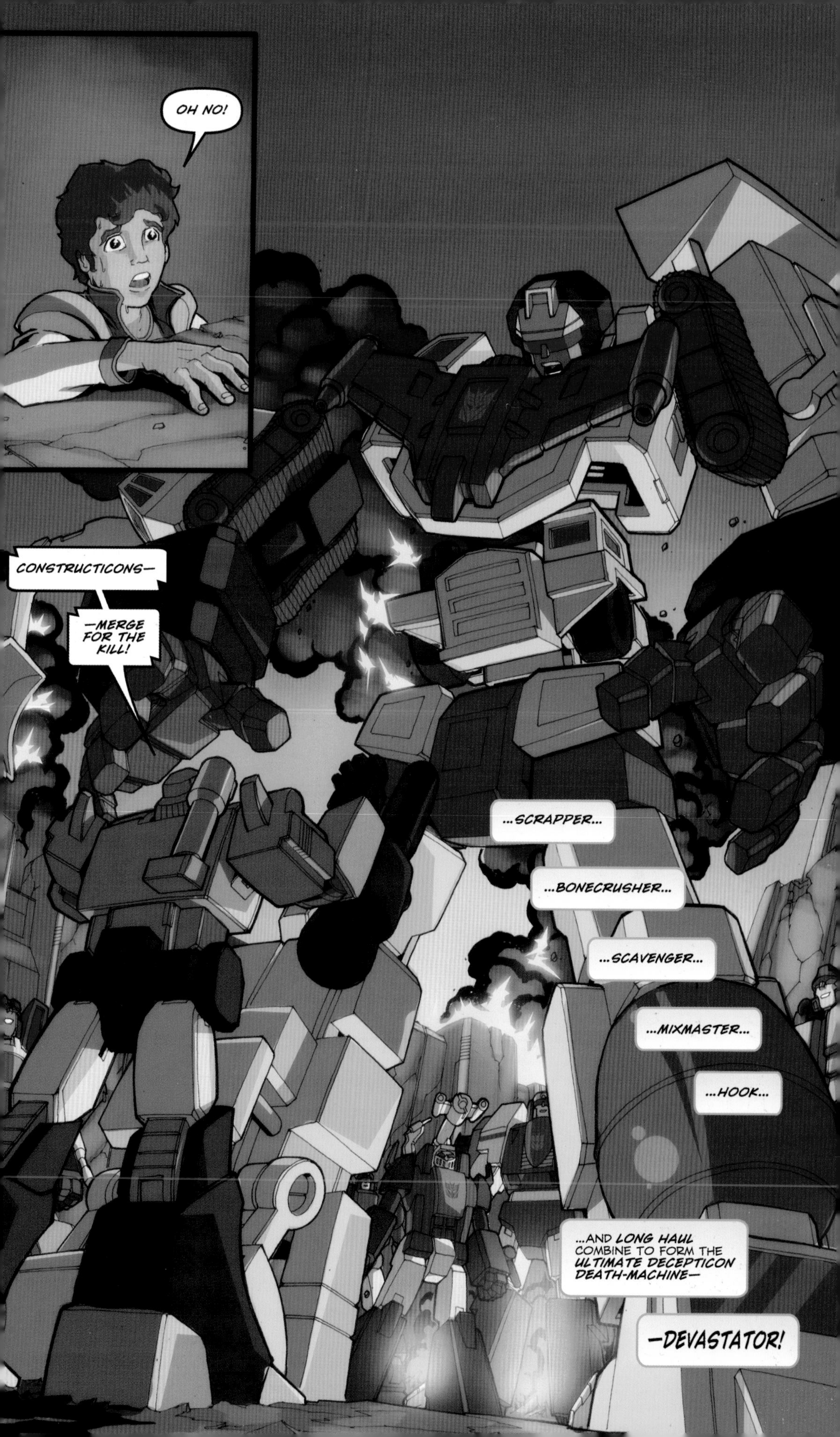
OH NO!
CONSTRUCTICONS—
—MERGE FOR THE KILL!
...SCRAPPER...
...BONECRUSHER...
...SCAVENGER...
...MIXMASTER...
...HOOK...
...AND LONG HAUL COMBINE TO FORM THE ULTIMATE DECEPTICON DEATH-MACHINE—
—DEVASTATOR!

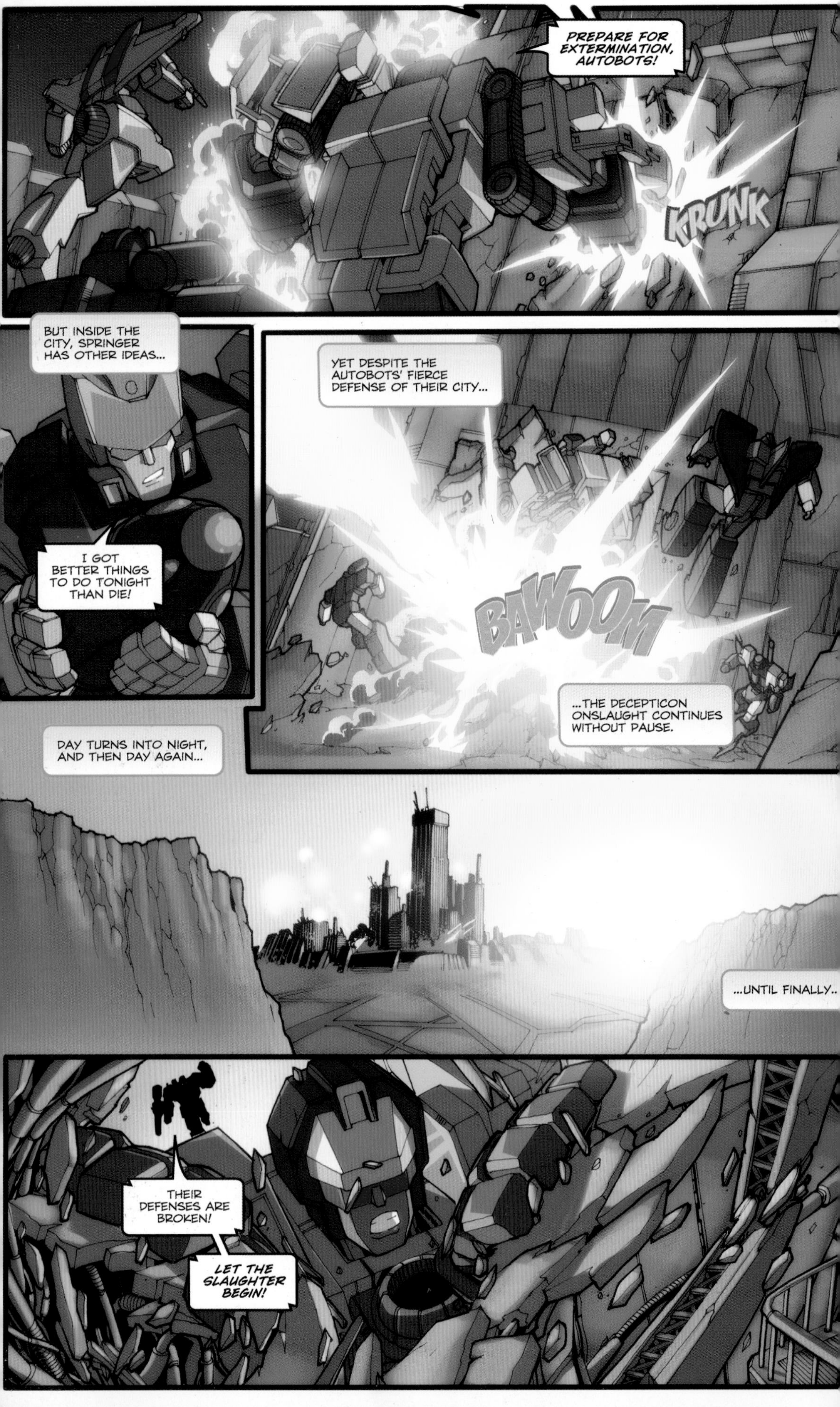
PREPARE FOR EXTERMINATION, AUTOBOTS!
KRUNK
BUT INSIDE THE CITY, SPRINGER HAS OTHER IDEAS...
I GOT BETTER THINGS TO DO TONIGHT THAN DIE!
YET DESPITE THE AUTOBOTS' FIERCE DEFENSE OF THEIR CITY...
BAWOOM
...THE DECEPTICON ONSLAUGHT CONTINUES WITHOUT PAUSE.
DAY TURNS INTO NIGHT, AND THEN DAY AGAIN...
...UNTIL FINALLY...
THEIR DEFENSES ARE BROKEN!
LET THE SLAUGHTER BEGIN!

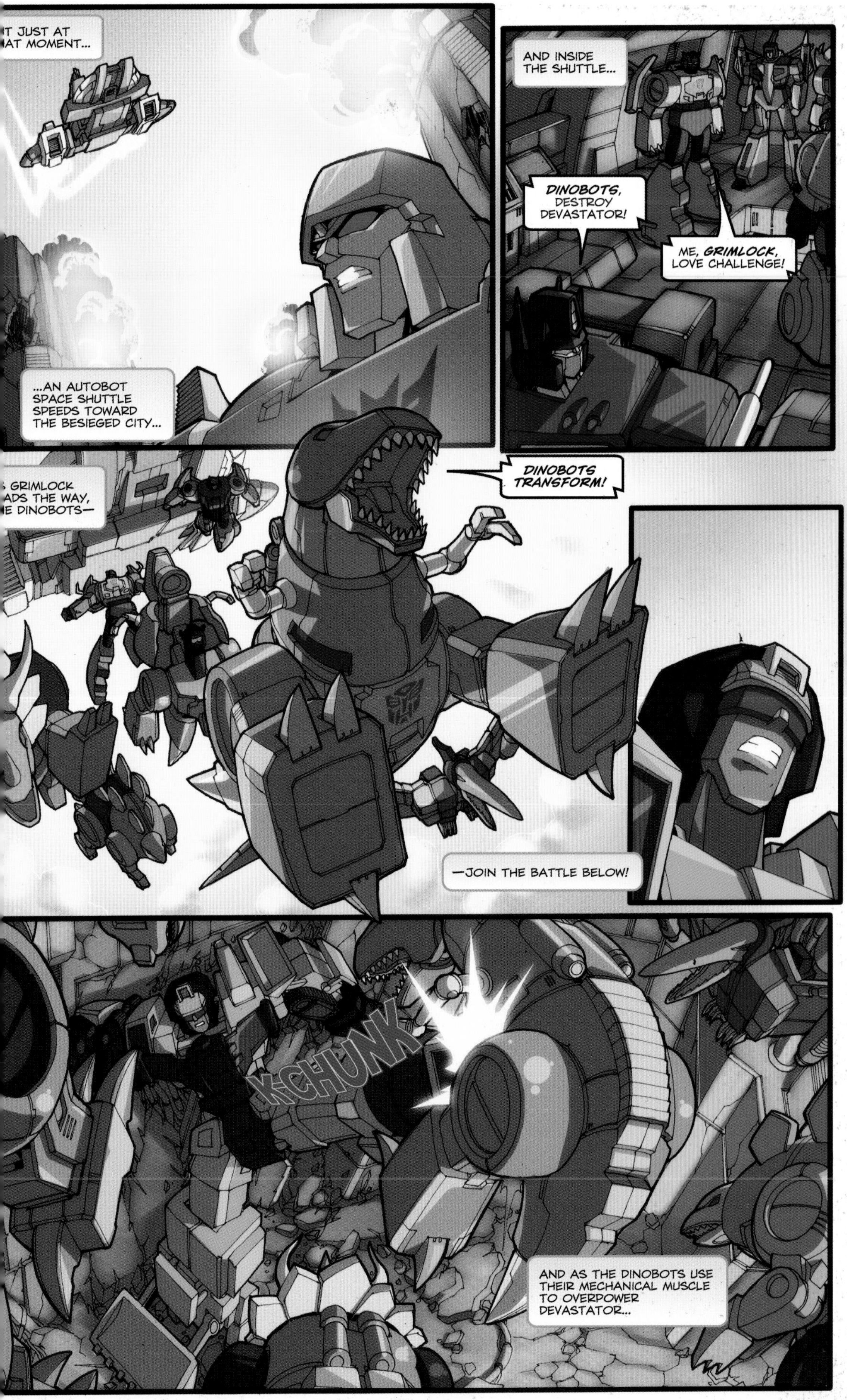
T JUST AT
AT MOMENT...
...AN AUTOBOT SPACE SHUTTLE SPEEDS TOWARD THE BESIEGED CITY...
AND INSIDE THE SHUTTLE...
DINOBOTS, DESTROY DEVASTATOR!
ME, GRIMLOCK, LOVE CHALLENGE!
S GRIMLOCK
ADS THE WAY,
E DINOBOTS—
DINOBOTS TRANSFORM!
—JOIN THE BATTLE BELOW!
K-CHUNK
AND AS THE DINOBOTS USE THEIR MECHANICAL MUSCLE TO OVERPOWER DEVASTATOR...

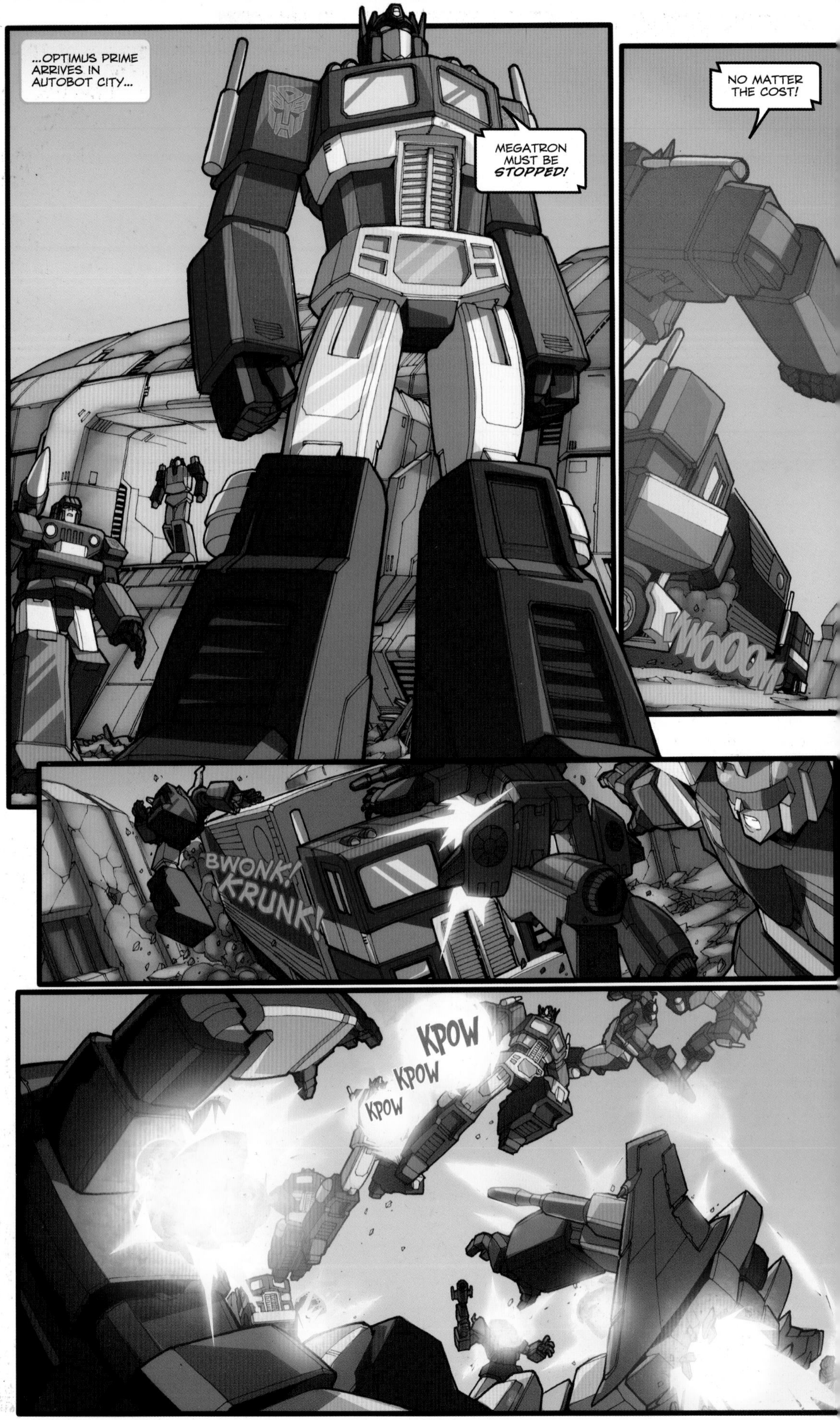
...OPTIMUS PRIME ARRIVES IN AUTOBOT CITY...
MEGATRON MUST BE STOPPED!
NO MATTER THE COST!
VWOOOM
BWONK!
KRUNK!
KPOW
KPOW
KPOW

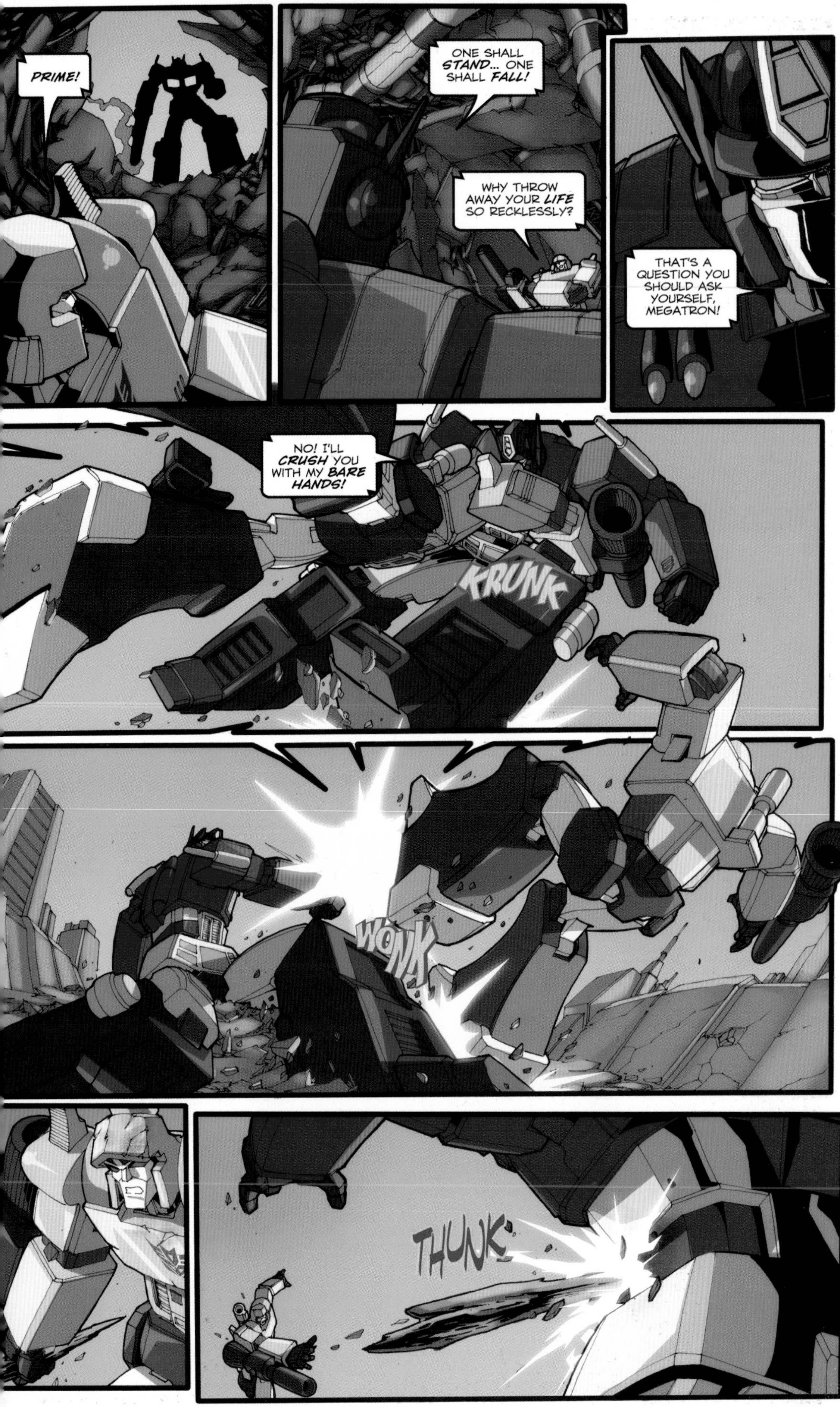
PRIME!
ONE SHALL STAND... ONE SHALL FALL!
WHY THROW AWAY YOUR LIFE SO RECKLESSLY?
THAT'S A QUESTION YOU SHOULD ASK YOURSELF, MEGATRON!
NO! I'LL CRUSH YOU WITH MY BARE HANDS!
KRUNK
WONK
THUNK

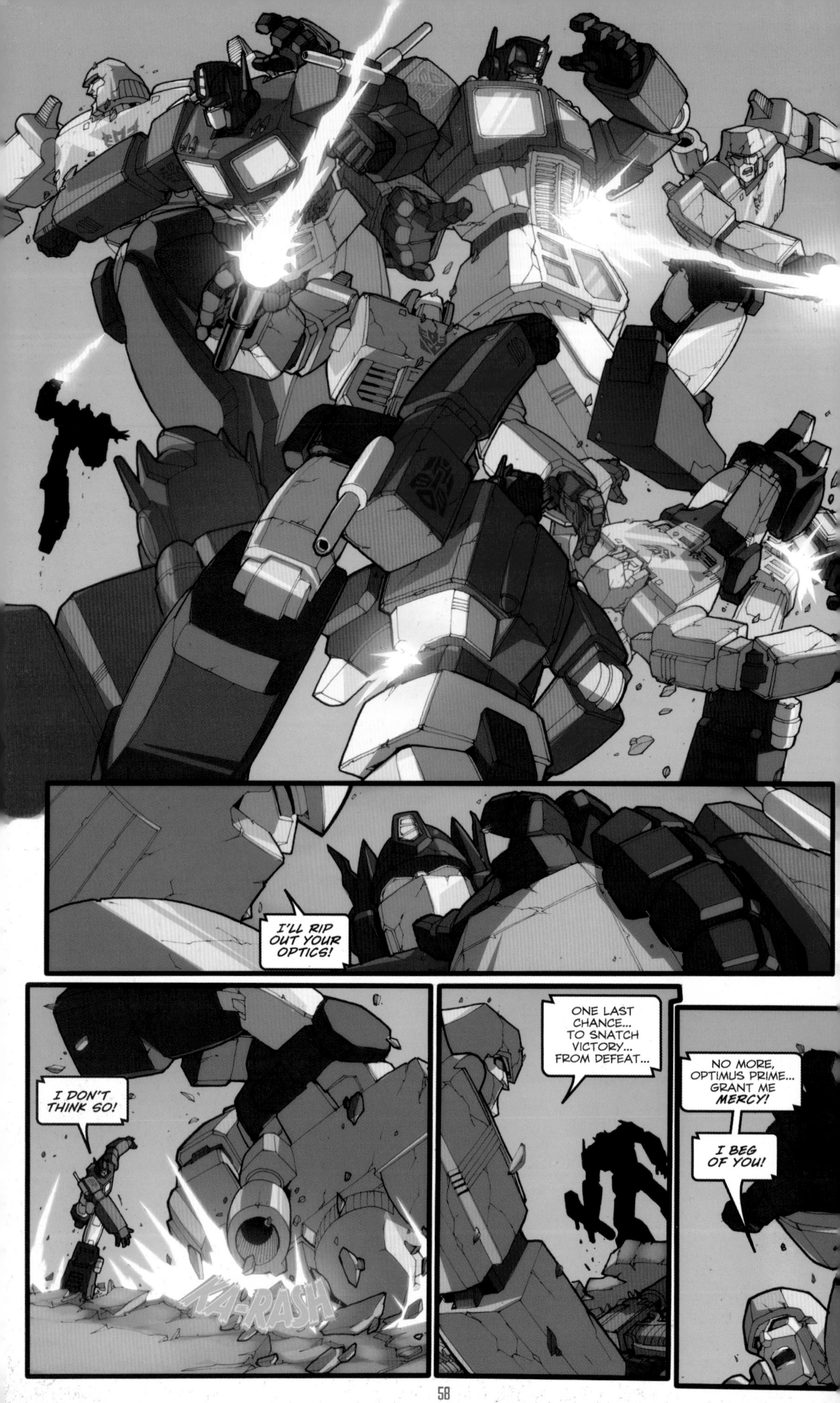

I'LL RIP OUT YOUR OPTICS!
I DON'T THINK SO!
KA-RASH
ONE LAST CHANCE... TO SNATCH VICTORY... FROM DEFEAT...
NO MORE, OPTIMUS PRIME... GRANT ME MERCY!
I BEG OF YOU!

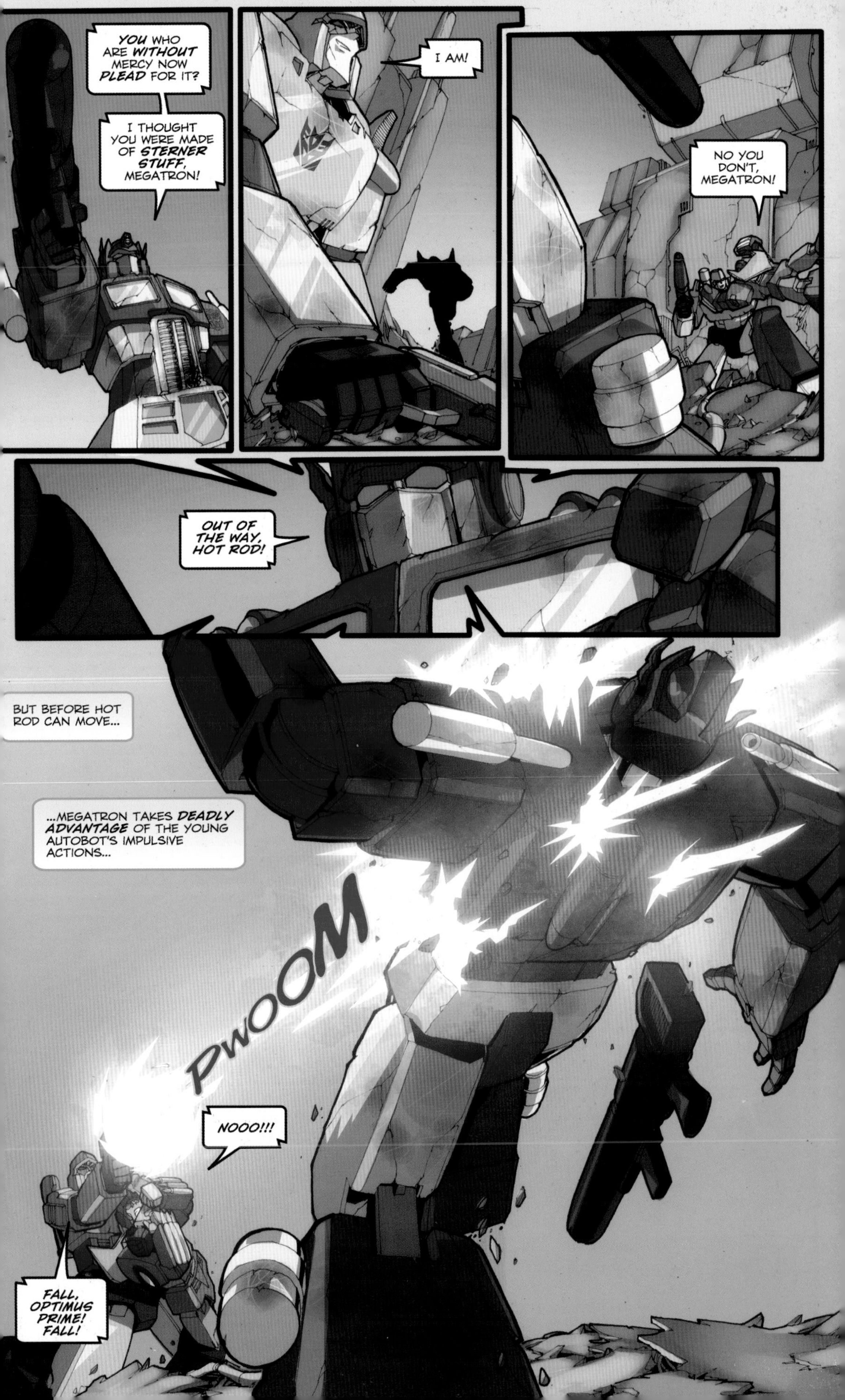
YOU WHO ARE WITHOUT MERCY NOW PLEAD FOR IT?
I THOUGHT YOU WERE MADE OF STERNER STUFF, MEGATRON!
I AM!
NO YOU DON'T, MEGATRON!
OUT OF THE WAY, HOT ROD!
BUT BEFORE HOT ROD CAN MOVE...
...MEGATRON TAKES DEADLY ADVANTAGE OF THE YOUNG AUTOBOT'S IMPULSIVE ACTIONS...
PWOOM
NOOO!!!
FALL, OPTIMUS PRIME! FALL!

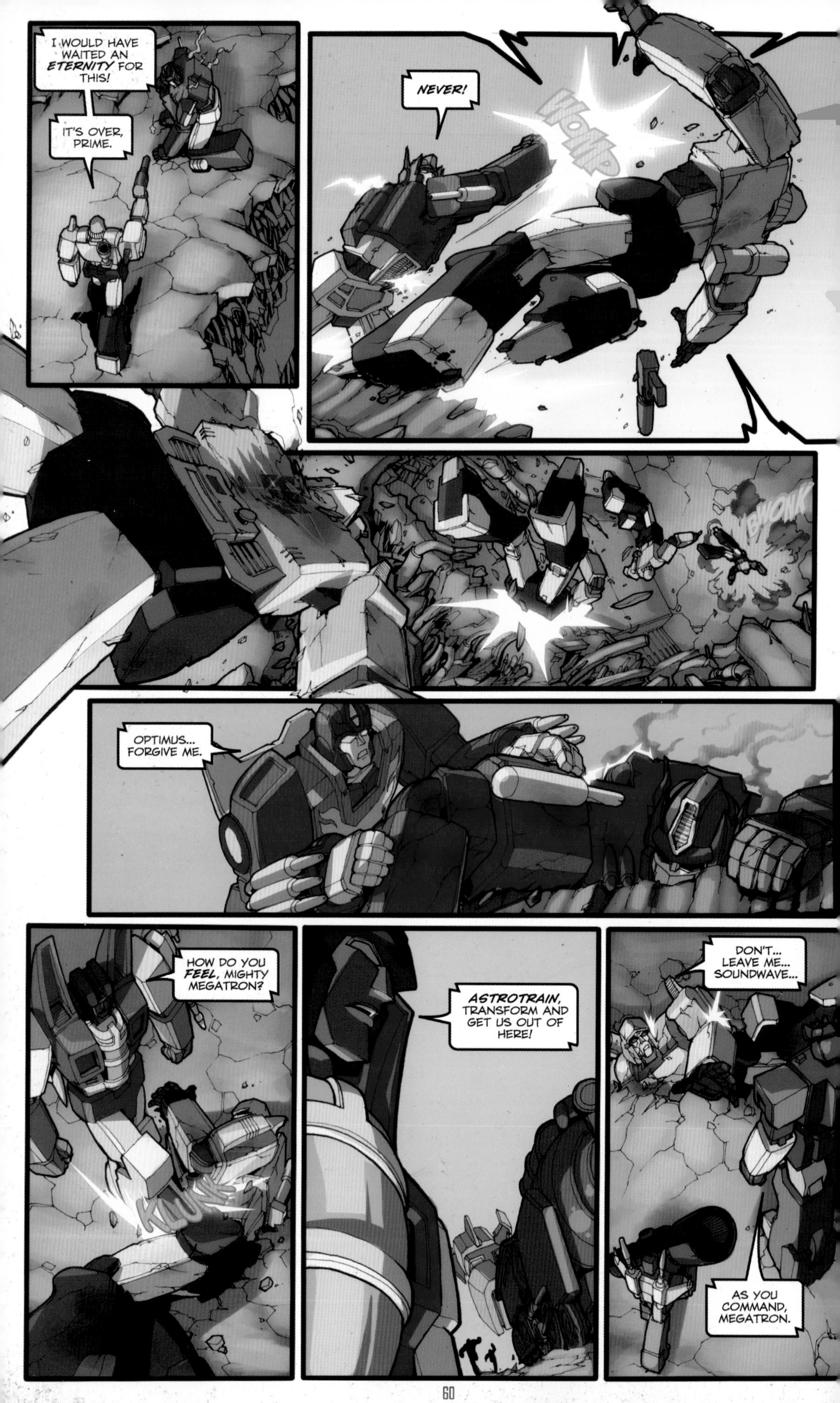
I WOULD HAVE WAITED AN *ETERNITY* FOR THIS!
IT'S OVER, PRIME.
NEVER!
WOMP
BWONK
OPTIMUS... FORGIVE ME.
HOW DO YOU *FEEL*, MIGHTY MEGATRON?
KLUNK
ASTROTRAIN, TRANSFORM AND GET US OUT OF HERE!
DON'T... LEAVE ME... SOUNDWAVE...
AS YOU COMMAND, MEGATRON.

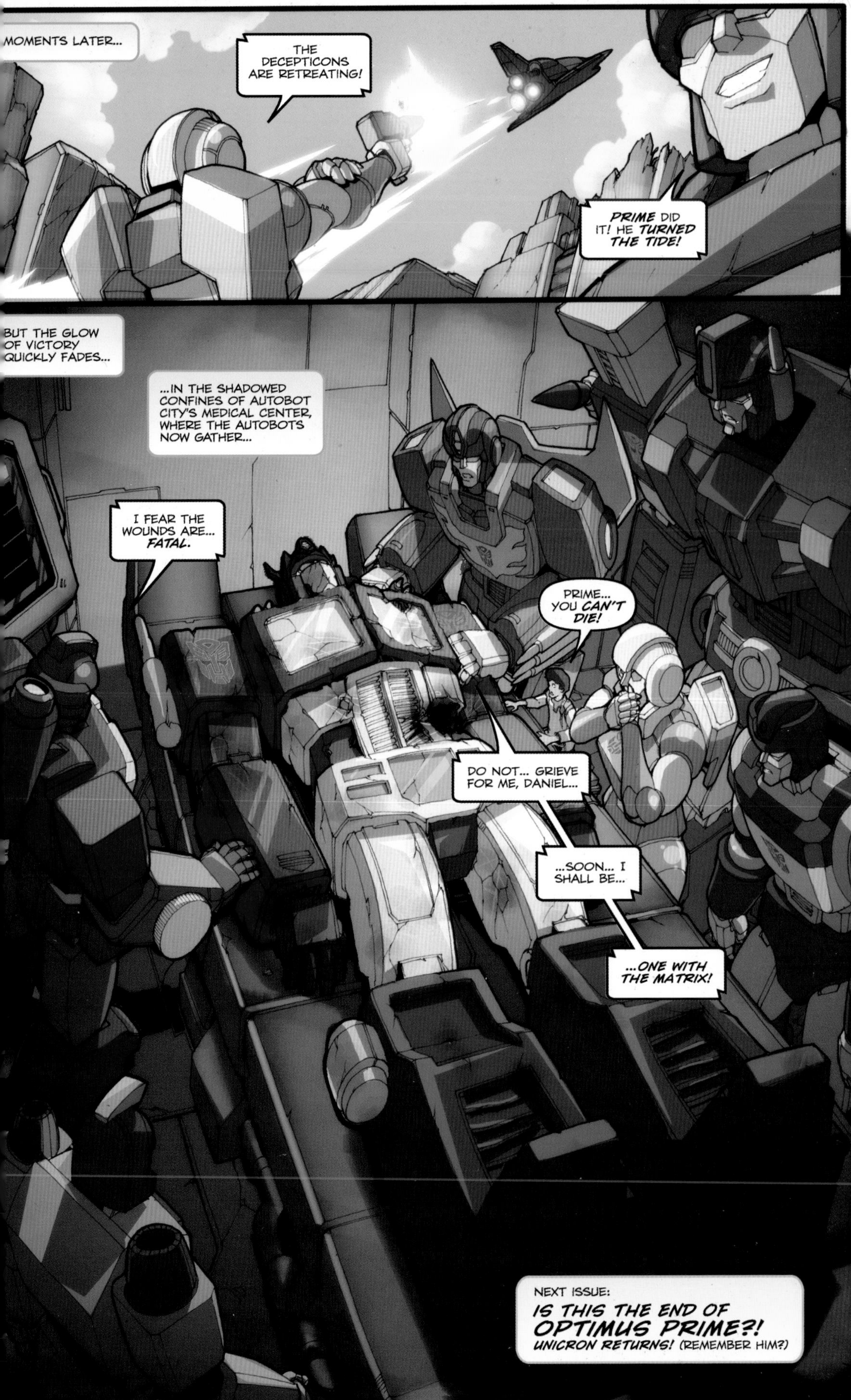

MOMENTS LATER...
THE DECEPTICONS ARE RETREATING!
PRIME DID IT! HE TURNED THE TIDE!
BUT THE GLOW OF VICTORY QUICKLY FADES...
...IN THE SHADOWED CONFINES OF AUTOBOT CITY'S MEDICAL CENTER, WHERE THE AUTOBOTS NOW GATHER...
I FEAR THE WOUNDS ARE... FATAL.
PRIME... YOU CAN'T DIE!
DO NOT... GRIEVE FOR ME, DANIEL...
...SOON... I SHALL BE...
...ONE WITH THE MATRIX!
NEXT ISSUE:
IS THIS THE END OF OPTIMUS PRIME?!
UNICRON RETURNS! (REMEMBER HIM?)

THE TRANSFORMERS
THE BEST OF OPTIMUS PRIME

THE WAR WITHIN #1

Taking things to a different level, Dreamwave assumed the TRANSFORMERS license and amidst the Generation One retelling—inspiring the REVOLTECH TRANSFORMERS line—deciding to bring a darker and much different perspective to the beginning of the Great War, and the ascension of PRIME to leadership.

One of the best things about this book, and a reason it was selected for this series, was the radically different take on PRIME's persona before assuming the mantle. This was the first time we saw a PRIME that wasn't a natural born leader, and had to learn who he really was in the midst of battle.

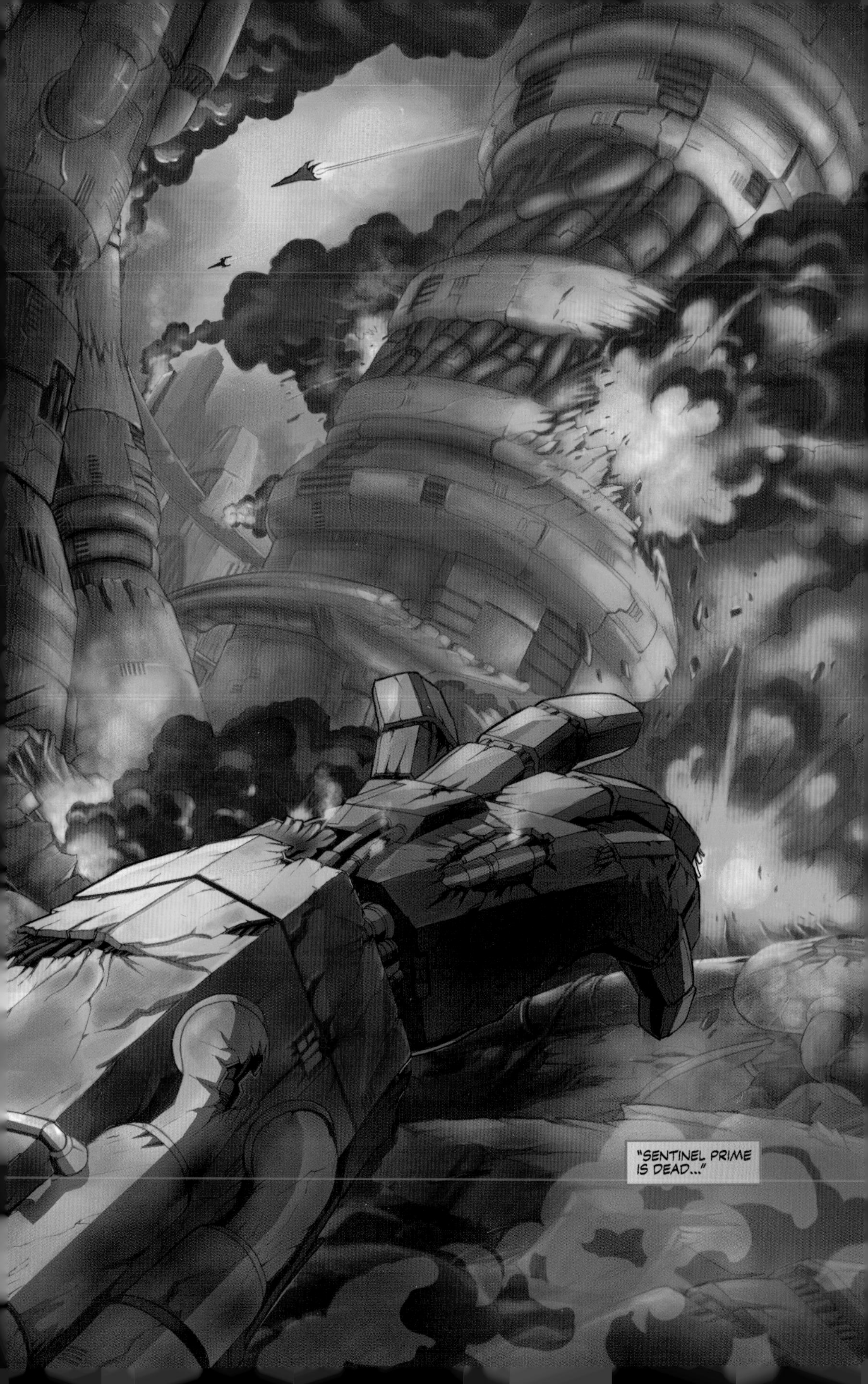
"SENTINEL PRIME IS DEAD..."

CYBERTRON, HUB CAPITAL IACON:

THE HIGH COUNCIL PAVILIONS:

THEY SAY *MEGATRON* HIMSELF *RIPPED* THE *SPARK CORE* FROM HIS SHATTERED TORSO.

THE VAULTS:

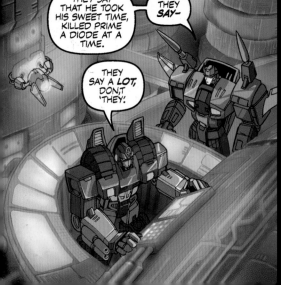

THEY SAY THAT HE TOOK HIS SWEET TIME, KILLED PRIME A DIODE AT A TIME.

THEY *SAY*—

THEY SAY A *LOT,* DON,T 'THEY!

I'M TRYING TO WORK HERE, *BLUESTREAK.* I HAVE SIXTY-THREE DATAFEEDS TO INPUT, WITH MORE INCOMING ON FIVE BREEM PULSES.

IF YOU BELIEVE EVERY EYE-WITNESS REPORT, MEGATRON HAS *PERSONALLY* DEVASTATED SIXTEEN PROVINCES AND ASSASSINATED THIRTY RANKING CUSTODIANS. ALL IN THE TIME IT'S TAKEN YOU TO TELL ME ABOUT SENTINEL PRIME.

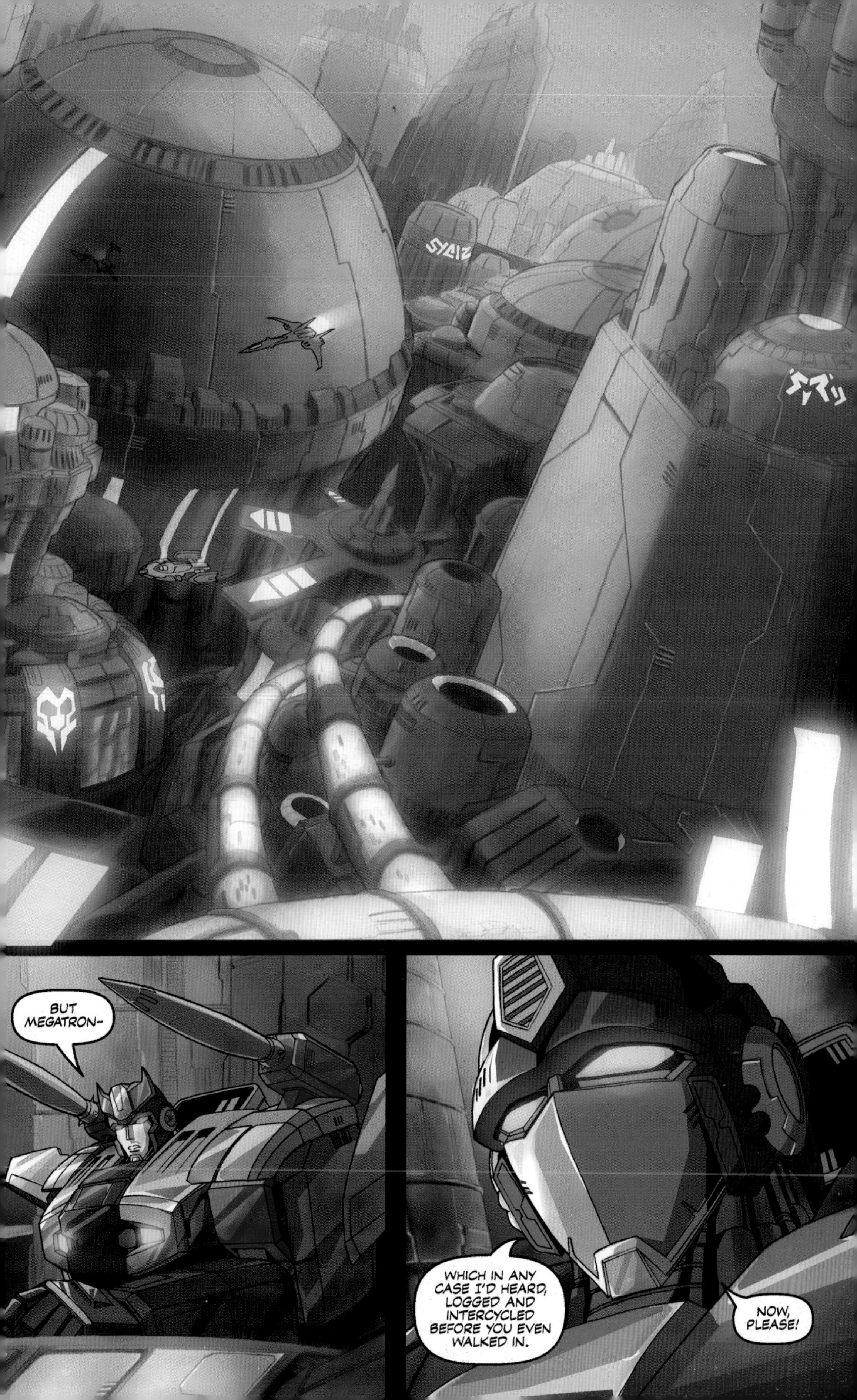
BUT MEGATRON-
WHICH IN ANY CASE I'D HEARD, LOGGED AND INTERCYCLED BEFORE YOU EVEN WALKED IN.
NOW, PLEASE!

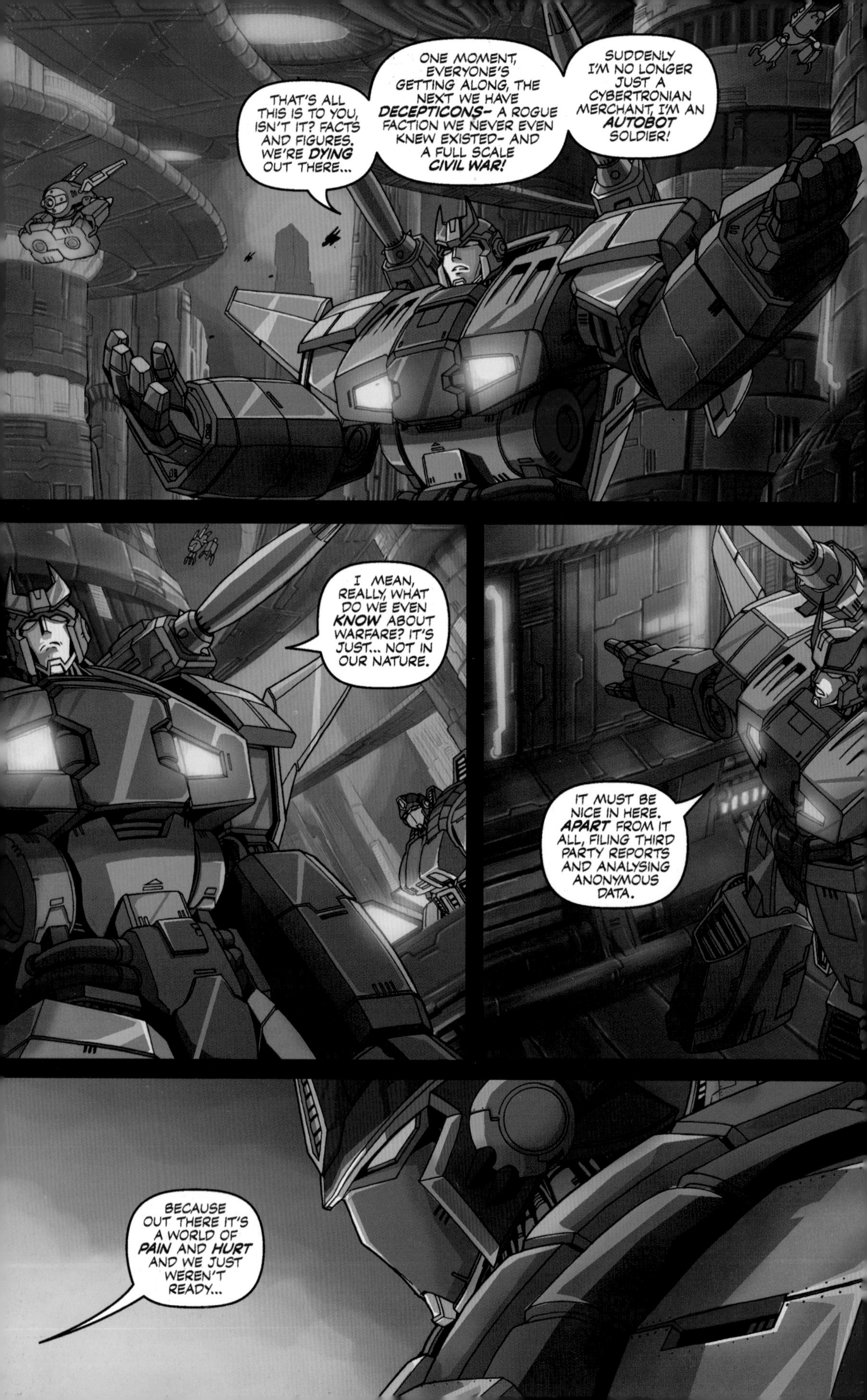
THAT'S ALL THIS IS TO YOU, ISN'T IT? FACTS AND FIGURES. WE'RE DYING OUT THERE...
ONE MOMENT, EVERYONE'S GETTING ALONG, THE NEXT WE HAVE DECEPTICONS- A ROGUE FACTION WE NEVER EVEN KNEW EXISTED- AND A FULL SCALE CIVIL WAR!
SUDDENLY I'M NO LONGER JUST A CYBERTRONIAN MERCHANT, I'M AN AUTOBOT SOLDIER!
I MEAN, REALLY, WHAT DO WE EVEN KNOW ABOUT WARFARE? IT'S JUST... NOT IN OUR NATURE.
IT MUST BE NICE IN HERE. APART FROM IT ALL, FILING THIRD PARTY REPORTS AND ANALYSING ANONYMOUS DATA.
BECAUSE OUT THERE IT'S A WORLD OF PAIN AND HURT AND WE JUST WEREN'T READY...

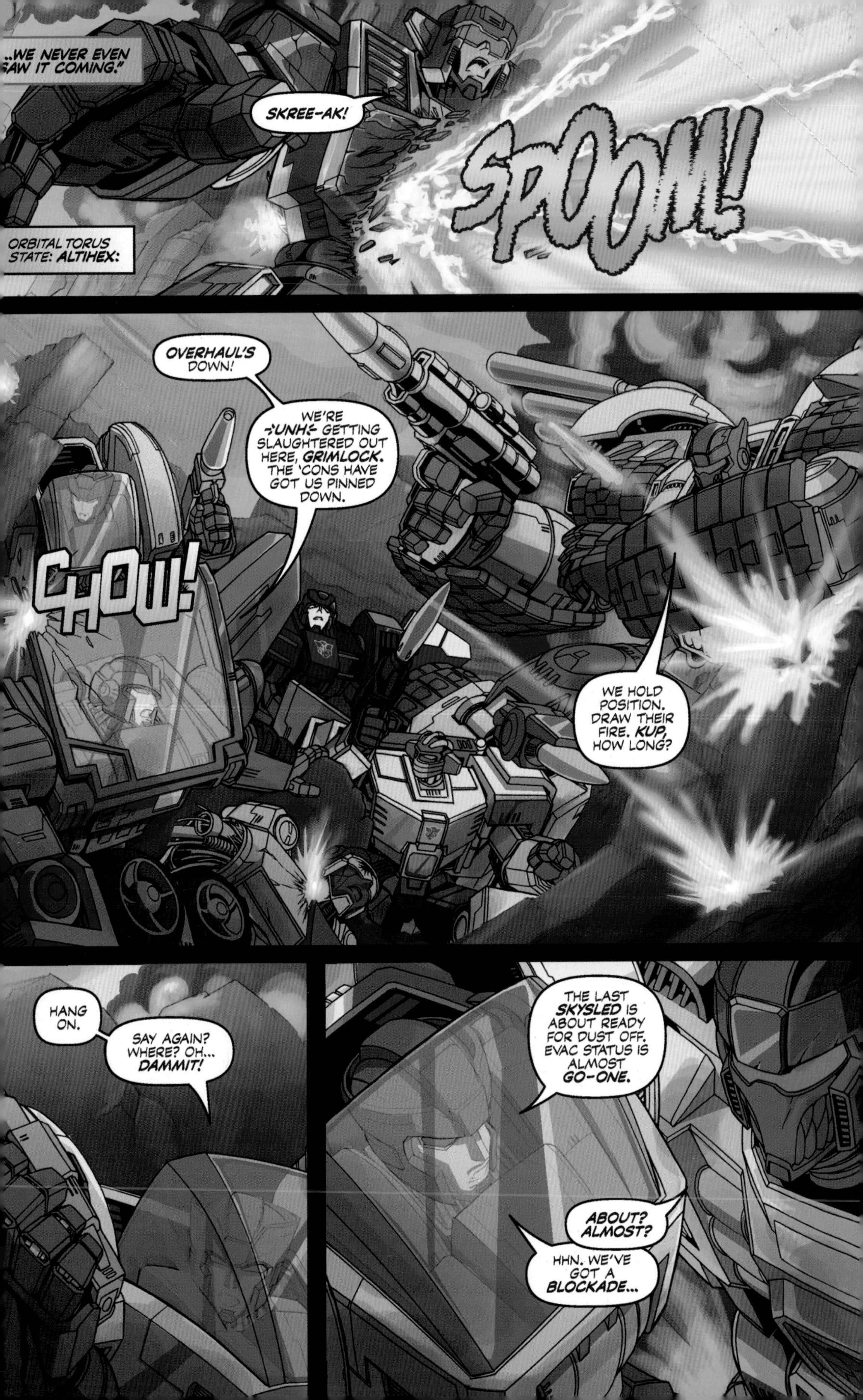

..WE NEVER EVEN SAW IT COMING."
SKREE-AK!
SPOOM!
ORBITAL TORUS STATE: ALTIHEX:
OVERHAUL'S DOWN!
WE'RE -UNH- GETTING SLAUGHTERED OUT HERE, GRIMLOCK. THE 'CONS HAVE GOT US PINNED DOWN.
CHOW!
WE HOLD POSITION. DRAW THEIR FIRE. KUP, HOW LONG?
HANG ON.
SAY AGAIN? WHERE? OH... DAMMIT!
THE LAST SKYSLED IS ABOUT READY FOR DUST OFF. EVAC STATUS IS ALMOST GO-ONE.
ABOUT? ALMOST?
HHN. WE'VE GOT A BLOCKADE...

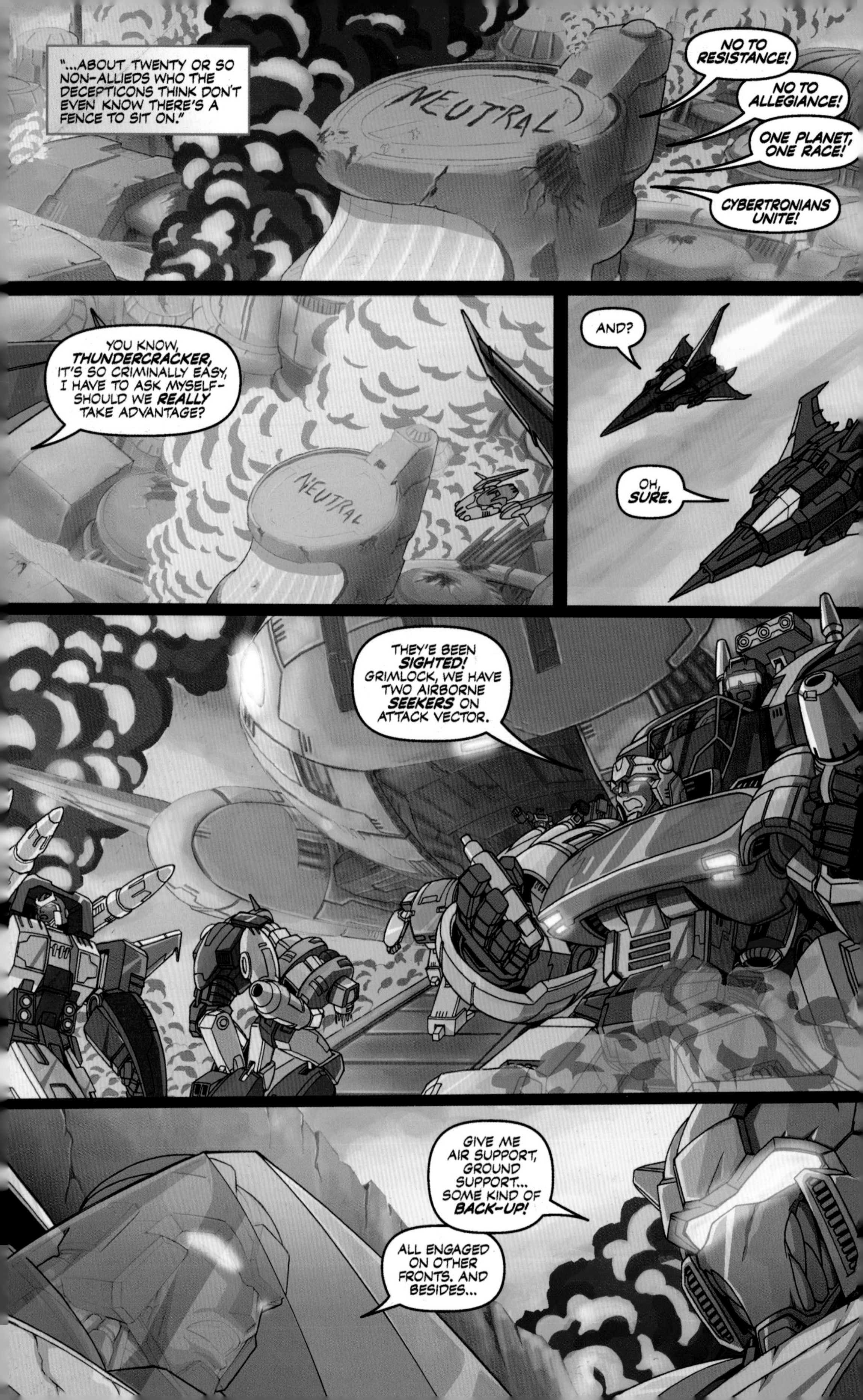
"...ABOUT TWENTY OR SO NON-ALLIEDS WHO THE DECEPTICONS THINK DON'T EVEN KNOW THERE'S A FENCE TO SIT ON."
NEUTRAL
NO TO RESISTANCE!
NO TO ALLEGIANCE!
ONE PLANET, ONE RACE!
CYBERTRONIANS UNITE!
YOU KNOW, THUNDERCRACKER, IT'S SO CRIMINALLY EASY, I HAVE TO ASK MYSELF-SHOULD WE REALLY TAKE ADVANTAGE?
NEUTRAL
AND?
OH, SURE.
THEY'VE BEEN SIGHTED! GRIMLOCK, WE HAVE TWO AIRBORNE SEEKERS ON ATTACK VECTOR.
GIVE ME AIR SUPPORT, GROUND SUPPORT... SOME KIND OF BACK-UP!
ALL ENGAGED ON OTHER FRONTS. AND BESIDES...

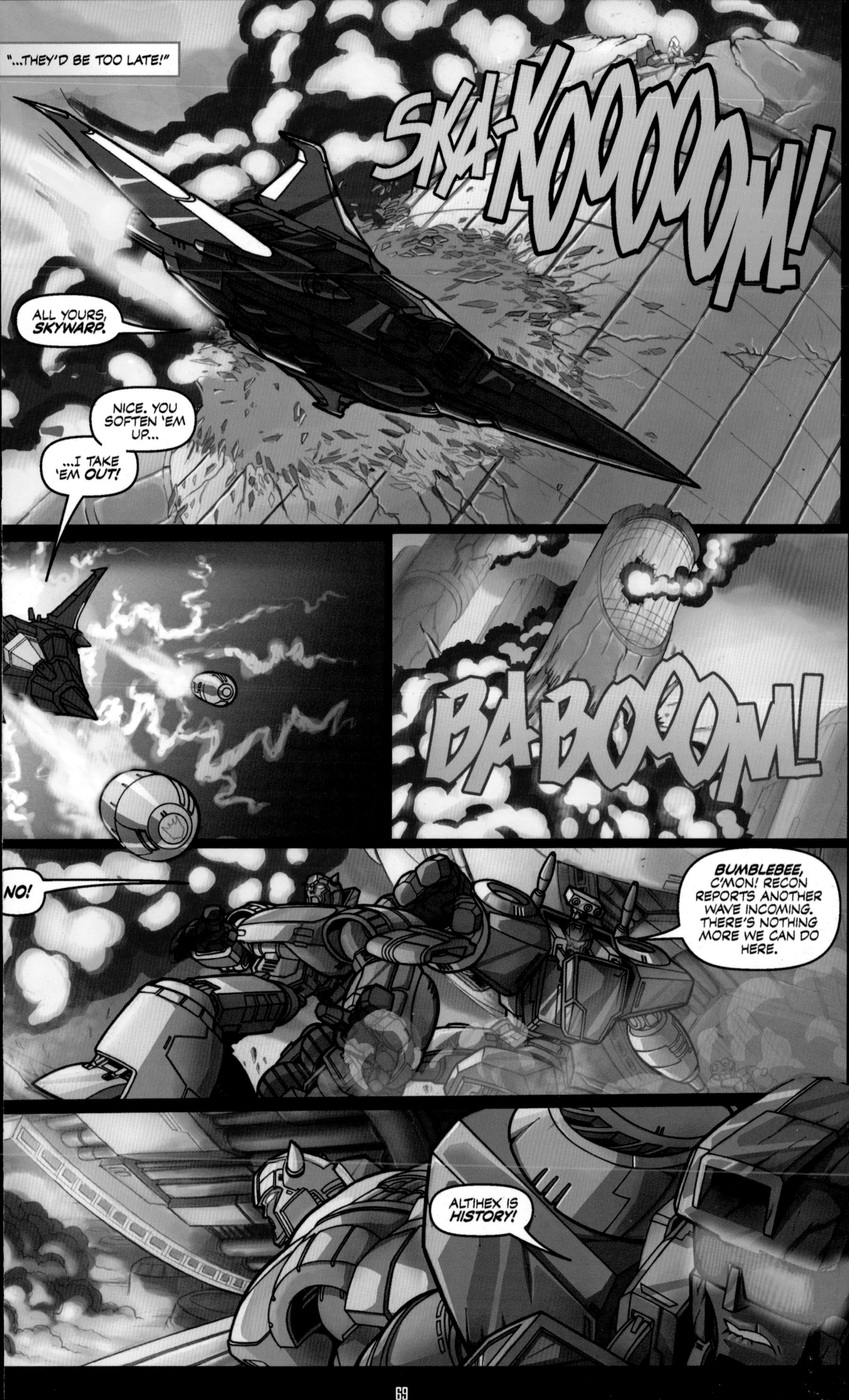

"...THEY'D BE TOO LATE!"
SKA-KOOOOOM!
ALL YOURS, SKYWARP.
NICE. YOU SOFTEN 'EM UP...
...I TAKE 'EM OUT!
BA-BOOOM!
NO!
BUMBLEBEE, C'MON! RECON REPORTS ANOTHER WAVE INCOMING. THERE'S NOTHING MORE WE CAN DO HERE.
ALTIHEX IS HISTORY!

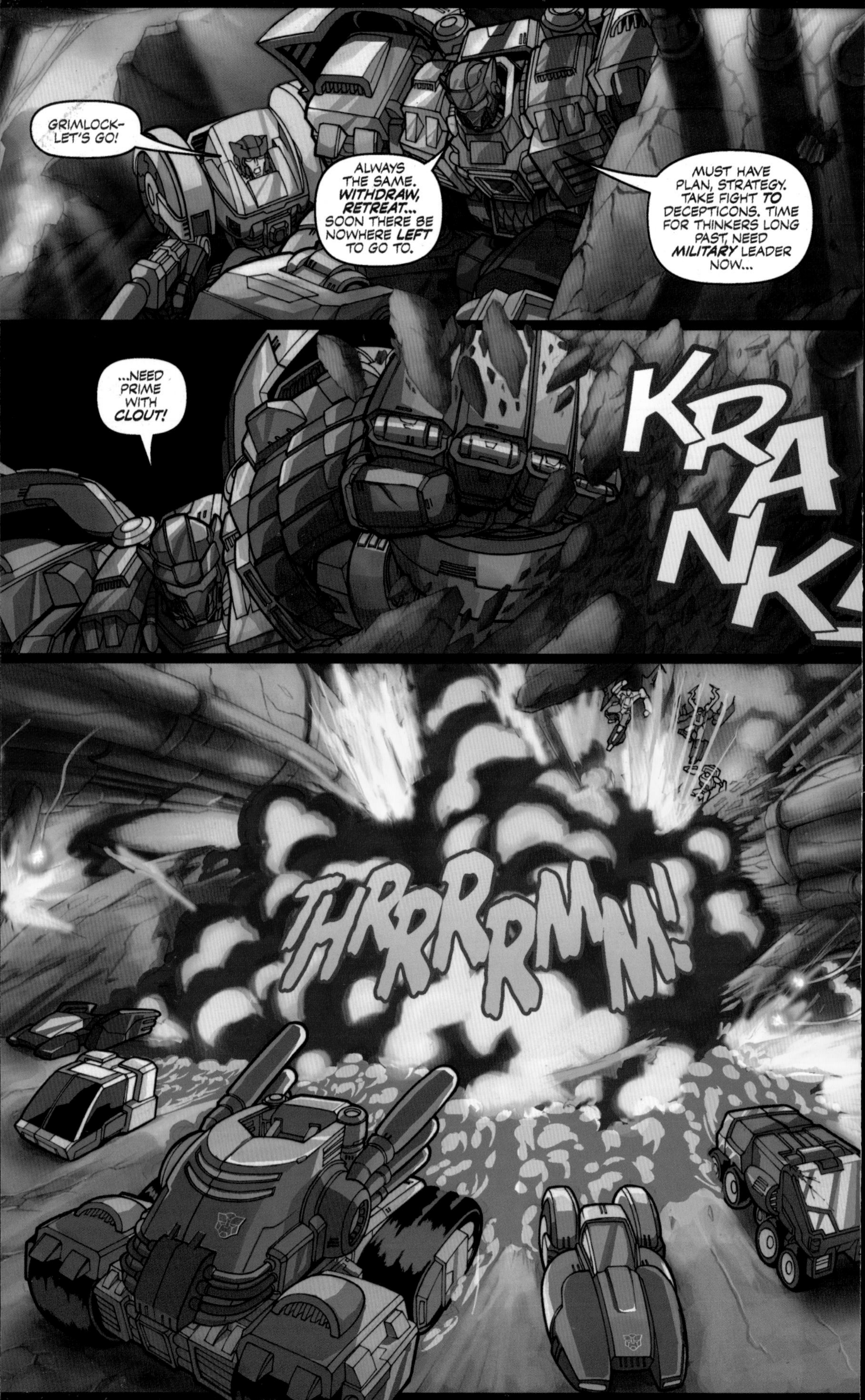
GRIMLOCK--LET'S GO!
ALWAYS THE SAME. WITHDRAW, RETREAT... SOON THERE BE NOWHERE LEFT TO GO TO.
MUST HAVE PLAN, STRATEGY. TAKE FIGHT TO DECEPTICONS. TIME FOR THINKERS LONG PAST, NEED MILITARY LEADER NOW...
...NEED PRIME WITH CLOUT!
KRANK!
THRRRMMM!

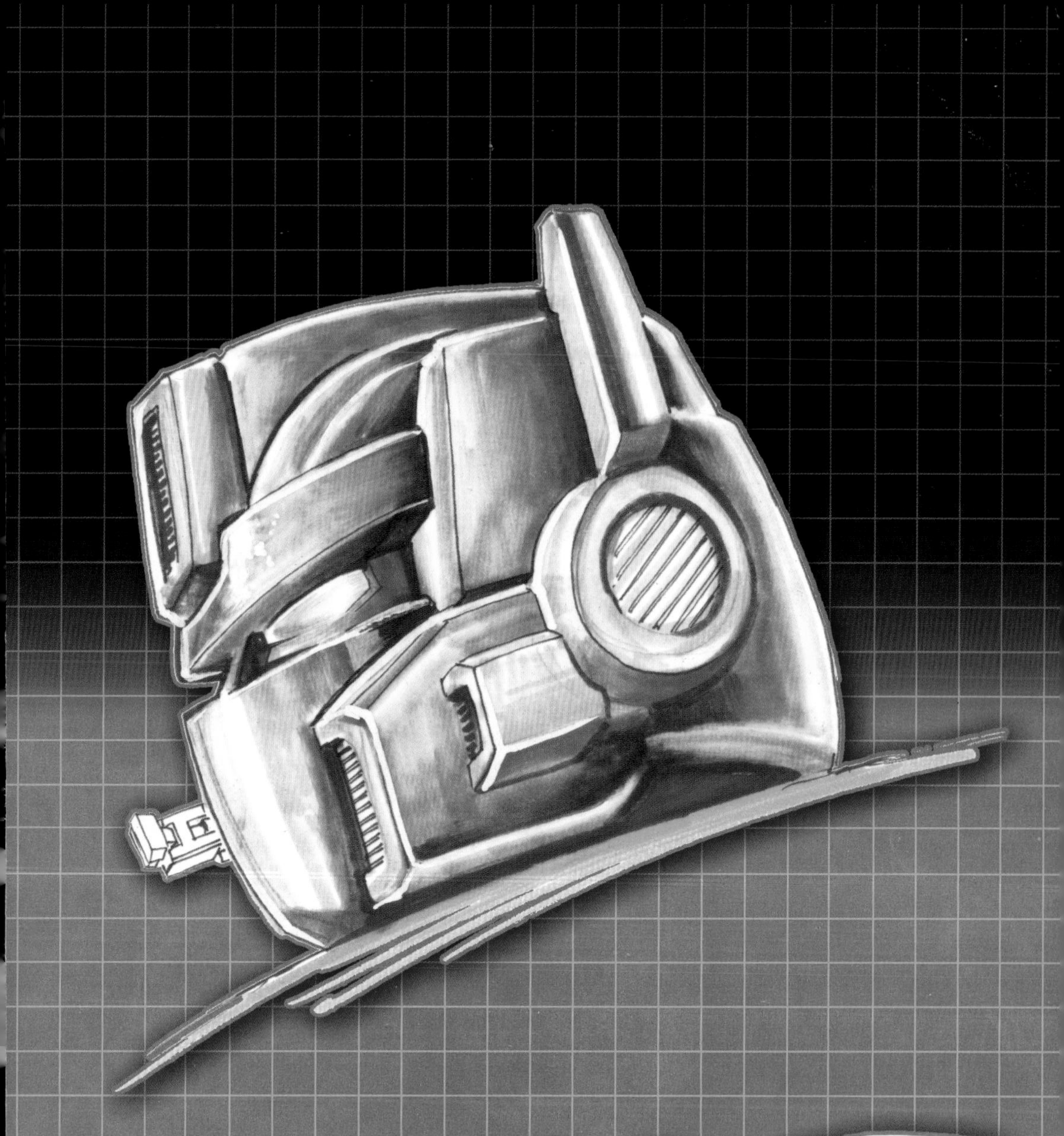

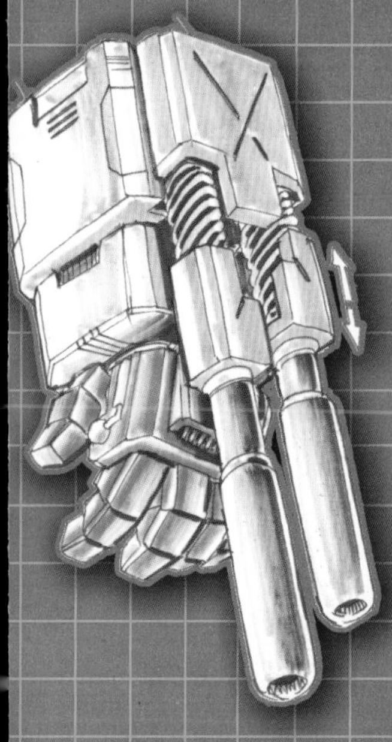

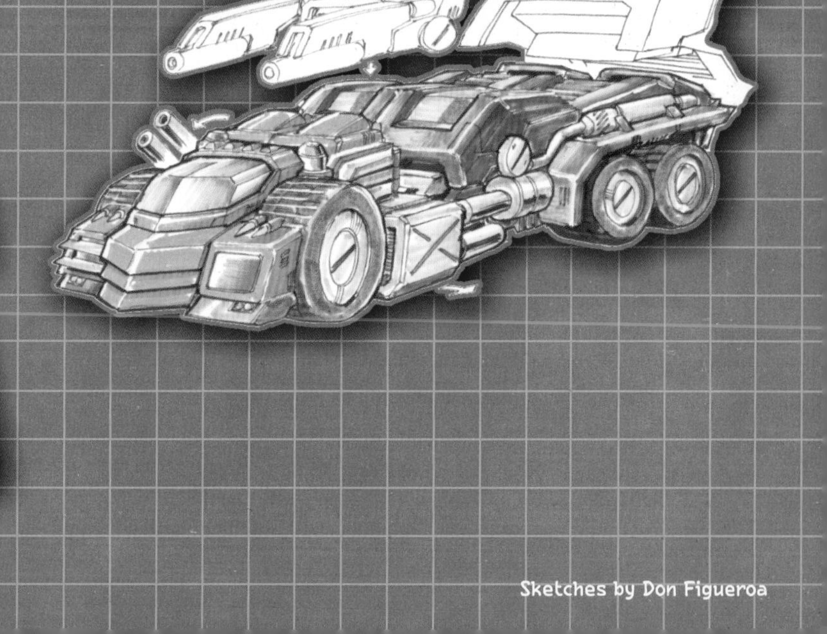

Sketches by Don Figueroa

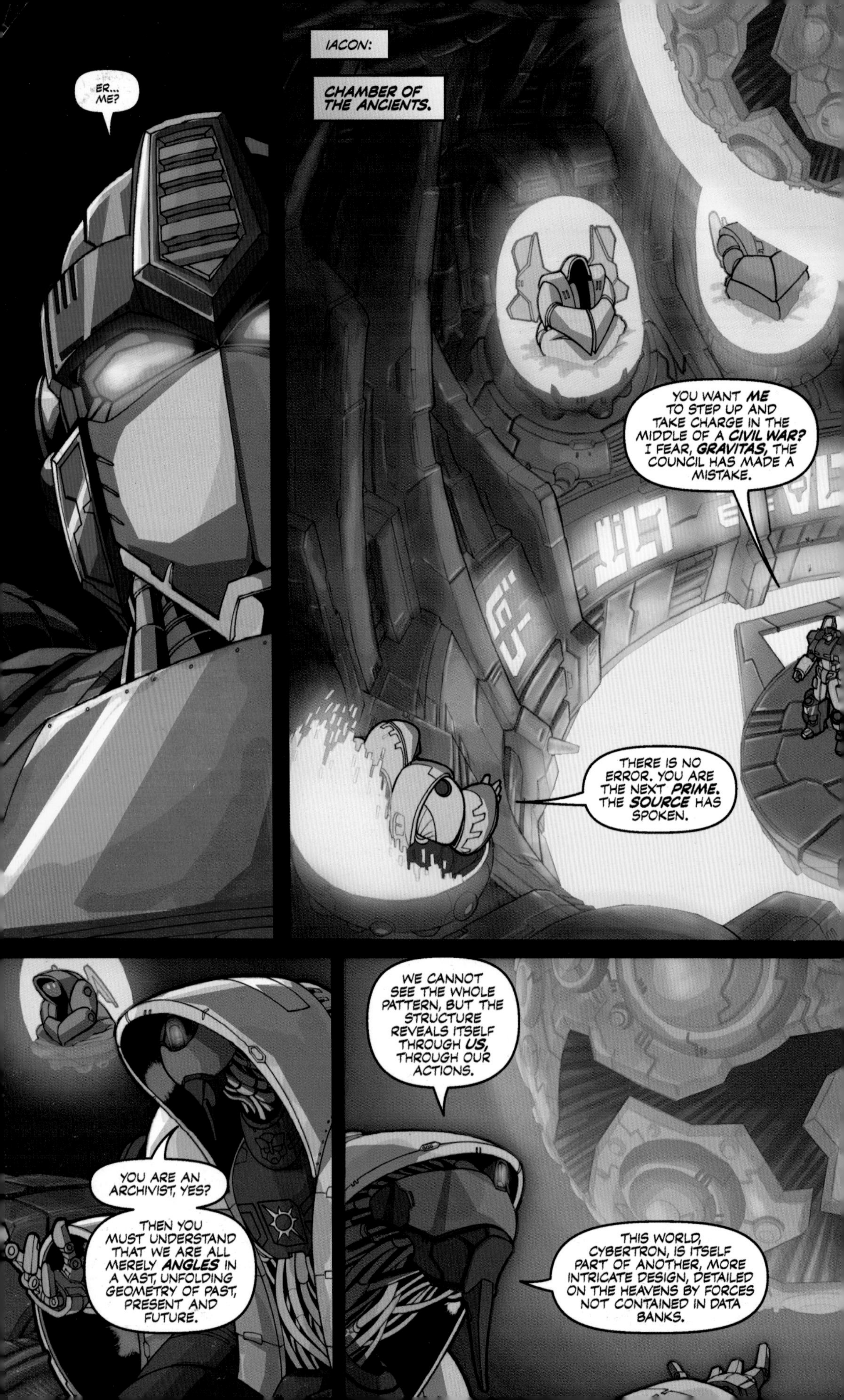
ER... ME?
IACON:
CHAMBER OF THE ANCIENTS.
YOU WANT ME TO STEP UP AND TAKE CHARGE IN THE MIDDLE OF A CIVIL WAR? I FEAR, GRAVITAS, THE COUNCIL HAS MADE A MISTAKE.
THERE IS NO ERROR. YOU ARE THE NEXT PRIME. THE SOURCE HAS SPOKEN.
YOU ARE AN ARCHIVIST, YES?
THEN YOU MUST UNDERSTAND THAT WE ARE ALL MERELY ANGLES IN A VAST, UNFOLDING GEOMETRY OF PAST, PRESENT AND FUTURE.
WE CANNOT SEE THE WHOLE PATTERN, BUT THE STRUCTURE REVEALS ITSELF THROUGH US, THROUGH OUR ACTIONS.
THIS WORLD, CYBERTRON, IS ITSELF PART OF ANOTHER, MORE INTRICATE DESIGN, DETAILED ON THE HEAVENS BY FORCES NOT CONTAINED IN DATA BANKS.

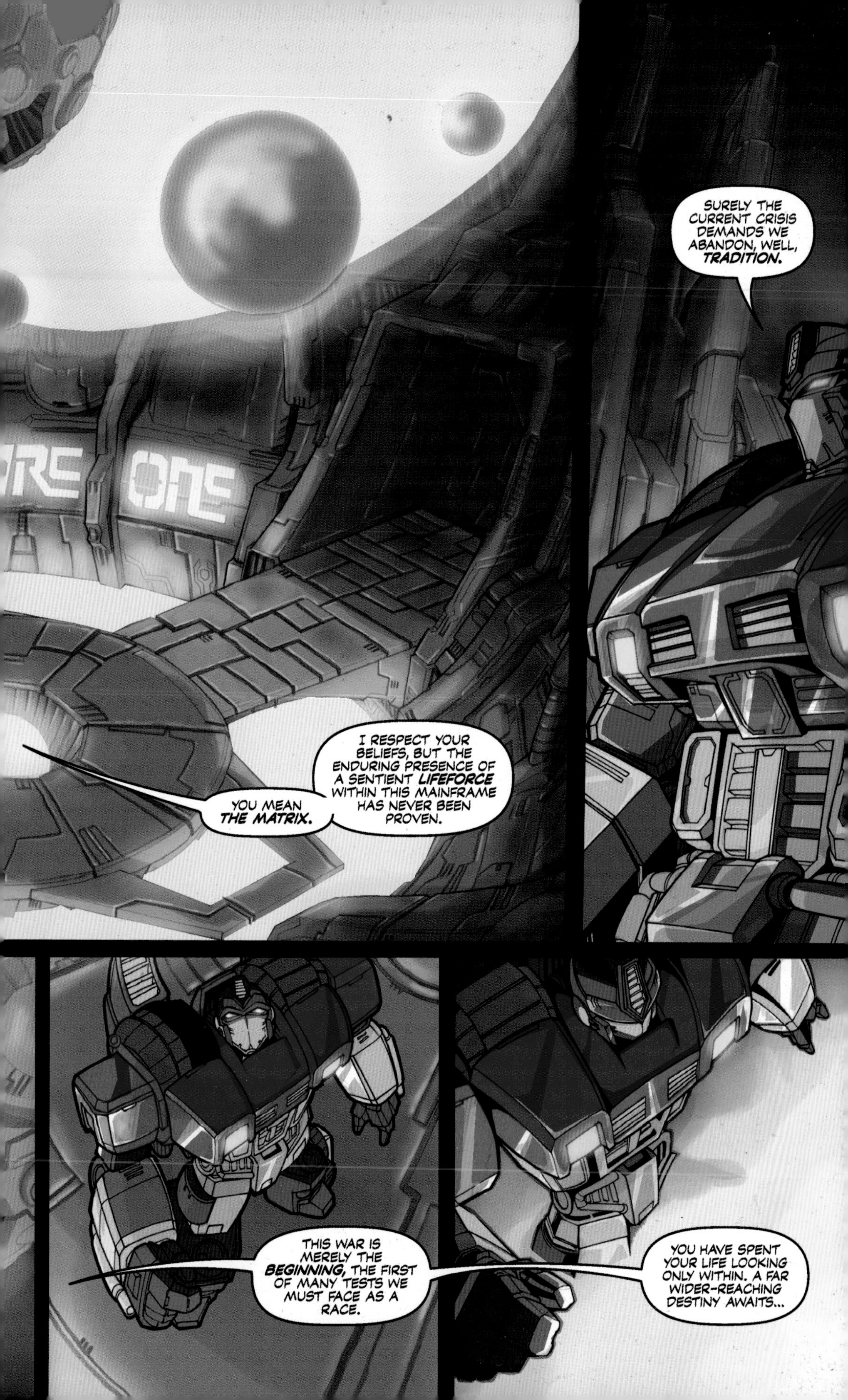
YOU MEAN *THE MATRIX.*
I RESPECT YOUR BELIEFS, BUT THE ENDURING PRESENCE OF A SENTIENT *LIFEFORCE* WITHIN THIS MAINFRAME HAS NEVER BEEN PROVEN.
SURELY THE CURRENT CRISIS DEMANDS WE ABANDON, WELL, *TRADITION.*
THIS WAR IS MERELY THE *BEGINNING,* THE FIRST OF MANY TESTS WE MUST FACE AS A RACE.
YOU HAVE SPENT YOUR LIFE LOOKING ONLY WITHIN. A FAR WIDER-REACHING DESTINY AWAITS...

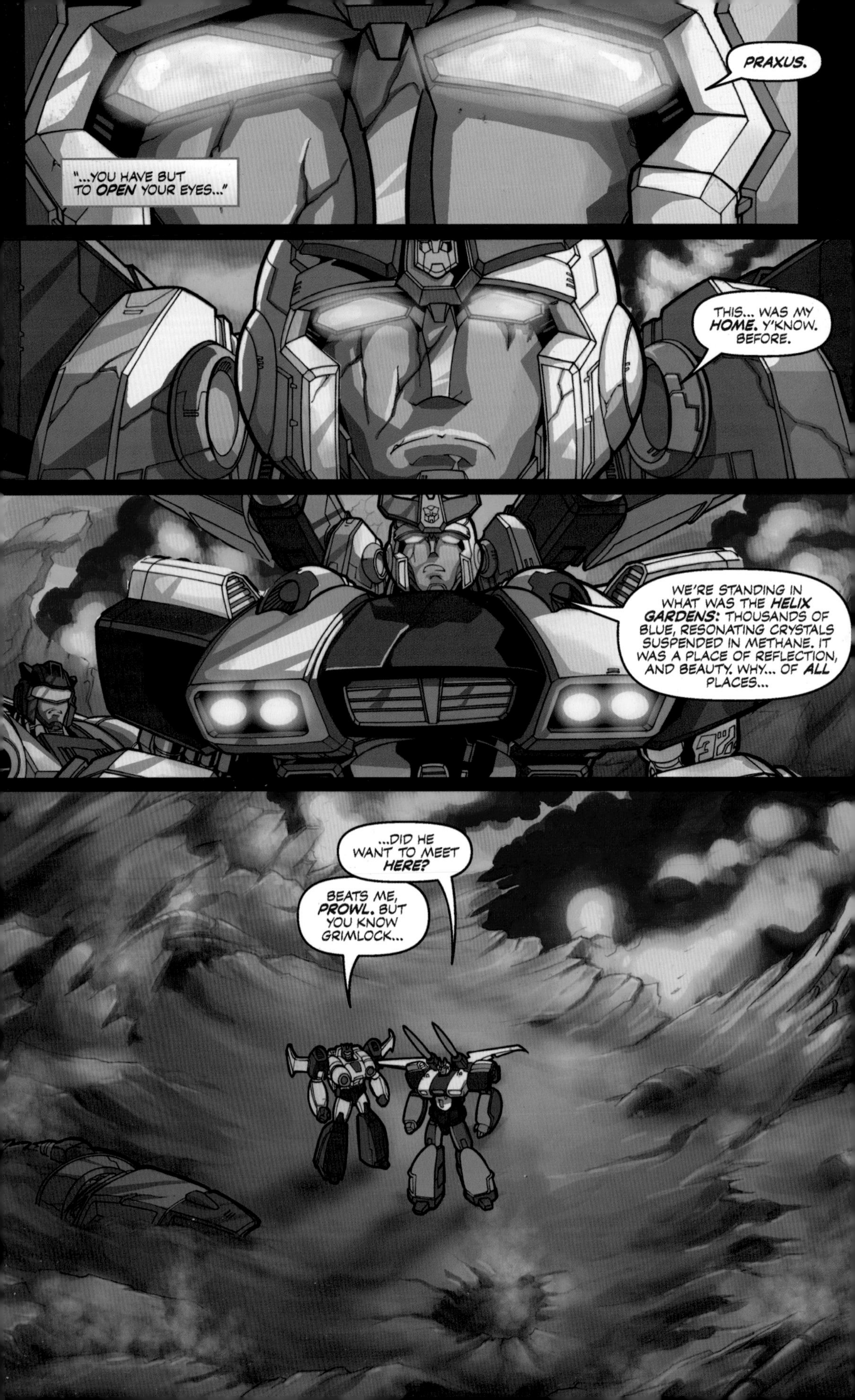
"...YOU HAVE BUT TO OPEN YOUR EYES..."
PRAXUS.
THIS... WAS MY HOME. Y'KNOW. BEFORE.
WE'RE STANDING IN WHAT WAS THE HELIX GARDENS: THOUSANDS OF BLUE, RESONATING CRYSTALS SUSPENDED IN METHANE. IT WAS A PLACE OF REFLECTION, AND BEAUTY. WHY... OF ALL PLACES...
...DID HE WANT TO MEET HERE?
BEATS ME, PROWL. BUT YOU KNOW GRIMLOCK...

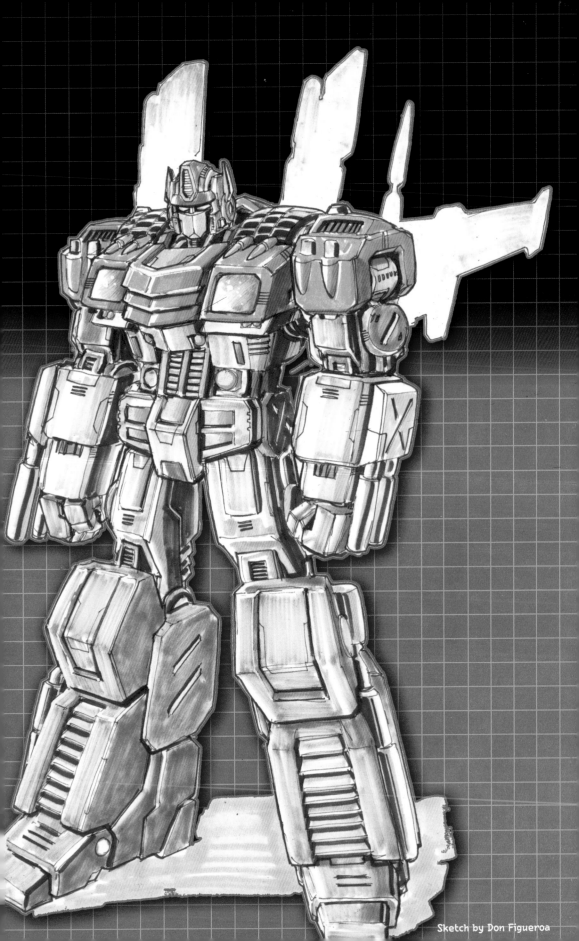

Sketch by Don Figueroa

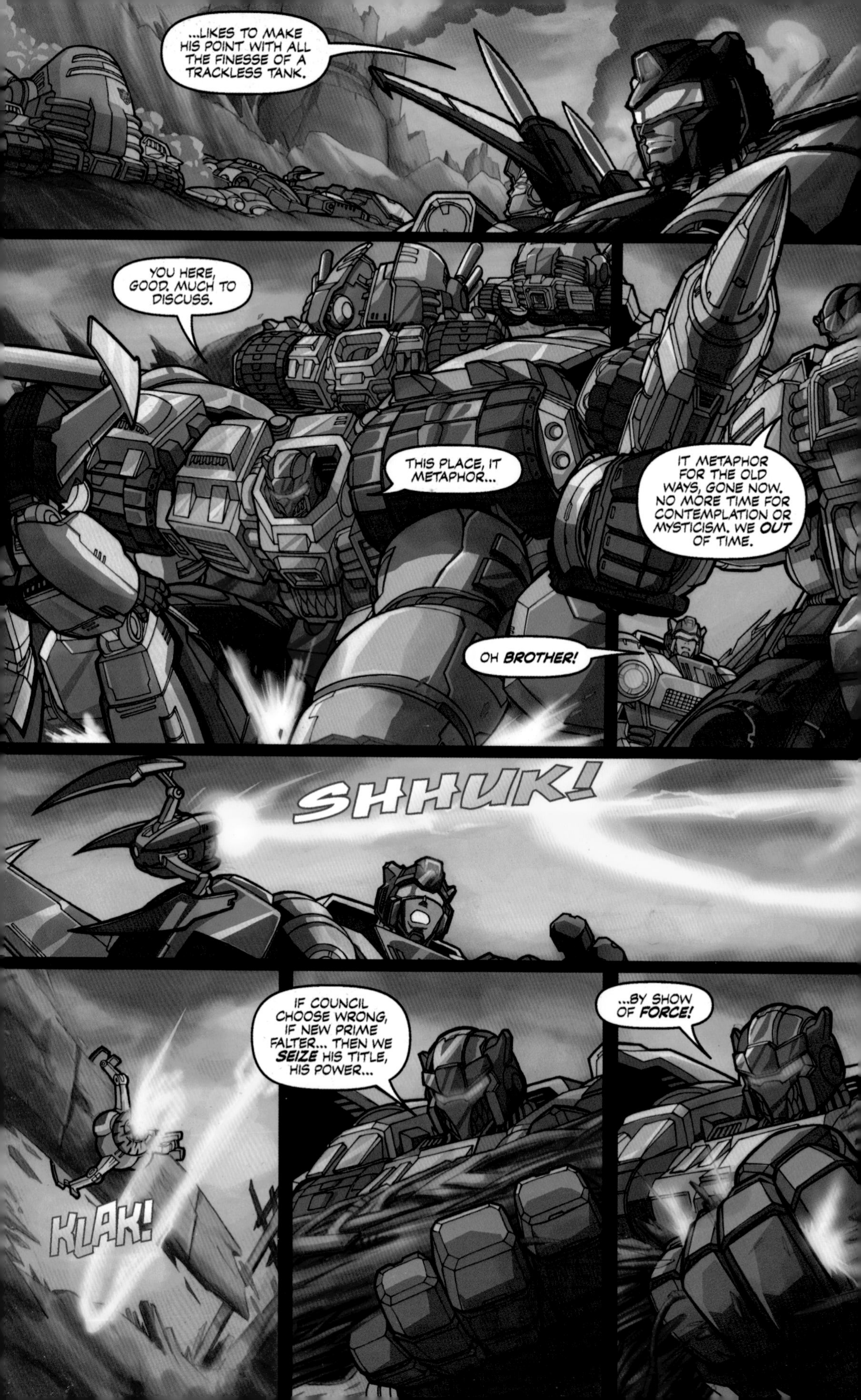
...LIKES TO MAKE HIS POINT WITH ALL THE FINESSE OF A TRACKLESS TANK.
YOU HERE, GOOD. MUCH TO DISCUSS.
THIS PLACE, IT METAPHOR...
IT METAPHOR FOR THE OLD WAYS, GONE NOW. NO MORE TIME FOR CONTEMPLATION OR MYSTICISM. WE OUT OF TIME.
OH BROTHER!
SHHUK!
KLAK!
IF COUNCIL CHOOSE WRONG, IF NEW PRIME FALTER... THEN WE SEIZE HIS TITLE, HIS POWER...
...BY SHOW OF FORCE!

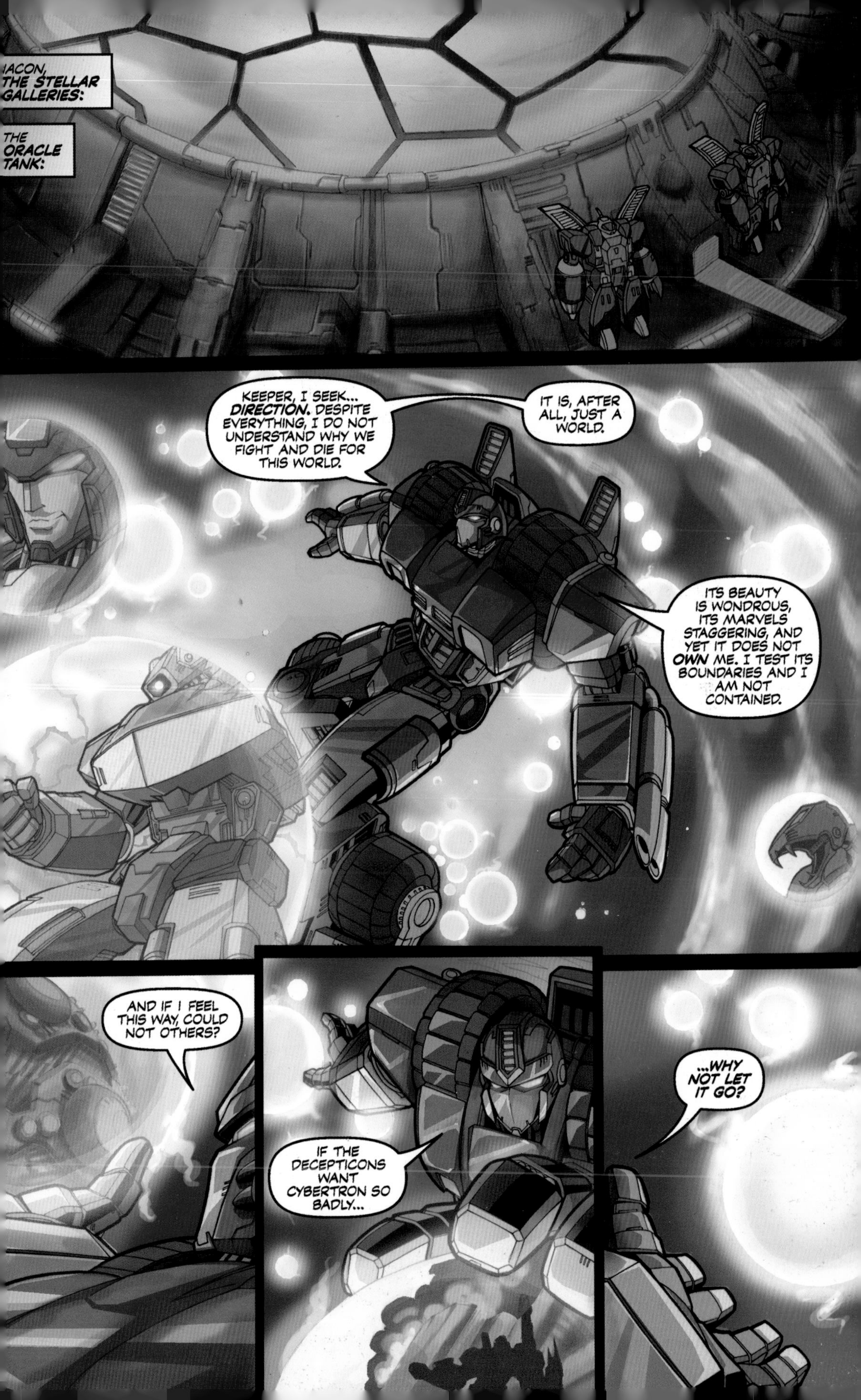
IACON, THE STELLAR GALLERIES:
THE ORACLE TANK:
KEEPER, I SEEK... **DIRECTION.** DESPITE EVERYTHING, I DO NOT UNDERSTAND WHY WE FIGHT AND DIE FOR THIS WORLD.
IT IS, AFTER ALL, JUST A WORLD.
ITS BEAUTY IS WONDROUS, ITS MARVELS STAGGERING, AND YET IT DOES NOT **OWN** ME. I TEST ITS BOUNDARIES AND I AM NOT CONTAINED.
AND IF I FEEL THIS WAY, COULD NOT OTHERS?
IF THE DECEPTICONS WANT CYBERTRON SO BADLY...
...WHY NOT LET IT GO?

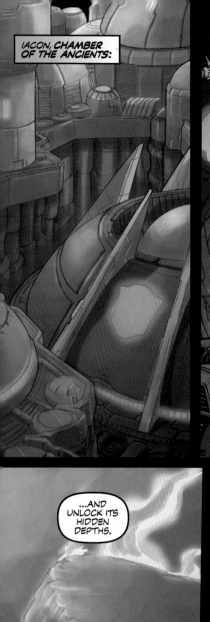

IACON, CHAMBER OF THE ANCIENTS:

WE ARE GATHERED HERE TODAY, ON THIS MOST SACRED OF OCCASIONS TO BEAR WITNESS...

...AS THE *TORCH* IS PASSED.

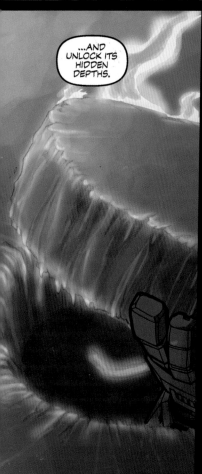

...AND UNLOCK ITS HIDDEN DEPTHS.

IN THESE DARK TIMES, MORE SO THAN EVER BEFORE, WE HAVE NEED OF A STRONG LEADER...

...TO GUIDE US INTO THE *LIGHT*.

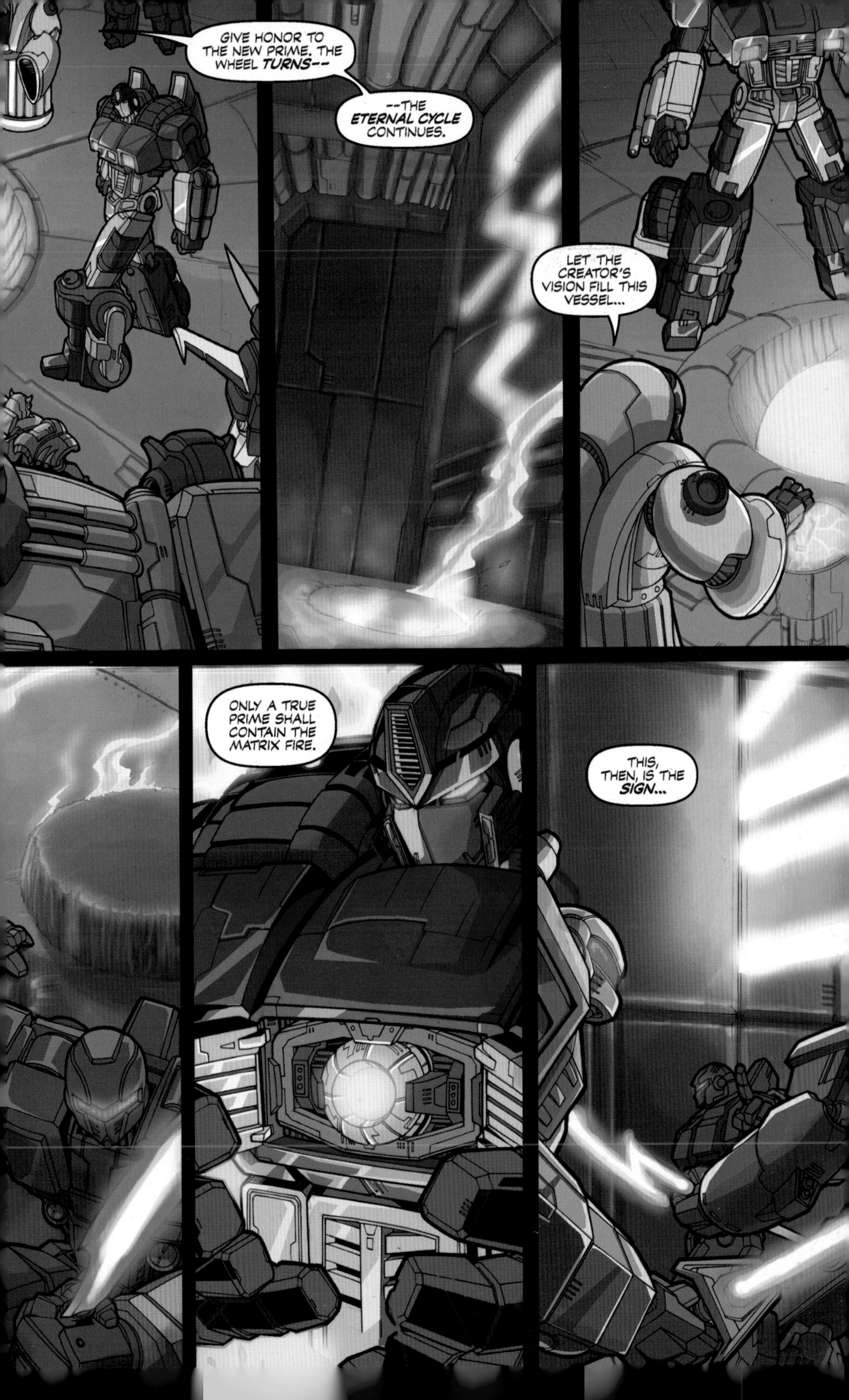
GIVE HONOR TO THE NEW PRIME. THE WHEEL *TURNS*--
--THE *ETERNAL CYCLE* CONTINUES.
LET THE CREATOR'S VISION FILL THIS VESSEL...
ONLY A TRUE PRIME SHALL CONTAIN THE MATRIX FIRE.
THIS, THEN, IS THE *SIGN*...

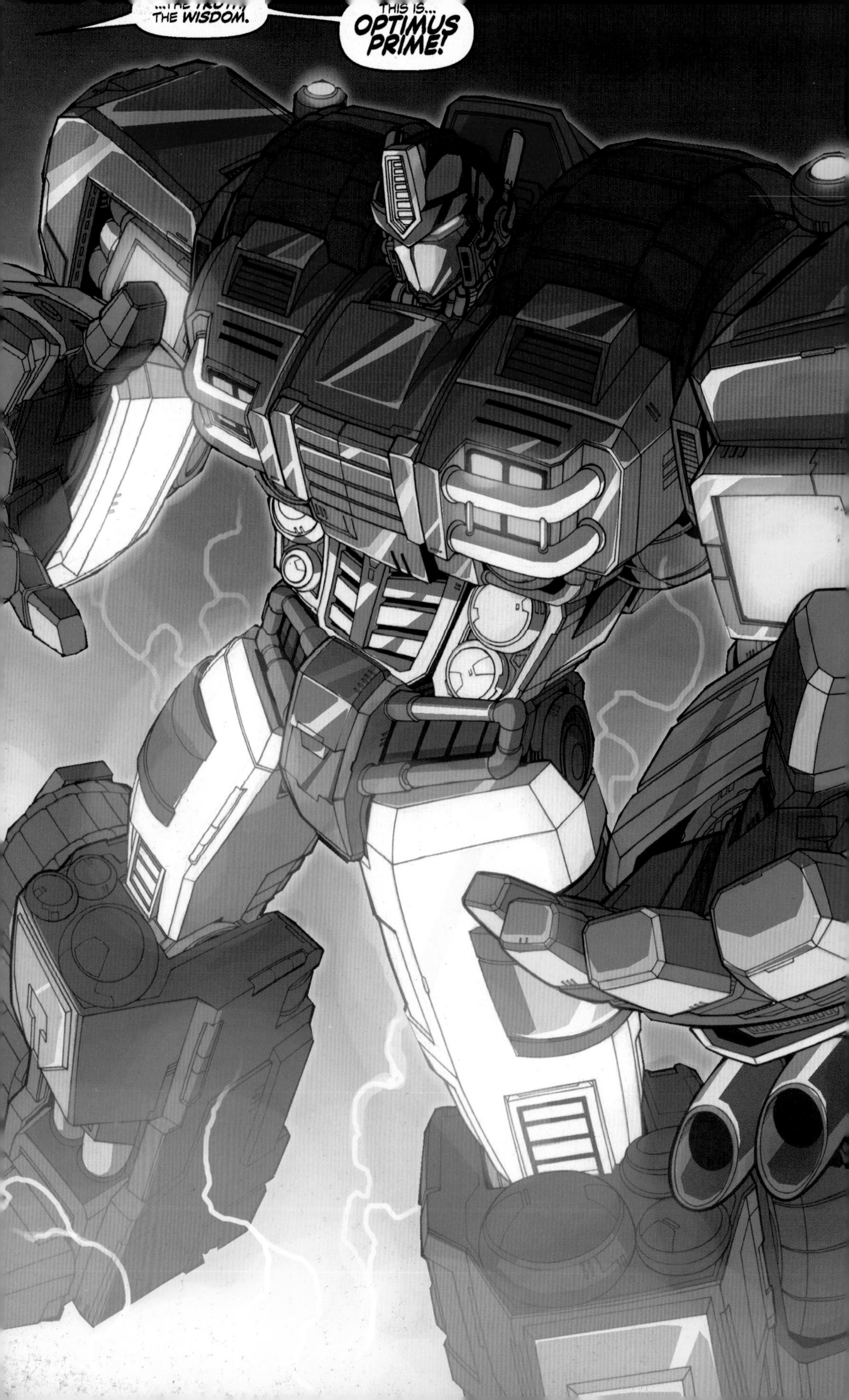
THE WISDOM.
THIS IS... OPTIMUS PRIME!

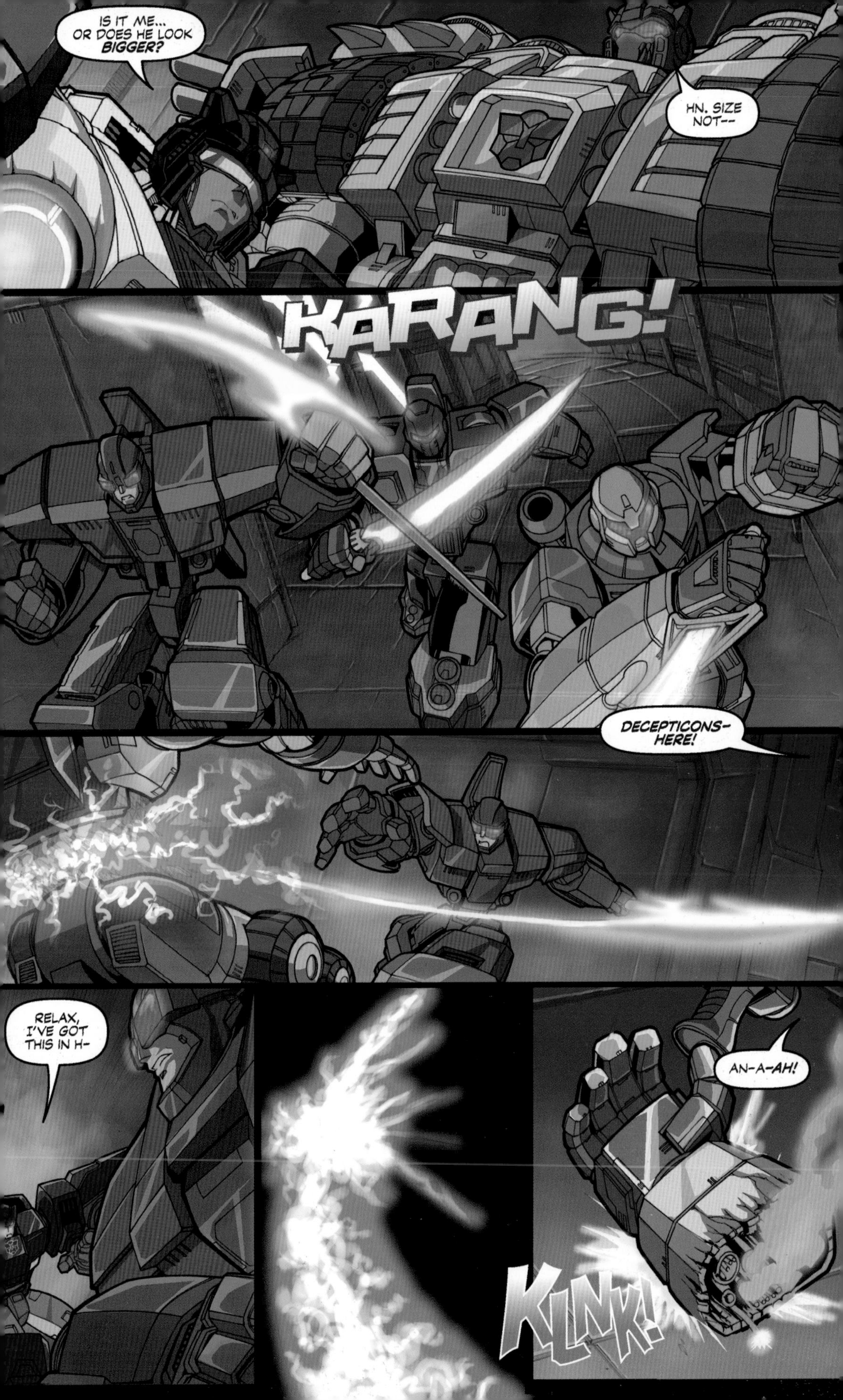
IS IT ME... OR DOES HE LOOK BIGGER?
HN. SIZE NOT--
KARANG!
DECEPTICONS-HERE!
RELAX, I'VE GOT THIS IN H-
AN-A-AH!
KLNK!

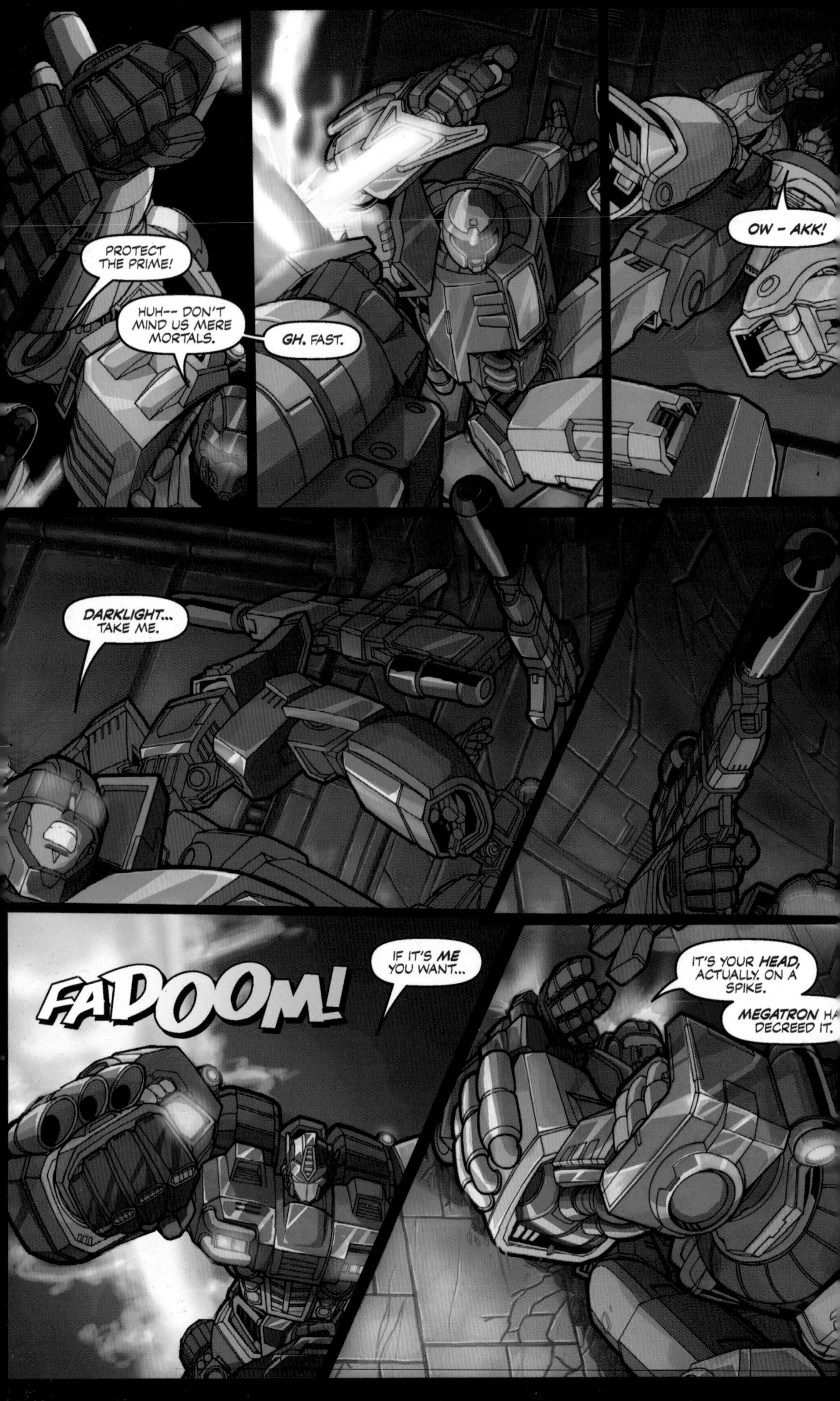
PROTECT THE PRIME!
HUH-- DON'T MIND US MERE MORTALS.
GH. FAST.
OW - AKK!
DARKLIGHT... TAKE ME.
FADOOM!
IF IT'S ME YOU WANT...
IT'S YOUR HEAD, ACTUALLY. ON A SPIKE.
MEGATRON HA DECREED IT.

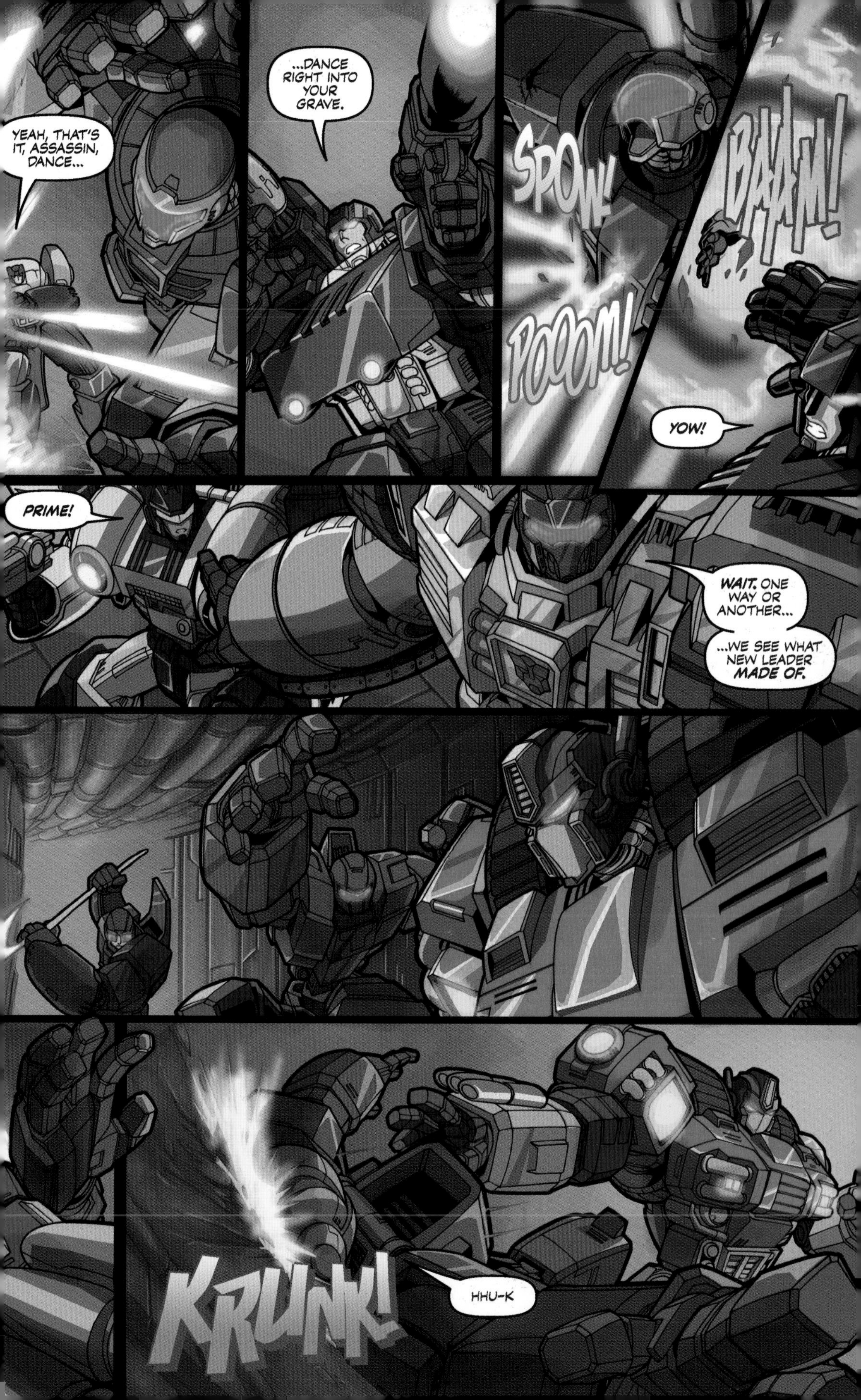
YEAH, THAT'S IT, ASSASSIN, DANCE...
...DANCE RIGHT INTO YOUR GRAVE.
SPOW!
POOOM!
BAAM!
YOW!
PRIME!
WAIT. ONE WAY OR ANOTHER...
...WE SEE WHAT NEW LEADER MADE OF.
KRUNK!
HHU-K

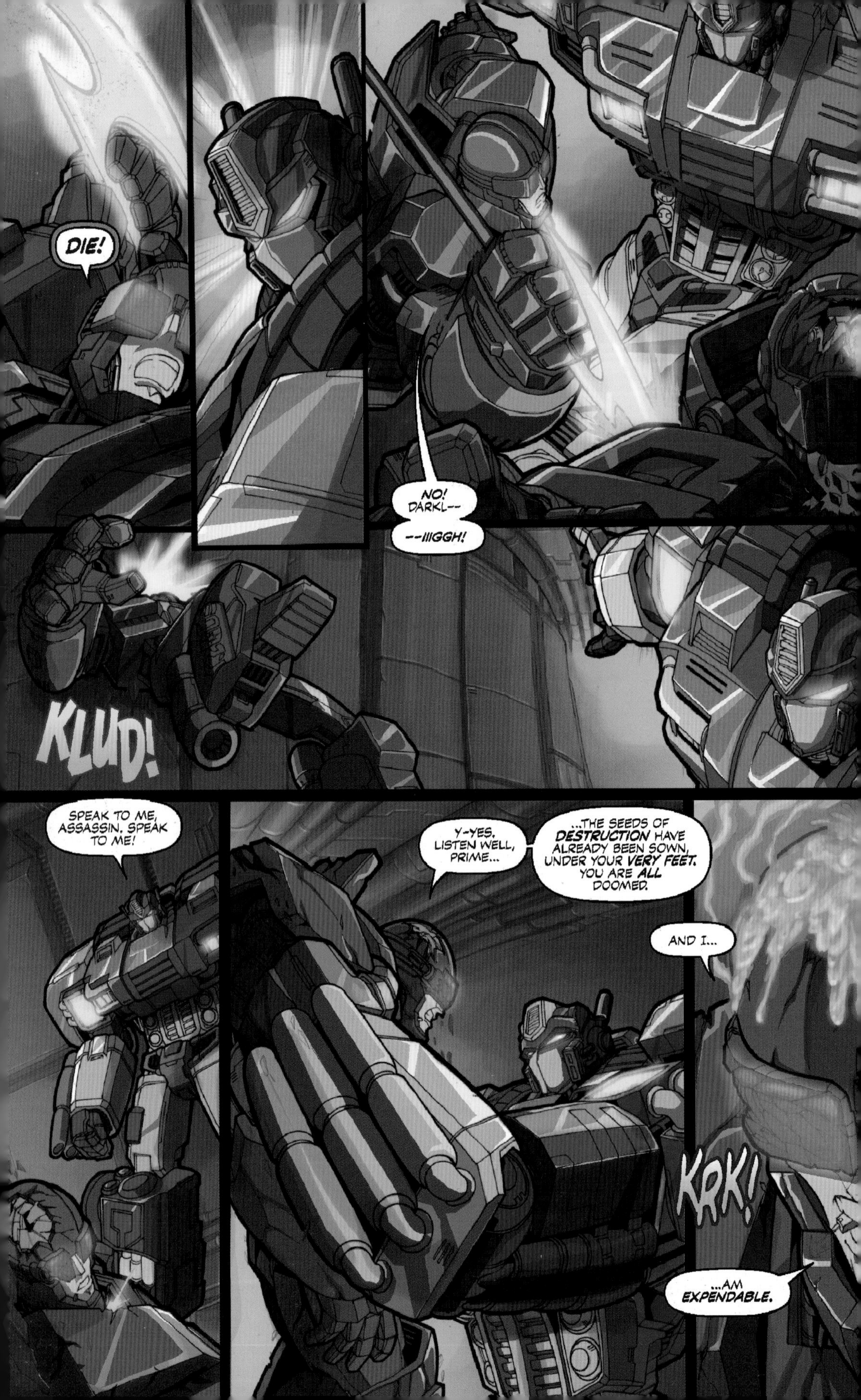
DIE!
NO! DARKL--
--IIIGGH!
KLUD!
SPEAK TO ME, ASSASSIN. SPEAK TO ME!
Y-YES, LISTEN WELL, PRIME...
...THE SEEDS OF DESTRUCTION HAVE ALREADY BEEN SOWN, UNDER YOUR VERY FEET. YOU ARE ALL DOOMED.
AND I...
KRK!
...AM EXPENDABLE.

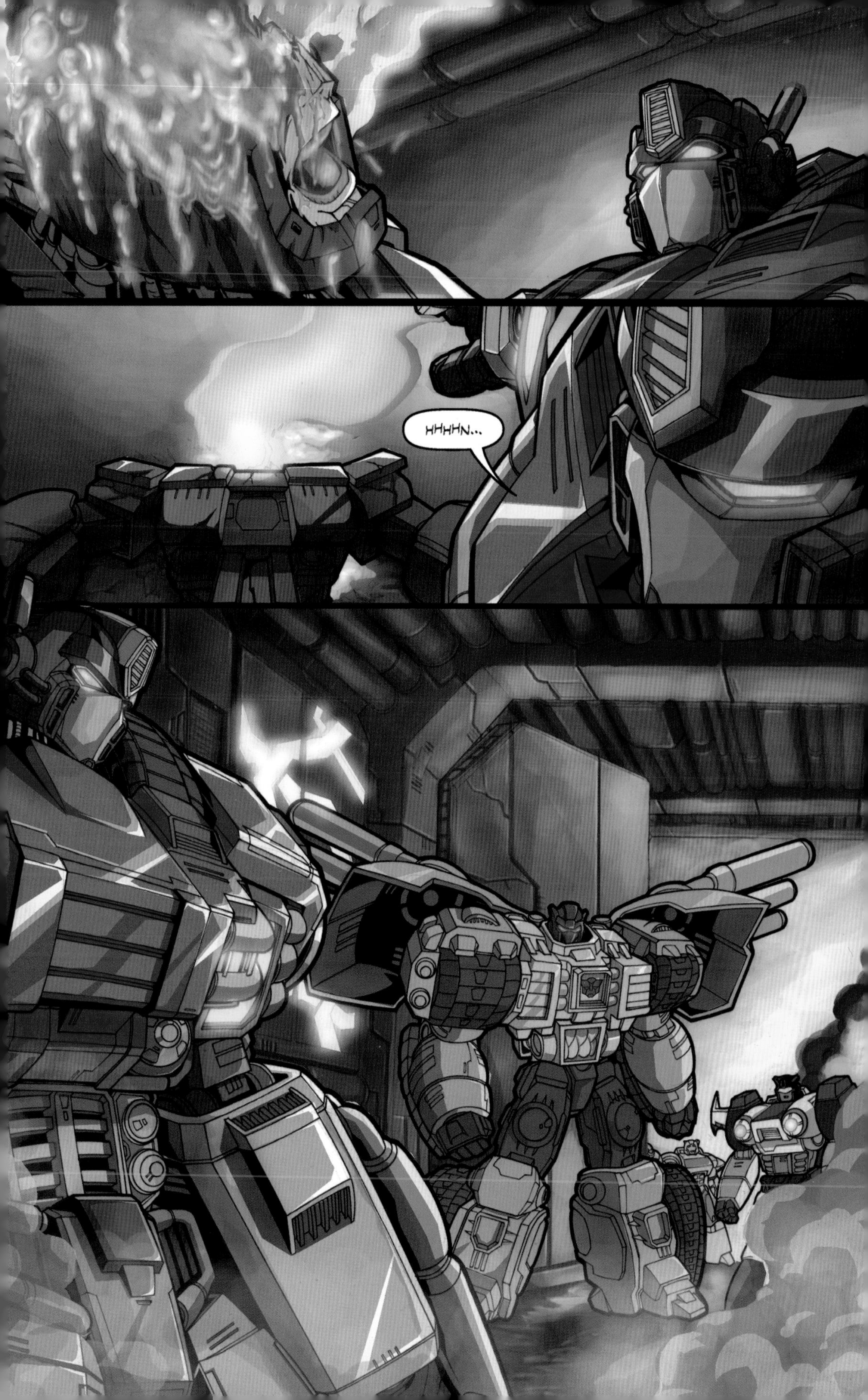
HHHHN...

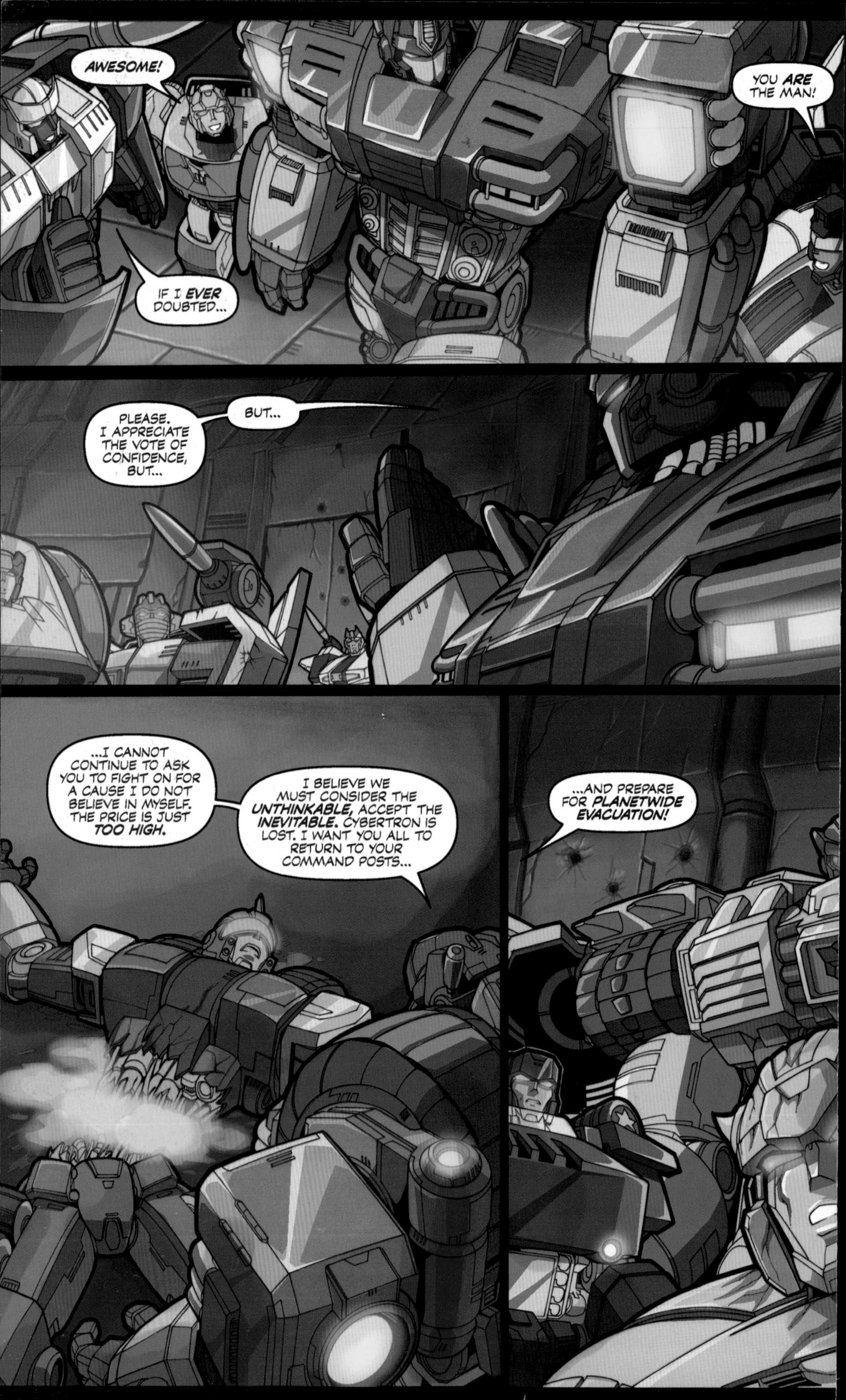
AWESOME!
IF I EVER DOUBTED...
YOU ARE THE MAN!
PLEASE. I APPRECIATE THE VOTE OF CONFIDENCE, BUT...
BUT...
...I CANNOT CONTINUE TO ASK YOU TO FIGHT ON FOR A CAUSE I DO NOT BELIEVE IN MYSELF. THE PRICE IS JUST TOO HIGH.
I BELIEVE WE MUST CONSIDER THE UNTHINKABLE, ACCEPT THE INEVITABLE. CYBERTRON IS LOST. I WANT YOU ALL TO RETURN TO YOUR COMMAND POSTS...
...AND PREPARE FOR PLANETWIDE EVACUATION!

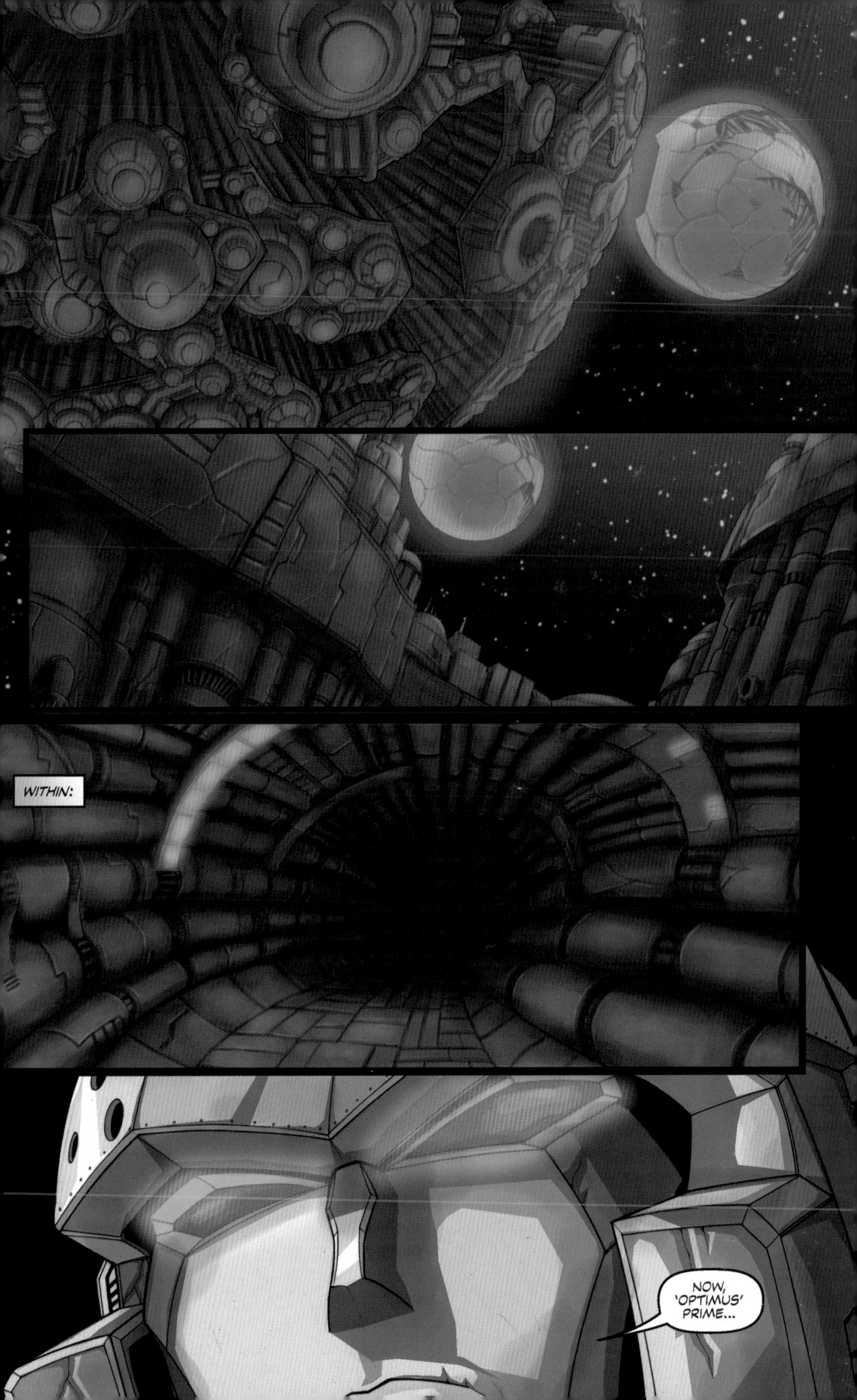
WITHIN:
NOW, 'OPTIMUS' PRIME...

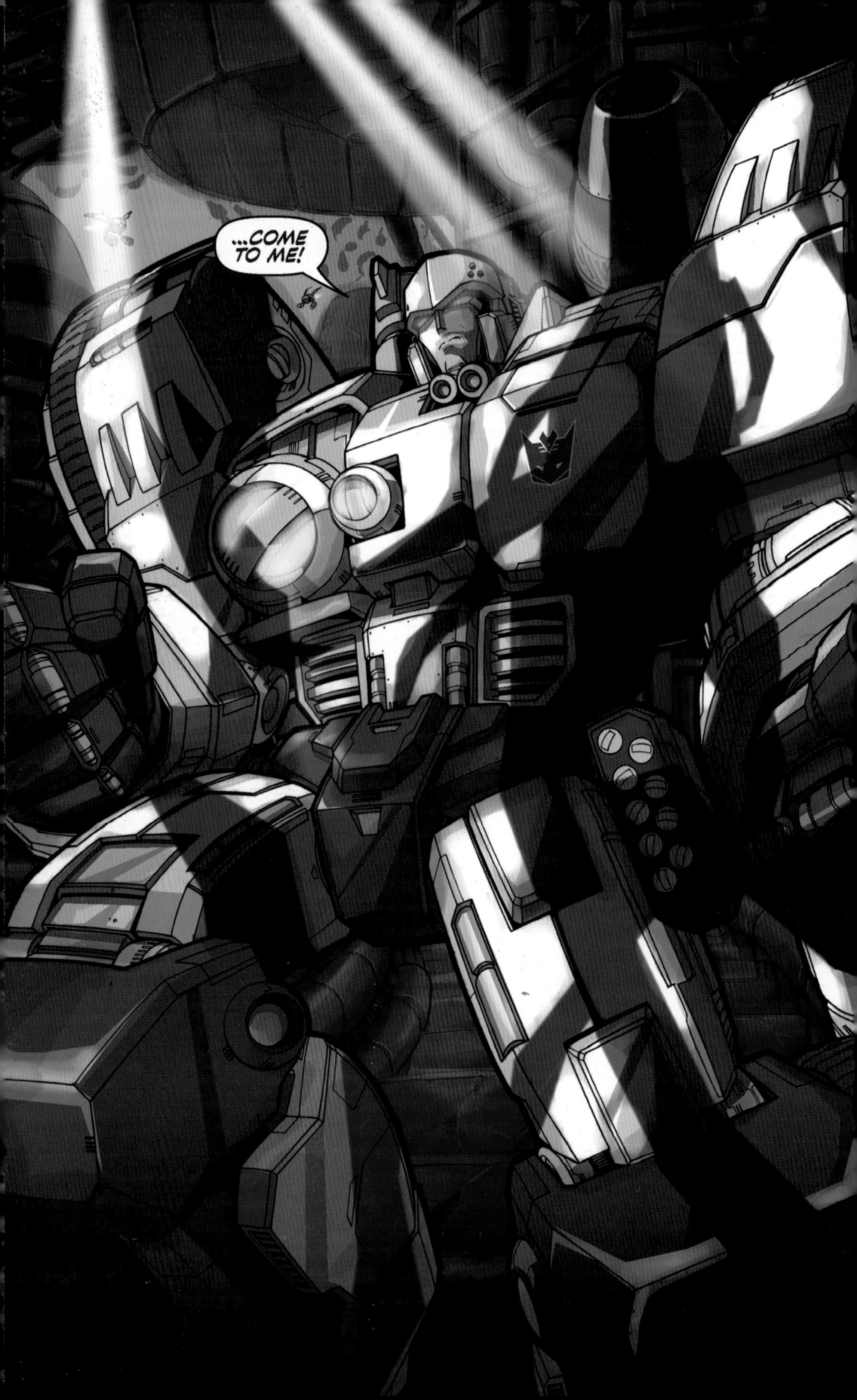
...COME TO ME!

THE TRANSFORMERS
THE BEST OF OPTIMUS PRIME

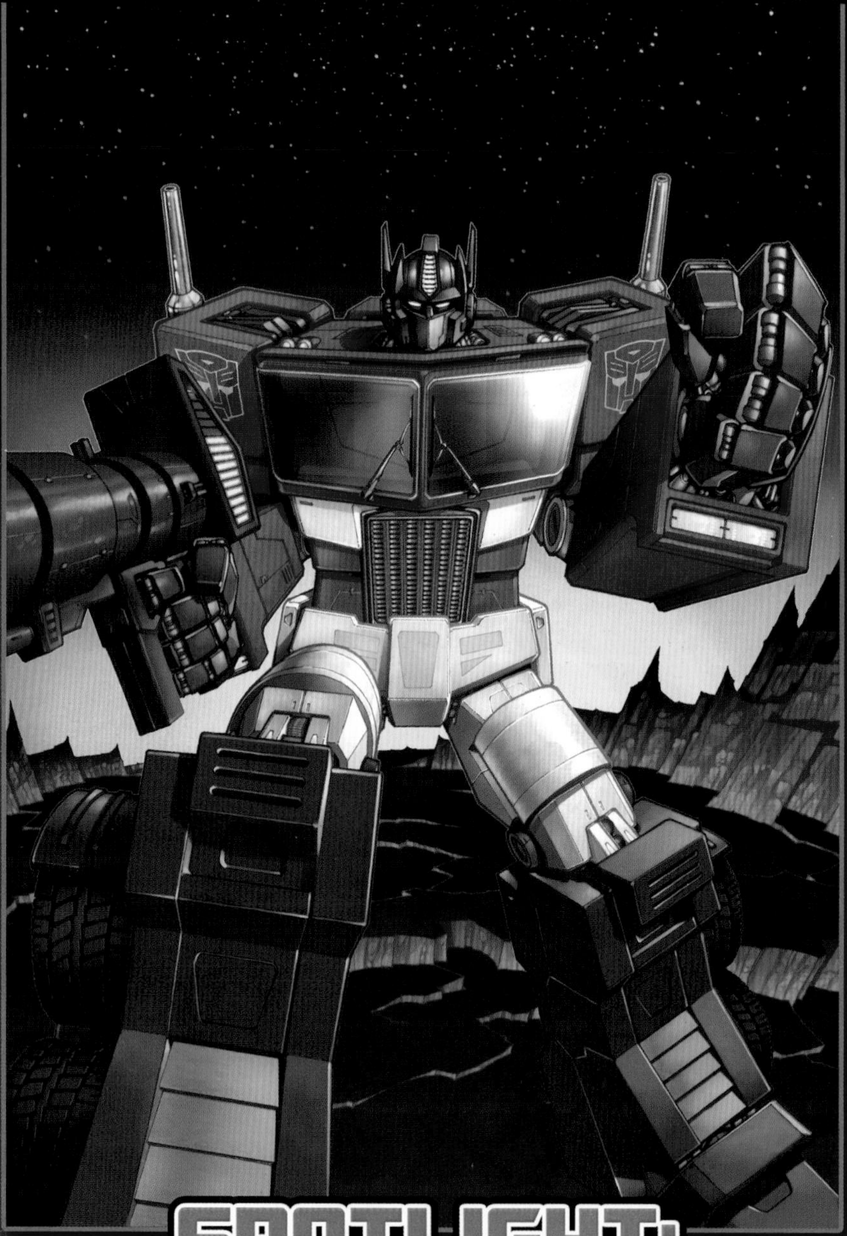

SPOTLIGHT: OPTIMUS PRIME

SPOTLIGHT: OPTIMUS PRIME brought forth some amazing revelations and rocked the foundation of the lineage of the PRIMEs.

Taking us within the mindset of OPTIMUS PRIME, we get a look at the fears that haunt the great leader, and the struggles he faces trying to balance being the strong, decisive leader that his AUTOBOTS look for him to be against the doubts of a soldier that is troubled by the unknown. In this story, he sees the truth behind one of the legendary AUTOBOT leaders, NOVA PRIME, and learns that the mantle of PRIME is not infallible.

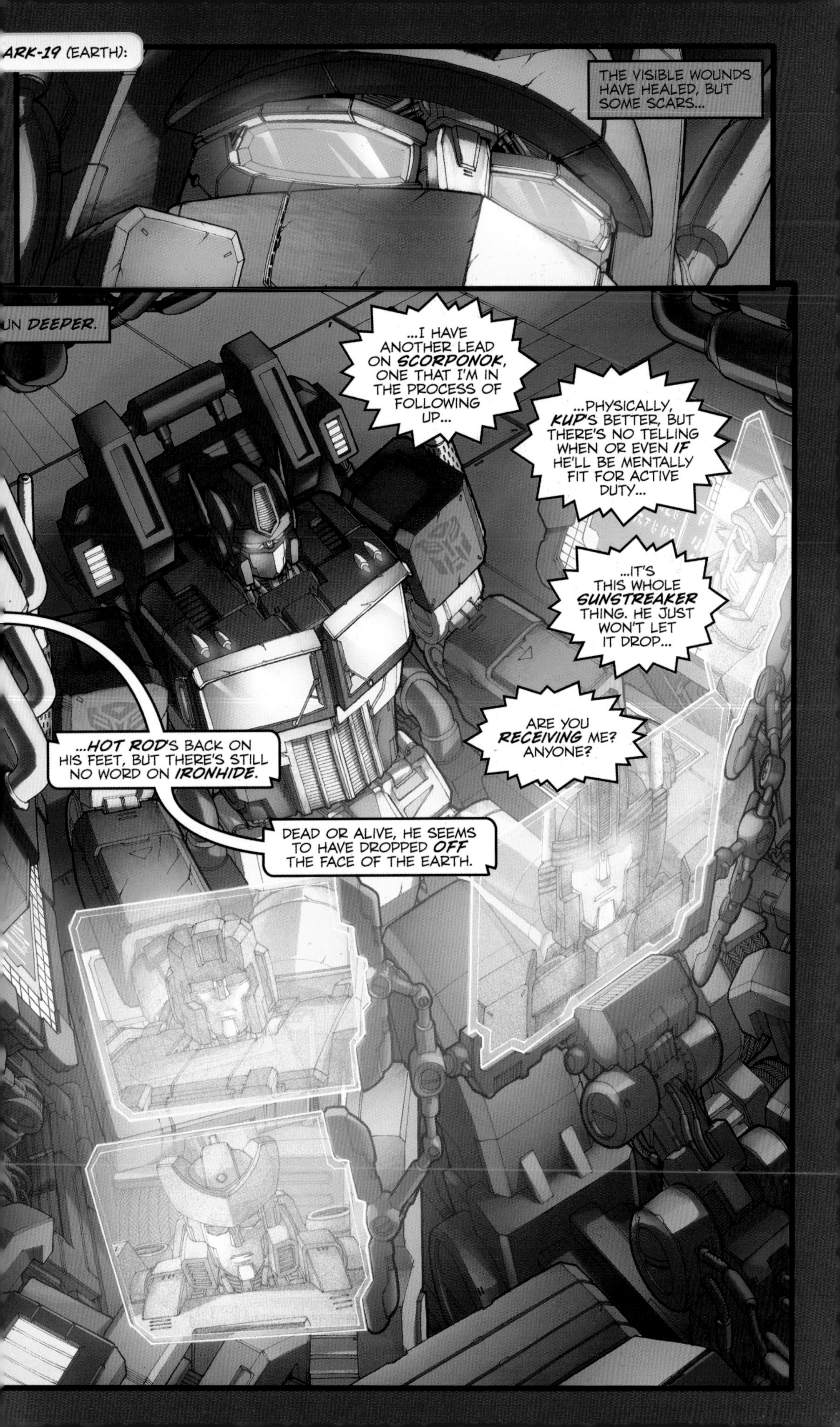

ARK-19 (EARTH):
THE VISIBLE WOUNDS HAVE HEALED, BUT SOME SCARS...
...UN DEEPER.
...I HAVE ANOTHER LEAD ON SCORPONOK, ONE THAT I'M IN THE PROCESS OF FOLLOWING UP...
...PHYSICALLY, KUP'S BETTER, BUT THERE'S NO TELLING WHEN OR EVEN IF HE'LL BE MENTALLY FIT FOR ACTIVE DUTY...
...IT'S THIS WHOLE SUNSTREAKER THING. HE JUST WON'T LET IT DROP...
ARE YOU RECEIVING ME? ANYONE?
...HOT ROD'S BACK ON HIS FEET, BUT THERE'S STILL NO WORD ON IRONHIDE.
DEAD OR ALIVE, HE SEEMS TO HAVE DROPPED OFF THE FACE OF THE EARTH.

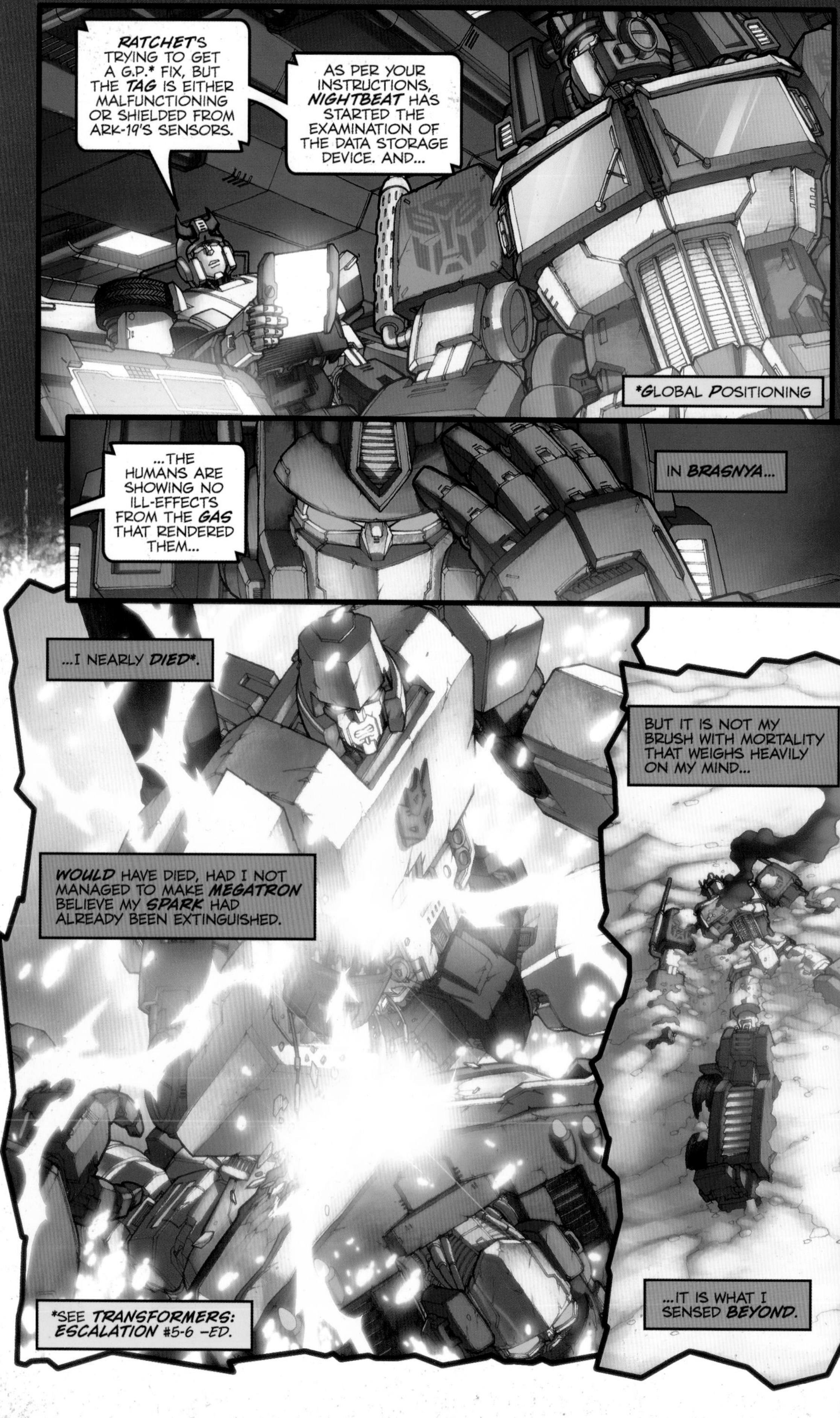
RATCHET'S TRYING TO GET A G.P.* FIX, BUT THE TAG IS EITHER MALFUNCTIONING OR SHIELDED FROM ARK-19'S SENSORS.
AS PER YOUR INSTRUCTIONS, NIGHTBEAT HAS STARTED THE EXAMINATION OF THE DATA STORAGE DEVICE. AND...
*GLOBAL POSITIONING
...THE HUMANS ARE SHOWING NO ILL-EFFECTS FROM THE GAS THAT RENDERED THEM...
IN BRASNYA...
...I NEARLY DIED*.
BUT IT IS NOT MY BRUSH WITH MORTALITY THAT WEIGHS HEAVILY ON MY MIND...
WOULD HAVE DIED, HAD I NOT MANAGED TO MAKE MEGATRON BELIEVE MY SPARK HAD ALREADY BEEN EXTINGUISHED.
*SEE TRANSFORMERS: ESCALATION #5-6 –ED.
...IT IS WHAT I SENSED BEYOND.

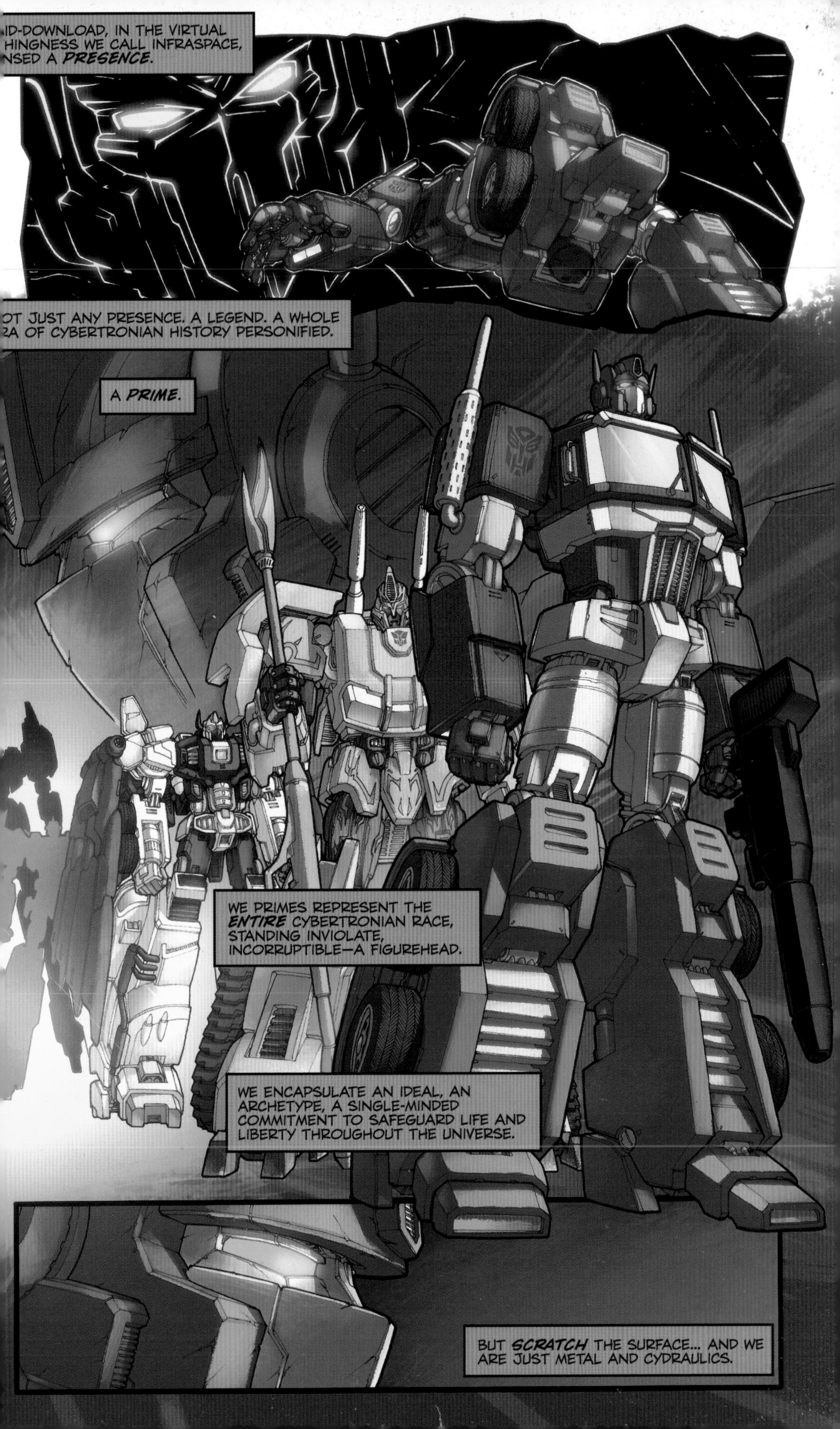
ID-DOWNLOAD, IN THE VIRTUAL HINGNESS WE CALL INFRASPACE, NSED A *PRESENCE*.
OT JUST ANY PRESENCE. A LEGEND. A WHOLE RA OF CYBERTRONIAN HISTORY PERSONIFIED.
A *PRIME*.
WE PRIMES REPRESENT THE *ENTIRE* CYBERTRONIAN RACE, STANDING INVIOLATE, INCORRUPTIBLE—A FIGUREHEAD.
WE ENCAPSULATE AN IDEAL, AN ARCHETYPE, A SINGLE-MINDED COMMITMENT TO SAFEGUARD LIFE AND LIBERTY THROUGHOUT THE UNIVERSE.
BUT *SCRATCH* THE SURFACE... AND WE ARE JUST METAL AND CYDRAULICS.

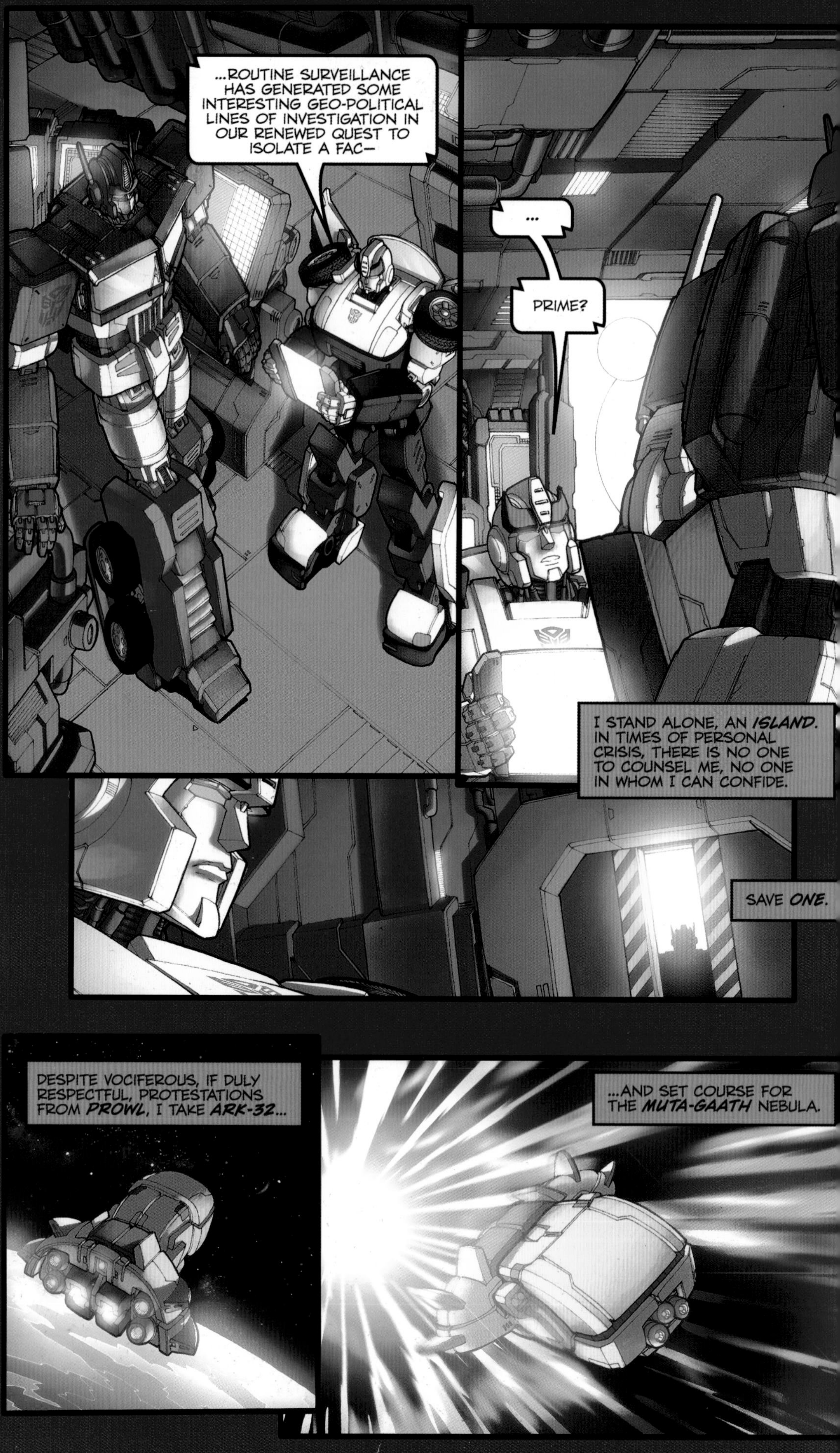
...ROUTINE SURVEILLANCE HAS GENERATED SOME INTERESTING GEO-POLITICAL LINES OF INVESTIGATION IN OUR RENEWED QUEST TO ISOLATE A FAC—
...
PRIME?
I STAND ALONE, AN *ISLAND*. IN TIMES OF PERSONAL CRISIS, THERE IS NO ONE TO COUNSEL ME, NO ONE IN WHOM I CAN CONFIDE.
SAVE *ONE*.
DESPITE VOCIFEROUS, IF DULY RESPECTFUL, PROTESTATIONS FROM *PROWL*, I TAKE *ARK-32*...
...AND SET COURSE FOR THE *MUTA-GAATH* NEBULA.

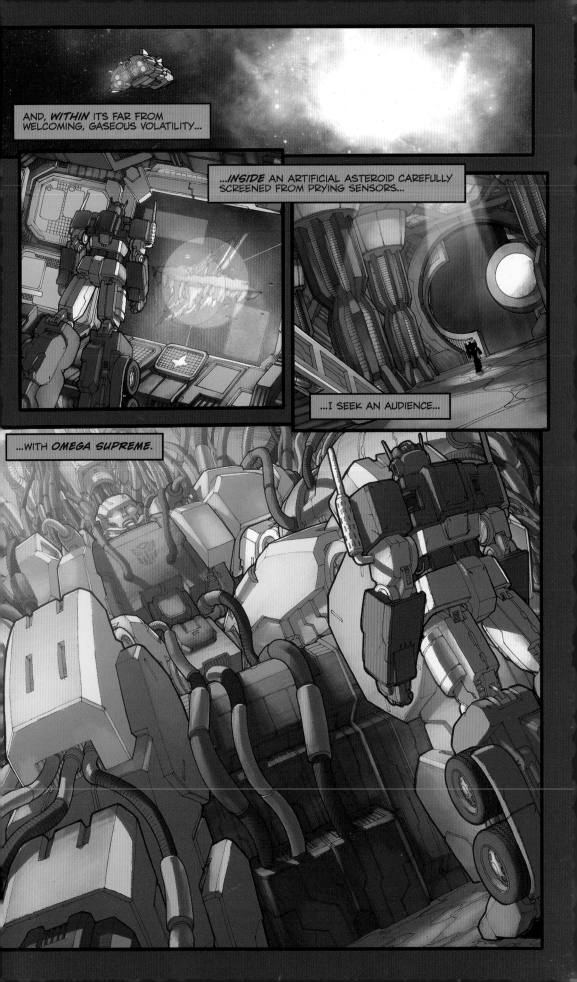

AND, *WITHIN* ITS FAR FROM WELCOMING, GASEOUS VOLATILITY...

...*INSIDE* AN ARTIFICIAL ASTEROID CAREFULLY SCREENED FROM PRYING SENSORS...

...I SEEK AN AUDIENCE...

...WITH *OMEGA SUPREME*.

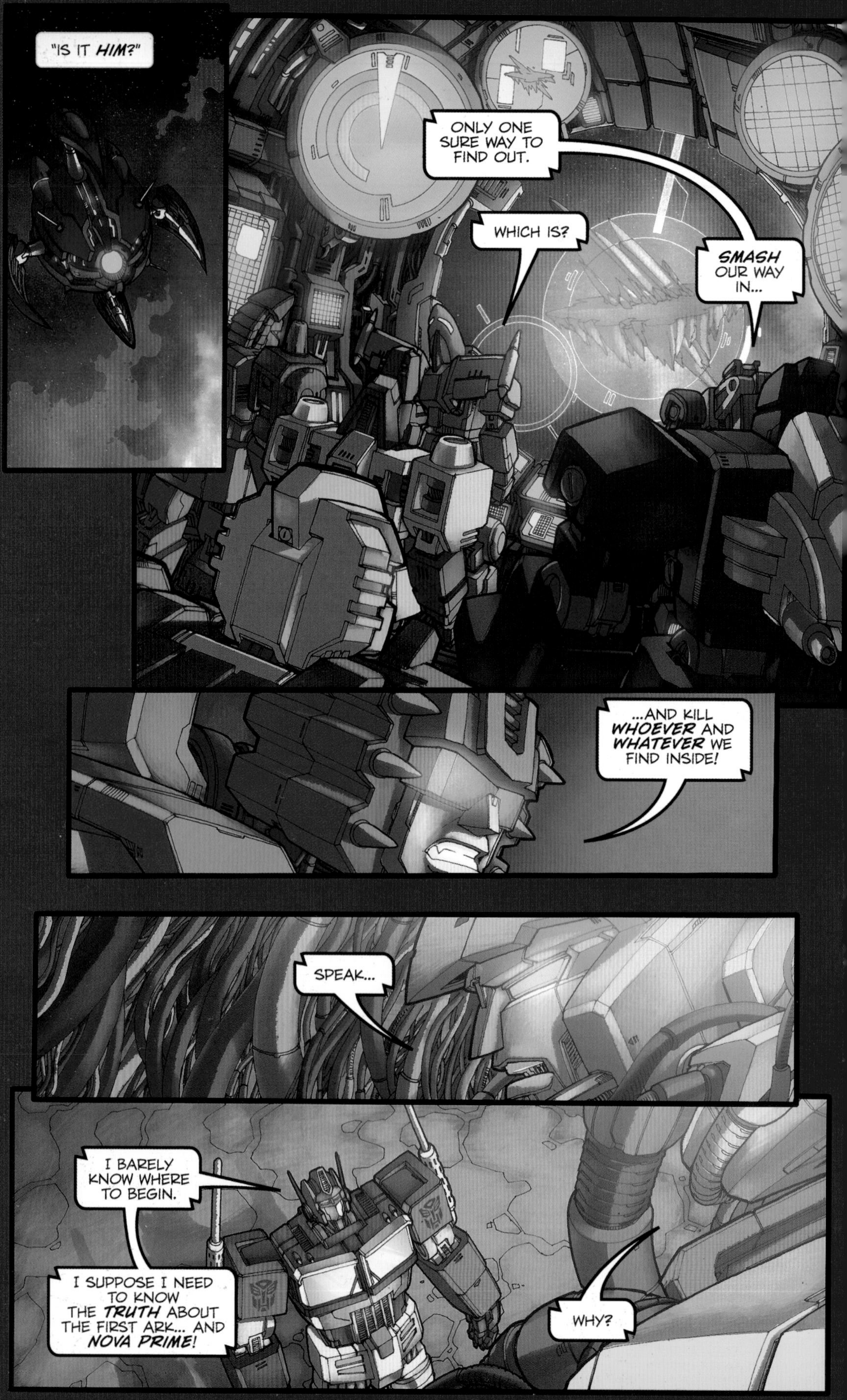
"IS IT *HIM?*"
ONLY ONE SURE WAY TO FIND OUT.
WHICH IS?
SMASH OUR WAY IN...
...AND KILL *WHOEVER* AND *WHATEVER* WE FIND INSIDE!
SPEAK...
I BARELY KNOW WHERE TO BEGIN.
I SUPPOSE I NEED TO KNOW THE *TRUTH* ABOUT THE FIRST ARK... AND *NOVA PRIME!*
WHY?

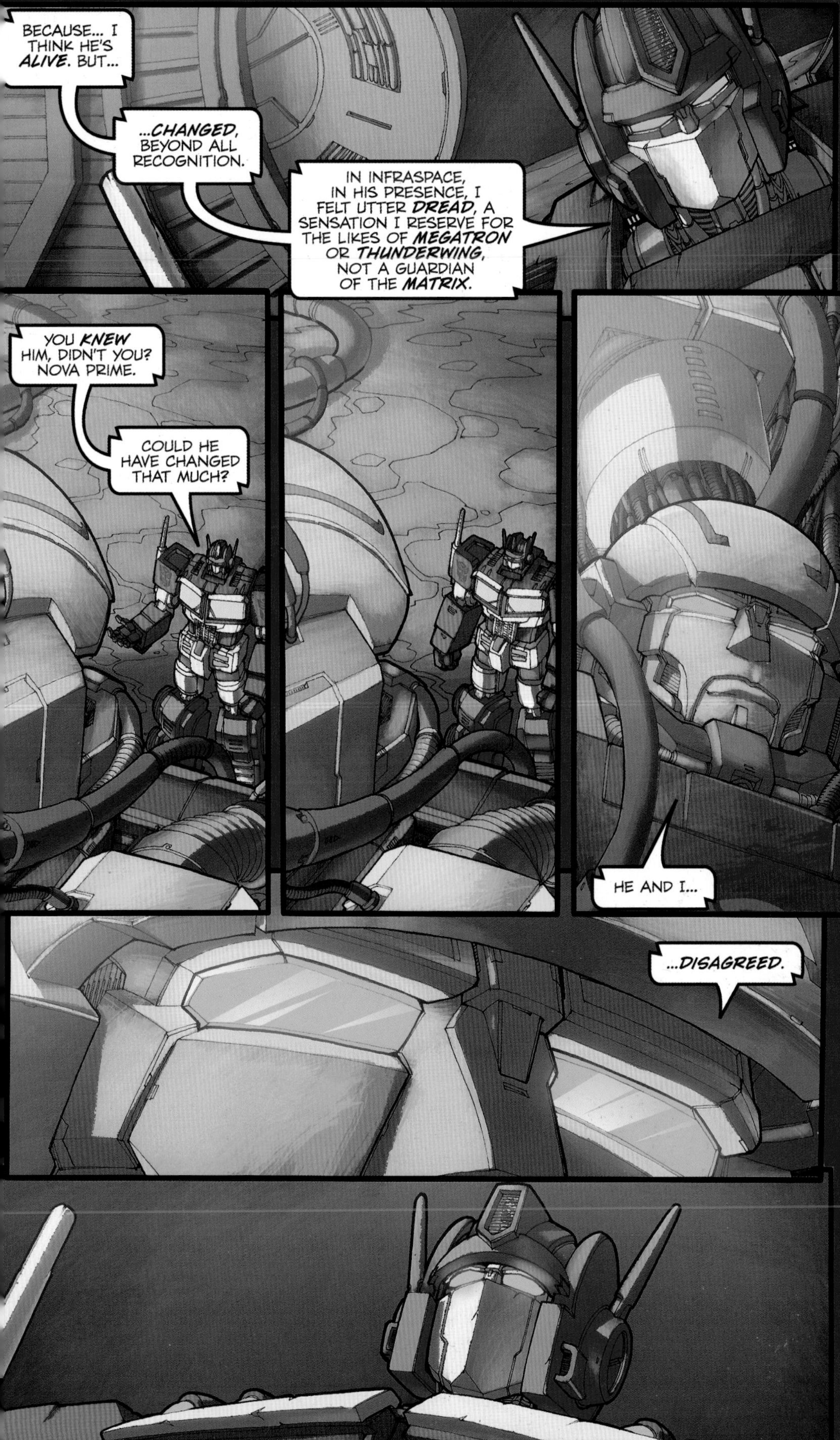
BECAUSE... I THINK HE'S ALIVE. BUT...
...CHANGED, BEYOND ALL RECOGNITION.
IN INFRASPACE, IN HIS PRESENCE, I FELT UTTER DREAD, A SENSATION I RESERVE FOR THE LIKES OF MEGATRON OR THUNDERWING, NOT A GUARDIAN OF THE MATRIX.
YOU KNEW HIM, DIDN'T YOU? NOVA PRIME.
COULD HE HAVE CHANGED THAT MUCH?
HE AND I...
...DISAGREED.

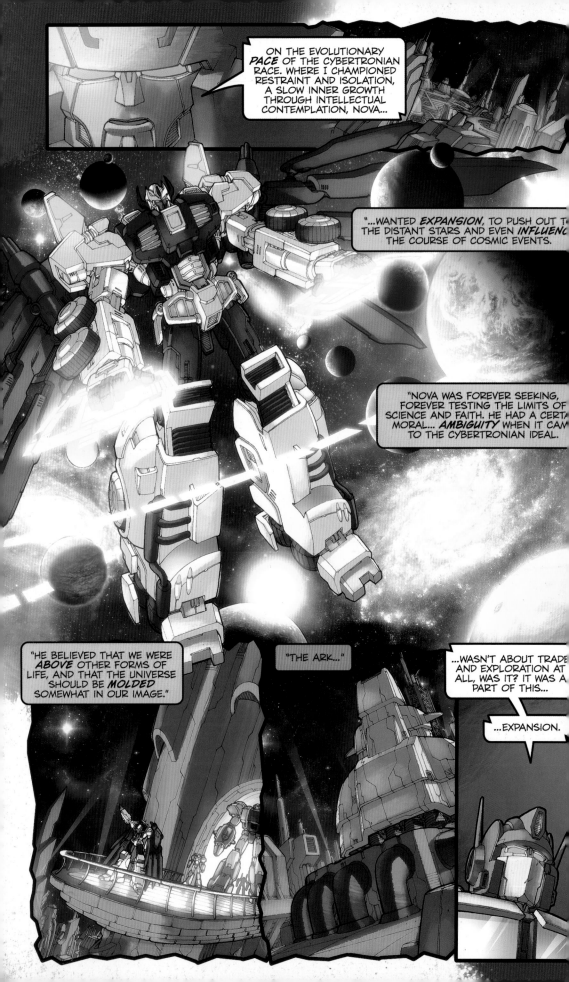

ON THE EVOLUTIONARY *PACE* OF THE CYBERTRONIAN RACE. WHERE I CHAMPIONED RESTRAINT AND ISOLATION, A SLOW INNER GROWTH THROUGH INTELLECTUAL CONTEMPLATION, NOVA...

"...WANTED *EXPANSION*, TO PUSH OUT T[O] THE DISTANT STARS AND EVEN *INFLUENC[E]* THE COURSE OF COSMIC EVENTS.

"NOVA WAS FOREVER SEEKING, FOREVER TESTING THE LIMITS OF SCIENCE AND FAITH. HE HAD A CERTA[IN] MORAL... *AMBIGUITY* WHEN IT CAM[E] TO THE CYBERTRONIAN IDEAL.

"HE BELIEVED THAT WE WERE *ABOVE* OTHER FORMS OF LIFE, AND THAT THE UNIVERSE SHOULD BE *MOLDED* SOMEWHAT IN OUR IMAGE."

"THE ARK..."

...WASN'T ABOUT TRADE AND EXPLORATION AT ALL, WAS IT? IT WAS A PART OF THIS...

...EXPANSION.

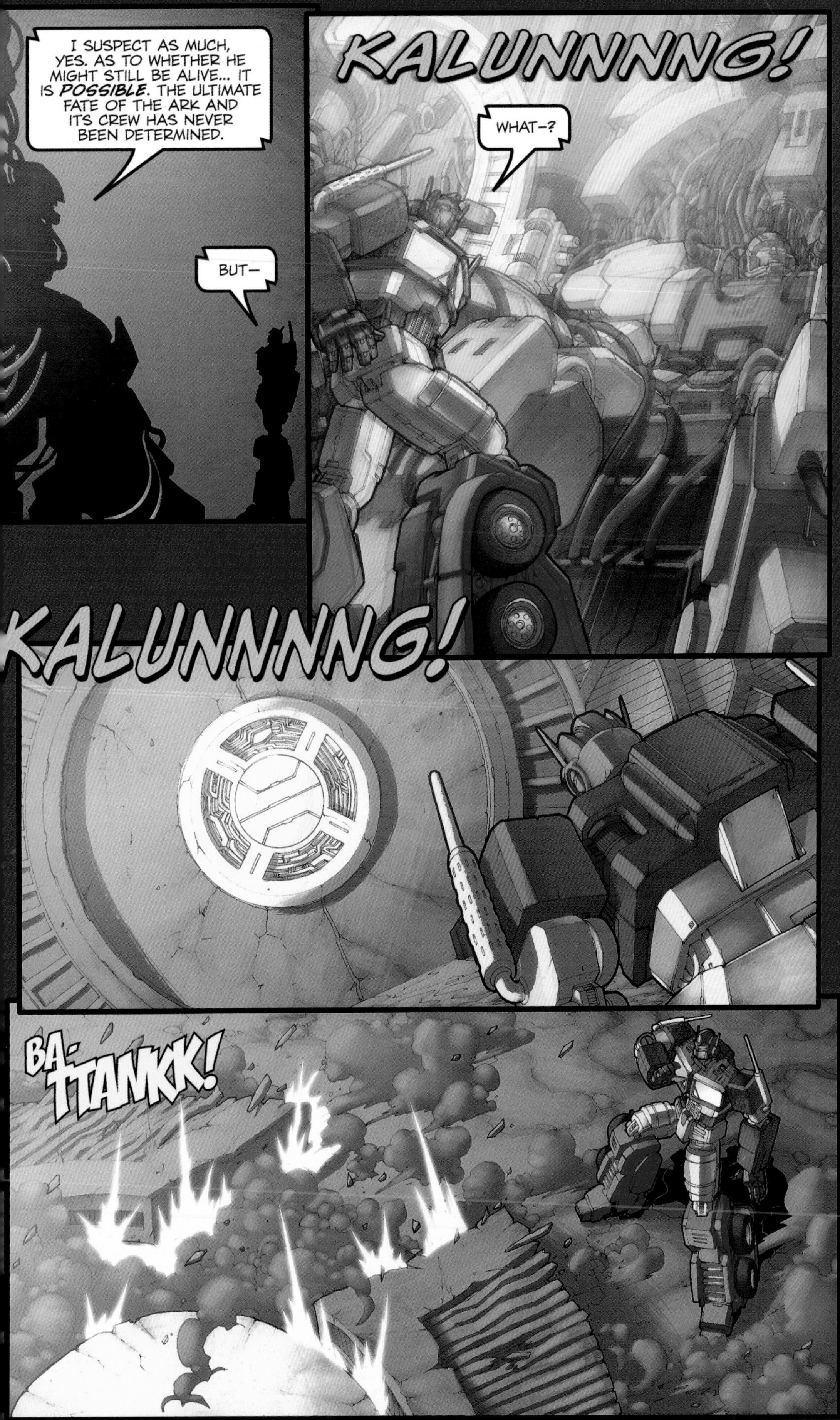
I SUSPECT AS MUCH, YES. AS TO WHETHER HE MIGHT STILL BE ALIVE... IT IS *POSSIBLE*. THE ULTIMATE FATE OF THE ARK AND ITS CREW HAS NEVER BEEN DETERMINED.
BUT—
KALUNNNNG!
WHAT-?
KALUNNNNG!
BA-TTANKK!

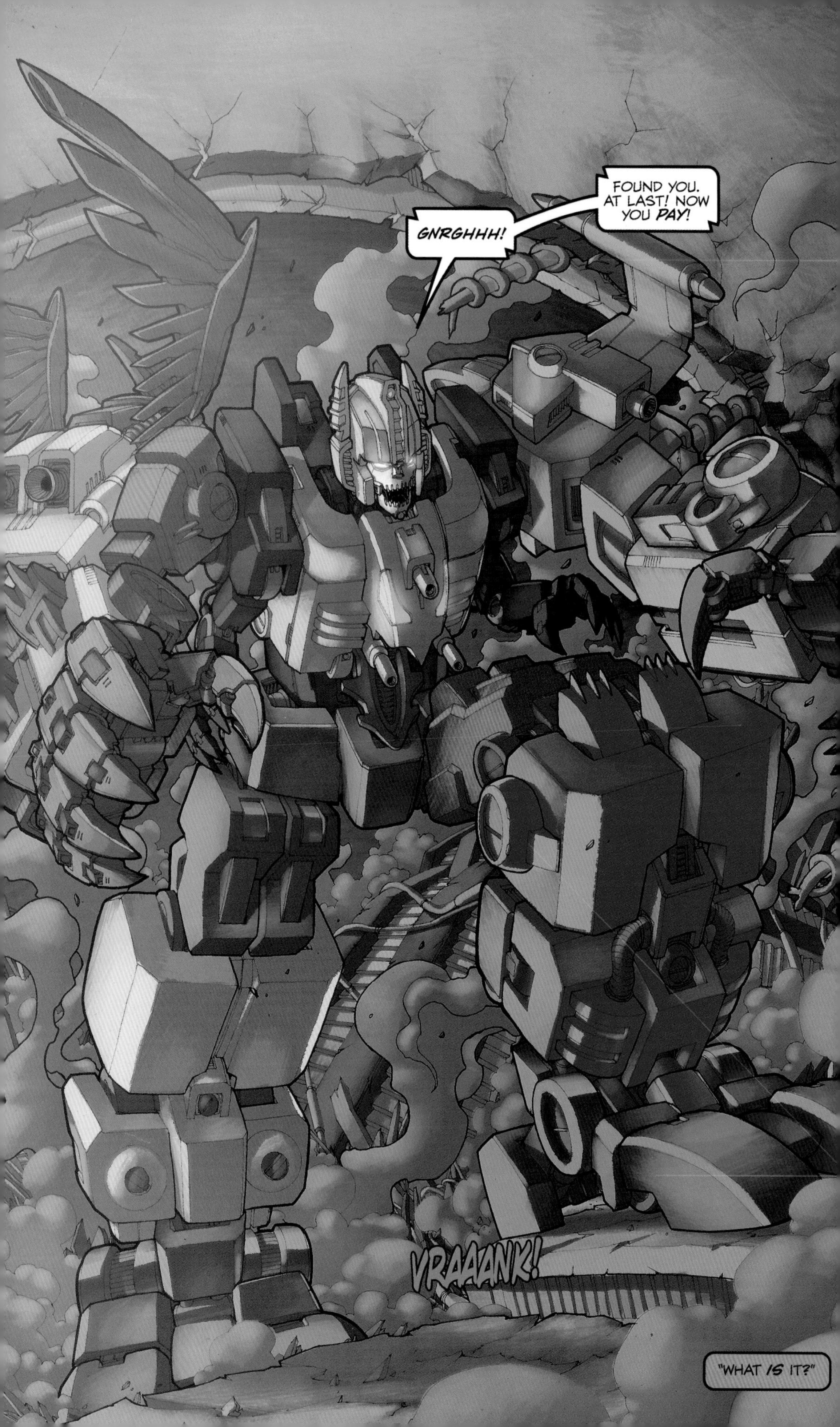
GNRGHHH!
FOUND YOU. AT LAST! NOW YOU *PAY*!
VRAAANK!
"WHAT *IS* IT?"

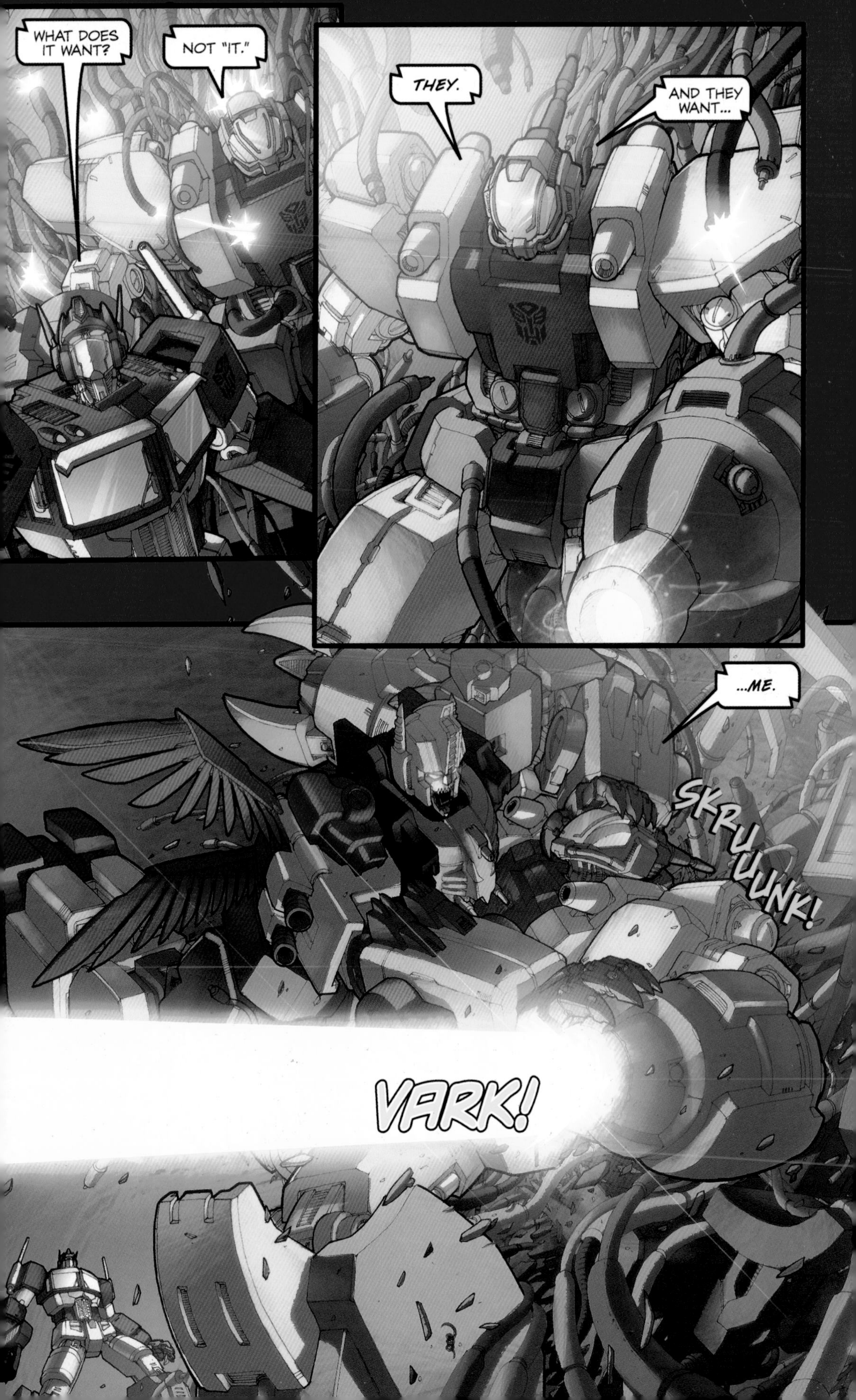
WHAT DOES IT WANT?
NOT "IT."
THEY.
AND THEY WANT...
...ME.
SKRUUUNK!
VARK!

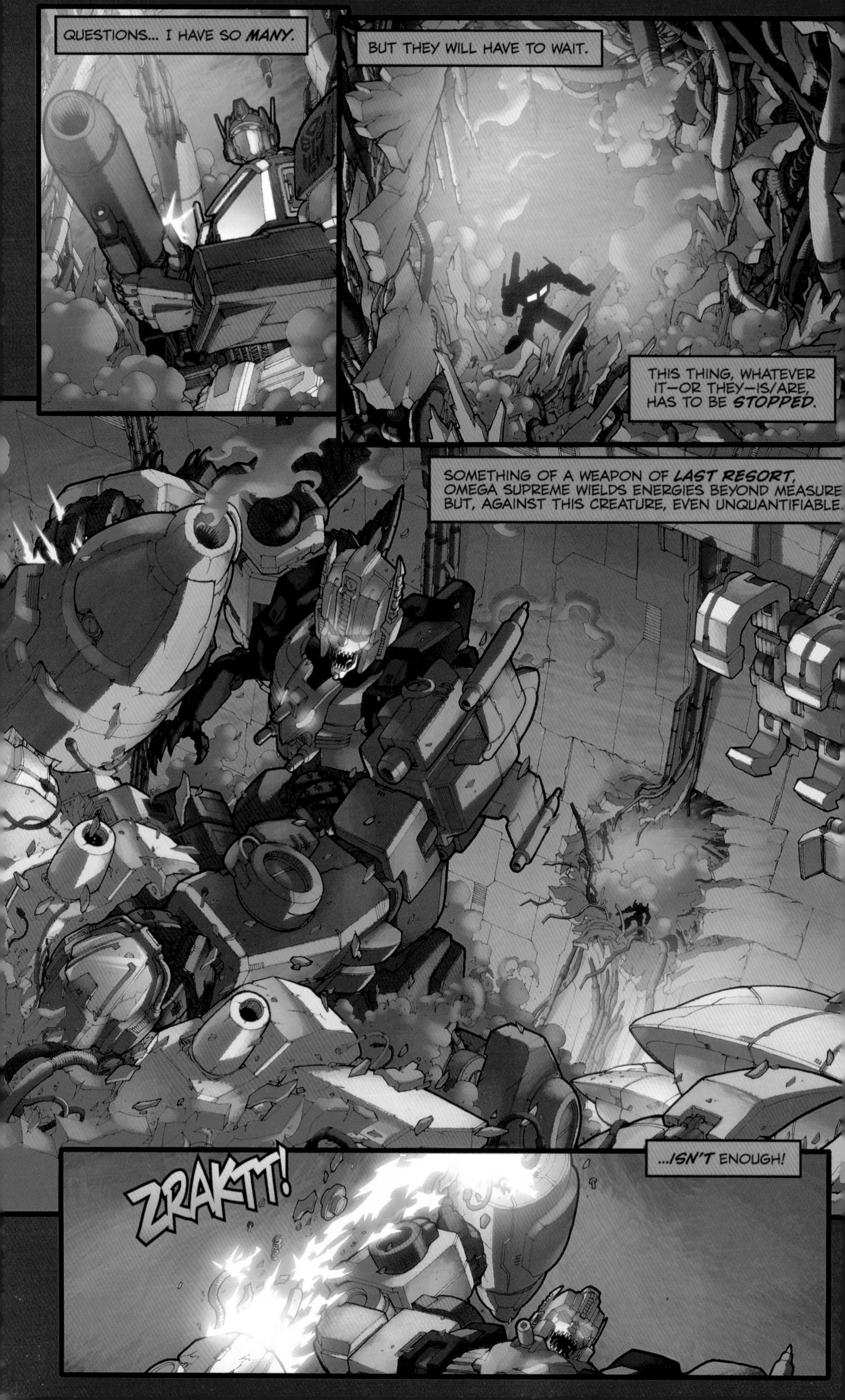
QUESTIONS... I HAVE SO MANY.
BUT THEY WILL HAVE TO WAIT.
THIS THING, WHATEVER IT—OR THEY—IS/ARE, HAS TO BE STOPPED.
SOMETHING OF A WEAPON OF LAST RESORT, OMEGA SUPREME WIELDS ENERGIES BEYOND MEASURE BUT, AGAINST THIS CREATURE, EVEN UNQUANTIFIABLE...
...ISN'T ENOUGH!
ZRAKTT!

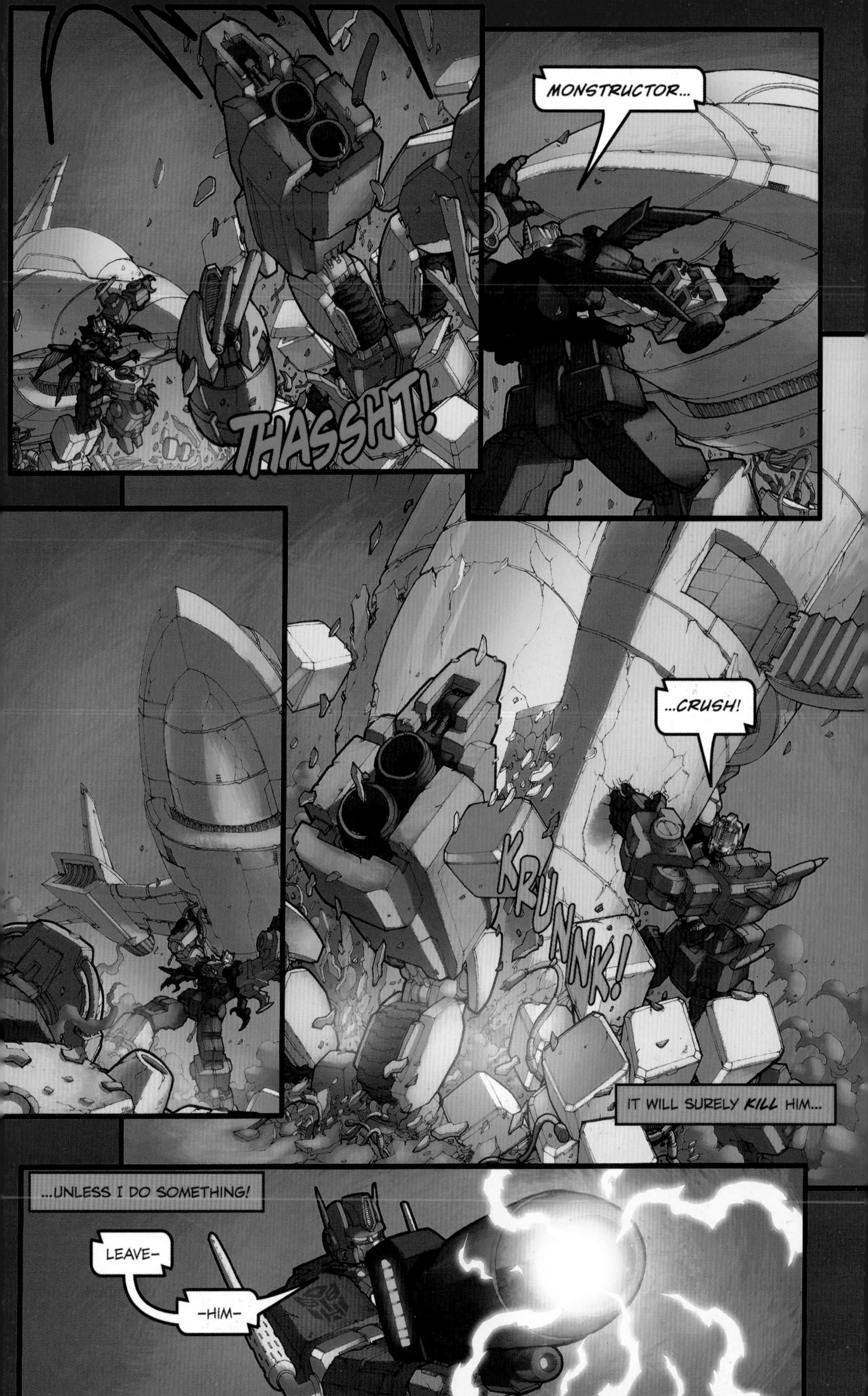
THASSHT!
MONSTRUCTOR...
...CRUSH!
KRUNNK!
IT WILL SURELY KILL HIM...
...UNLESS I DO SOMETHING!
LEAVE-
-HIM-

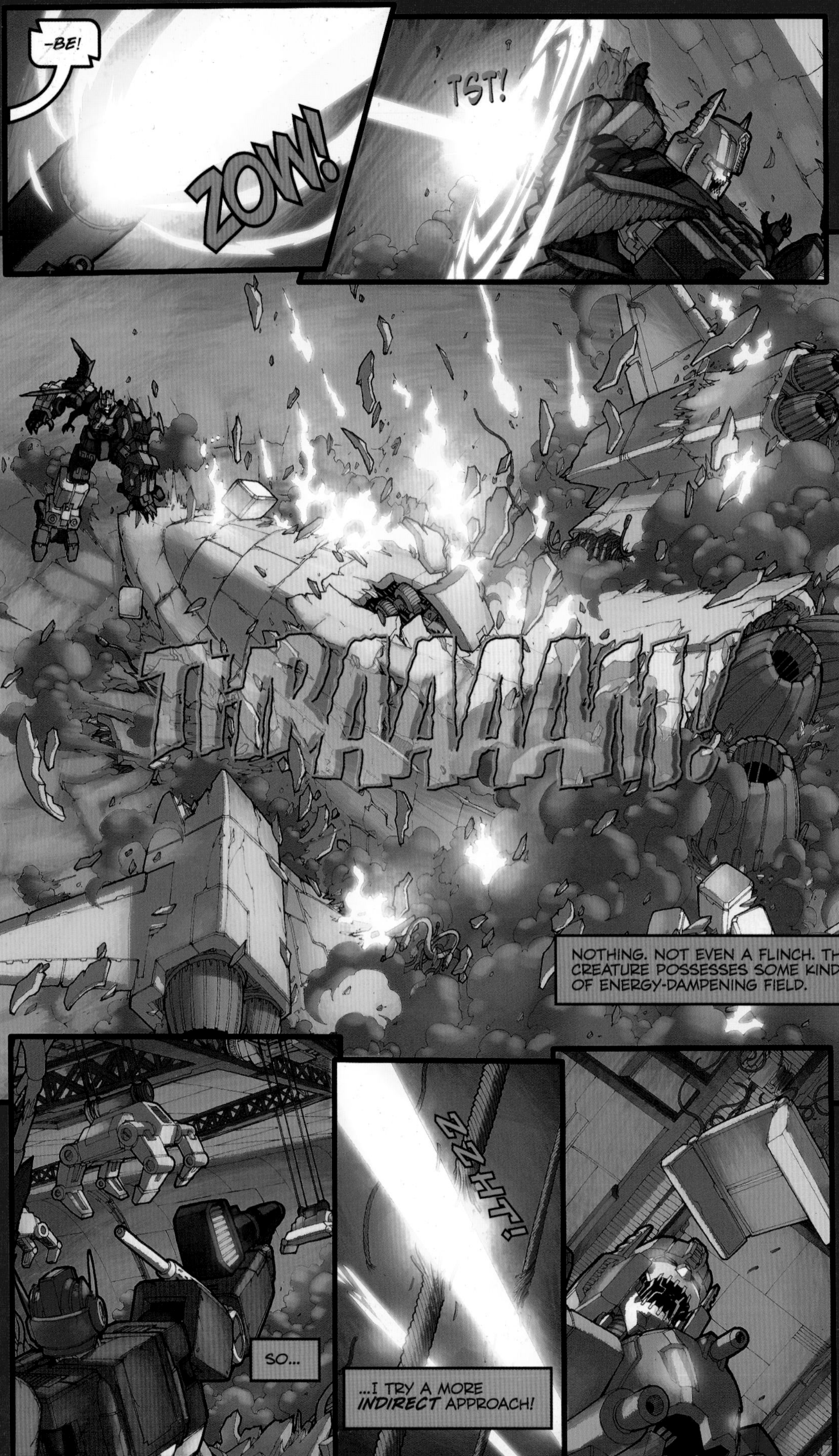
-BE!
ZOW!
TST!
THRAAAM!
NOTHING. NOT EVEN A FLINCH. THE CREATURE POSSESSES SOME KIND OF ENERGY-DAMPENING FIELD.
SO...
ZZHT!
...I TRY A MORE INDIRECT APPROACH!

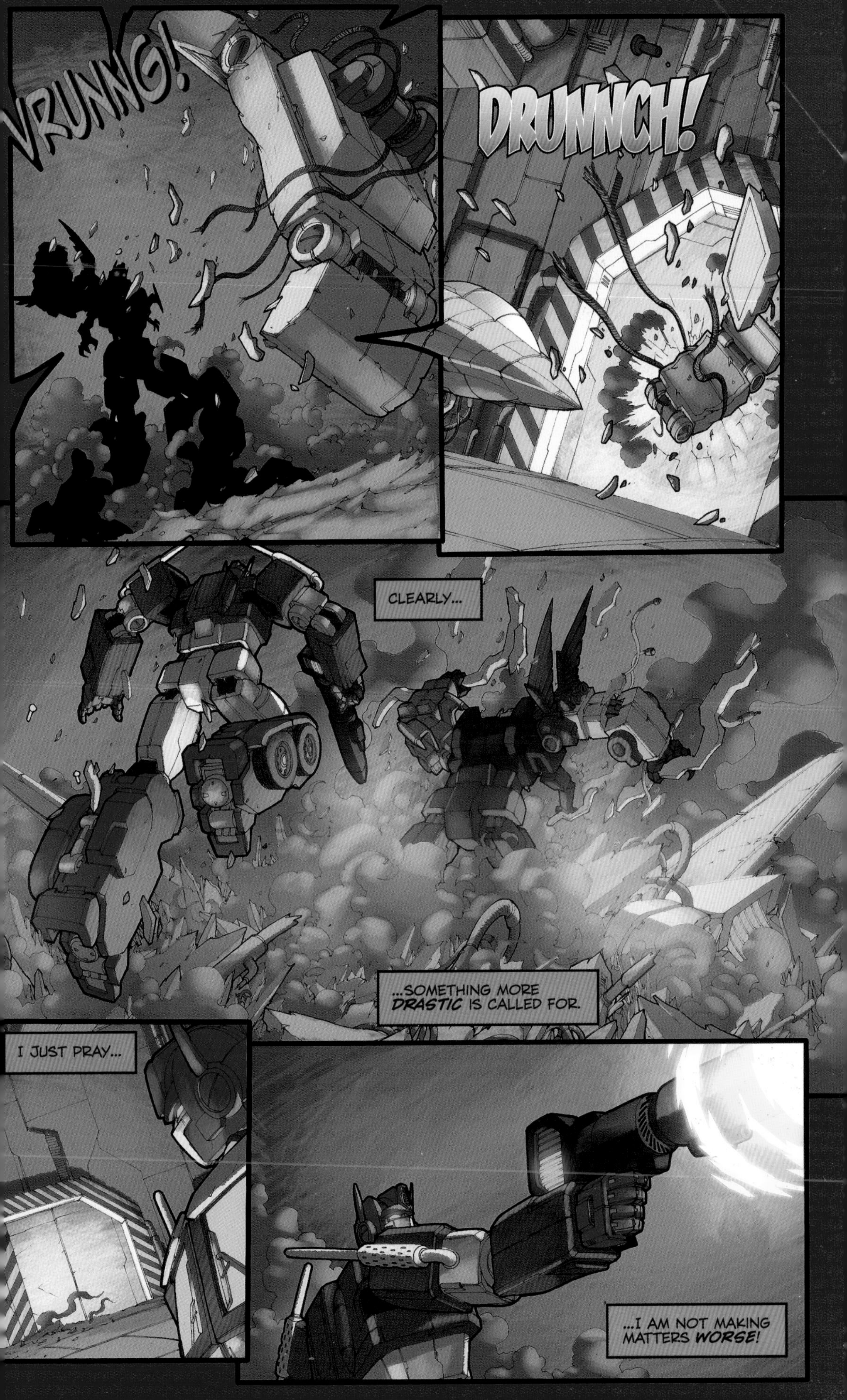
VRUNNG!
DRUNNCH!
CLEARLY...
...SOMETHING MORE DRASTIC IS CALLED FOR.
I JUST PRAY...
...I AM NOT MAKING MATTERS WORSE!

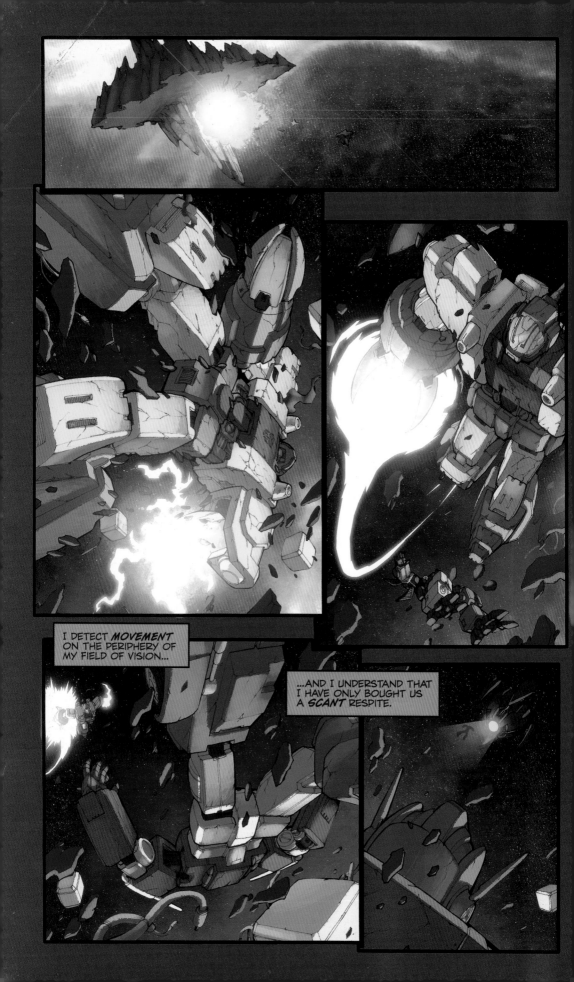

I DETECT **MOVEMENT** ON THE PERIPHERY OF MY FIELD OF VISION...

...AND I UNDERSTAND THAT I HAVE ONLY BOUGHT US A **SCANT** RESPITE.

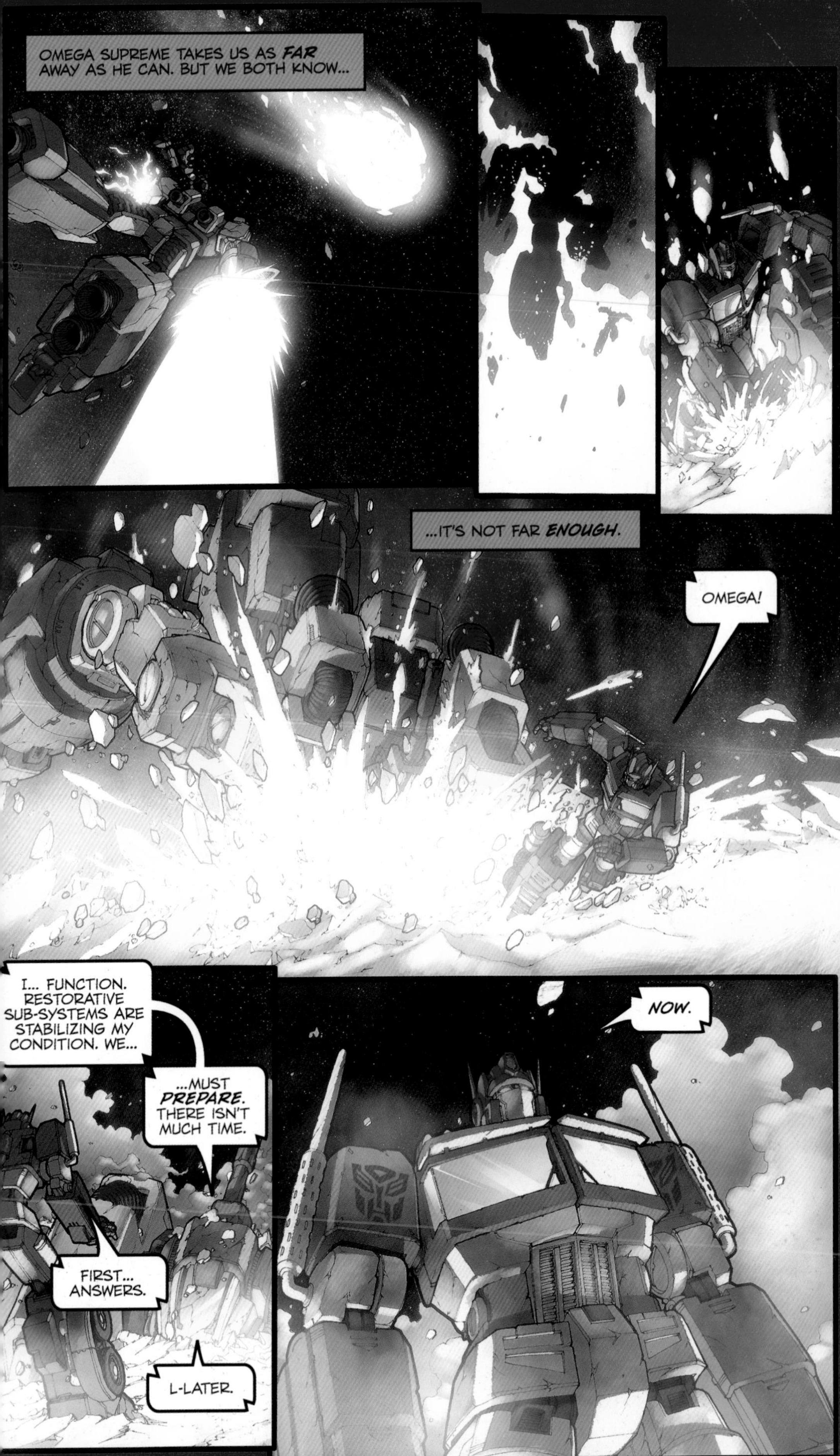
OMEGA SUPREME TAKES US AS FAR AWAY AS HE CAN. BUT WE BOTH KNOW...
...IT'S NOT FAR ENOUGH.
OMEGA!
I... FUNCTION. RESTORATIVE SUB-SYSTEMS ARE STABILIZING MY CONDITION. WE...
...MUST PREPARE. THERE ISN'T MUCH TIME.
FIRST... ANSWERS.
L-LATER.
NOW.

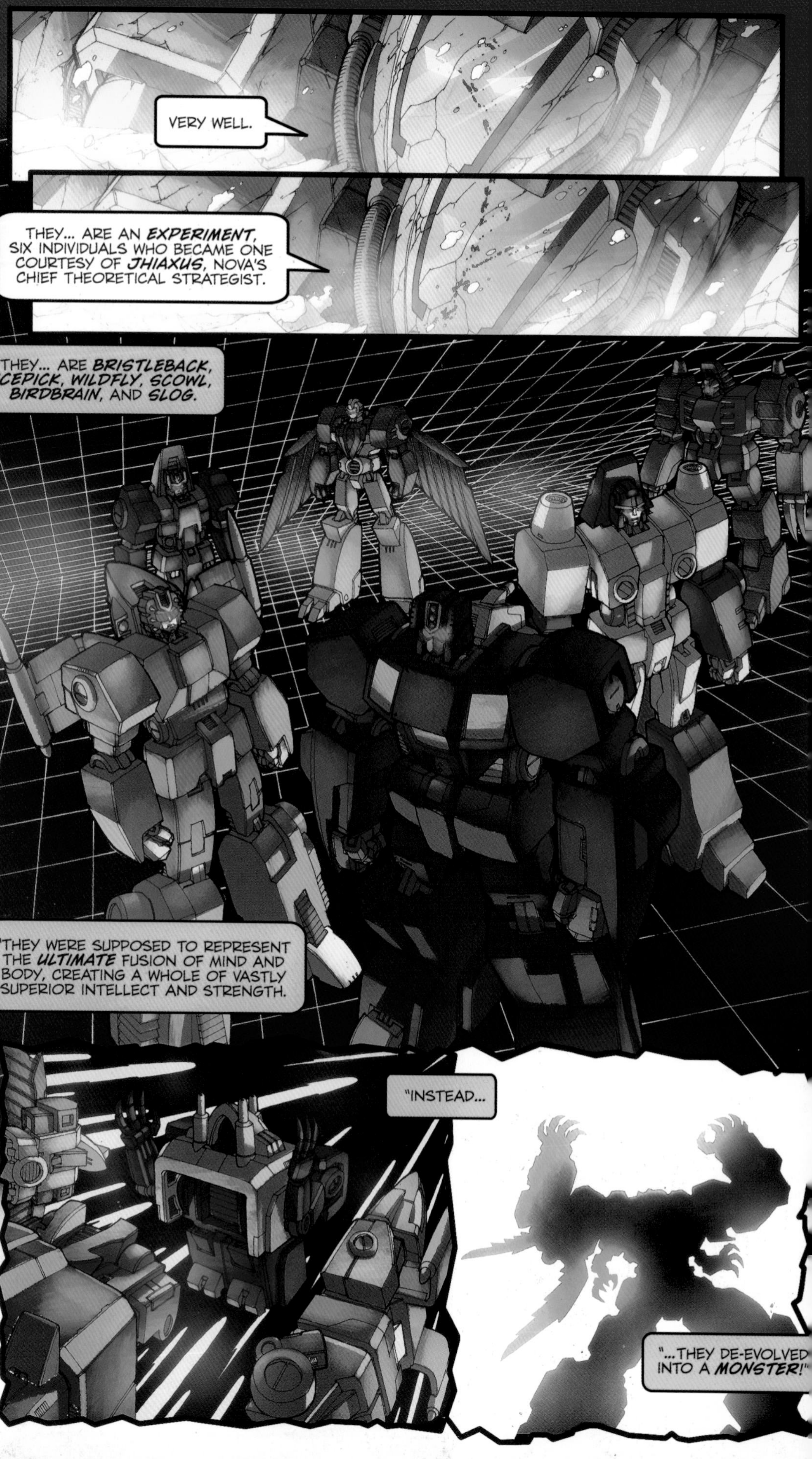
VERY WELL.
THEY... ARE AN EXPERIMENT, SIX INDIVIDUALS WHO BECAME ONE COURTESY OF JHIAXUS, NOVA'S CHIEF THEORETICAL STRATEGIST.
"THEY... ARE BRISTLEBACK, ICEPICK, WILDFLY, SCOWL, BIRDBRAIN, AND SLOG.
"THEY WERE SUPPOSED TO REPRESENT THE ULTIMATE FUSION OF MIND AND BODY, CREATING A WHOLE OF VASTLY SUPERIOR INTELLECT AND STRENGTH.
"INSTEAD...
"...THEY DE-EVOLVED INTO A MONSTER!"

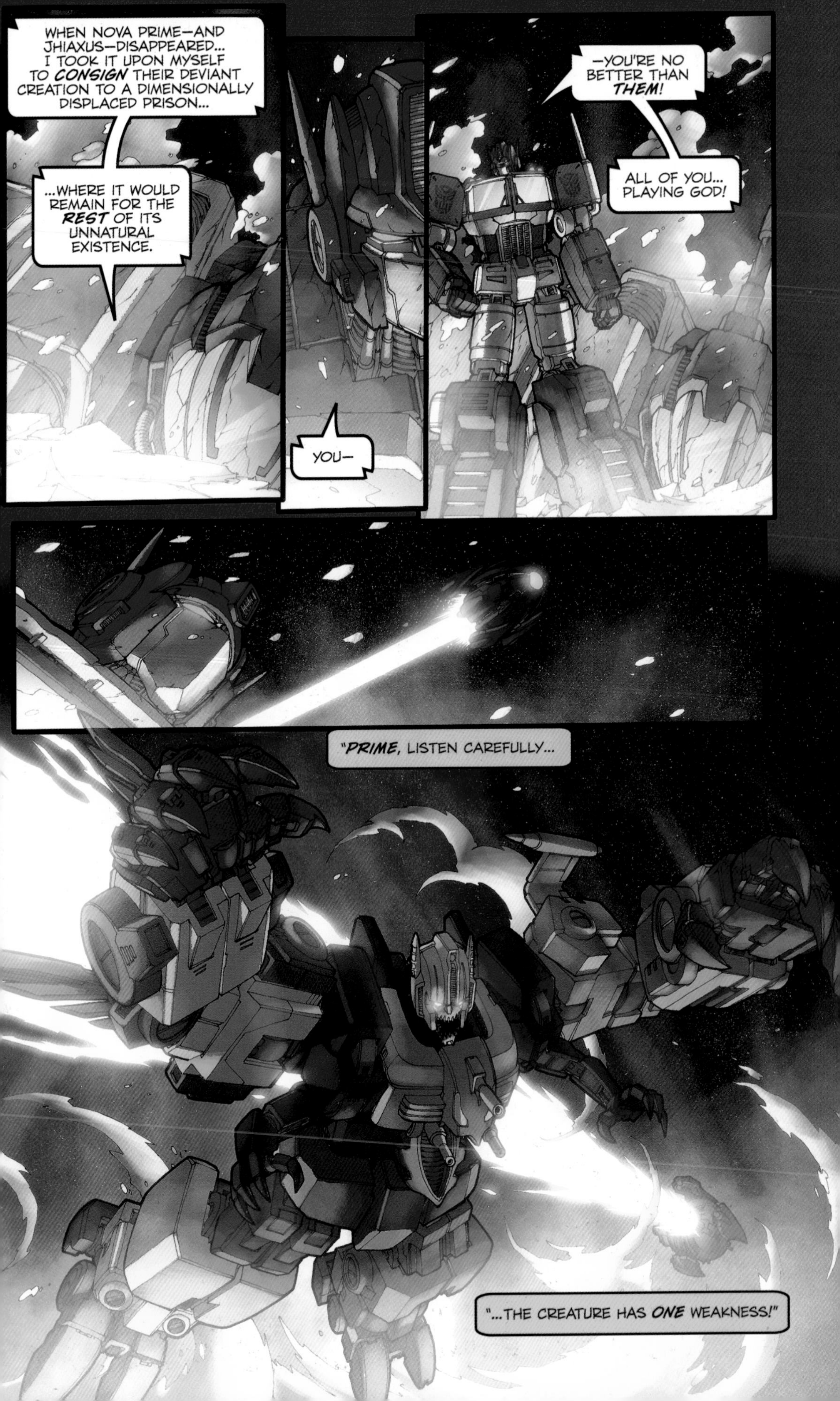
WHEN NOVA PRIME—AND JHIAXUS—DISAPPEARED... I TOOK IT UPON MYSELF TO *CONSIGN* THEIR DEVIANT CREATION TO A DIMENSIONALLY DISPLACED PRISON...
...WHERE IT WOULD REMAIN FOR THE *REST* OF ITS UNNATURAL EXISTENCE.
YOU—
—YOU'RE NO BETTER THAN *THEM*!
ALL OF YOU... PLAYING GOD!
"*PRIME*, LISTEN CAREFULLY...
"...THE CREATURE HAS *ONE* WEAKNESS!"

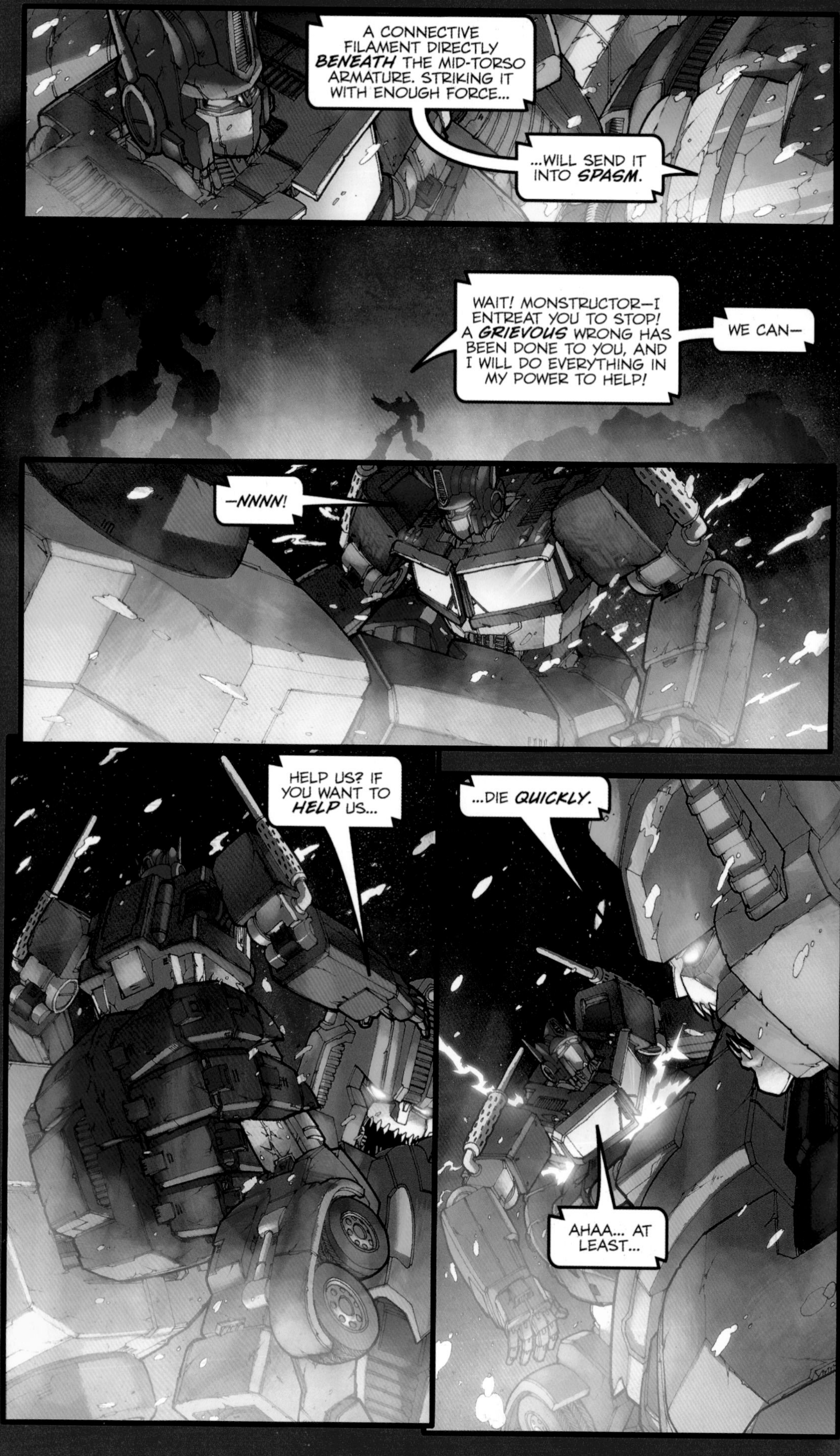
A CONNECTIVE FILAMENT DIRECTLY BENEATH THE MID-TORSO ARMATURE. STRIKING IT WITH ENOUGH FORCE...
...WILL SEND IT INTO SPASM.
WAIT! MONSTRUCTOR—I ENTREAT YOU TO STOP! A GRIEVOUS WRONG HAS BEEN DONE TO YOU, AND I WILL DO EVERYTHING IN MY POWER TO HELP!
WE CAN—
—NNNN!
HELP US? IF YOU WANT TO HELP US...
...DIE QUICKLY.
AHAA... AT LEAST...

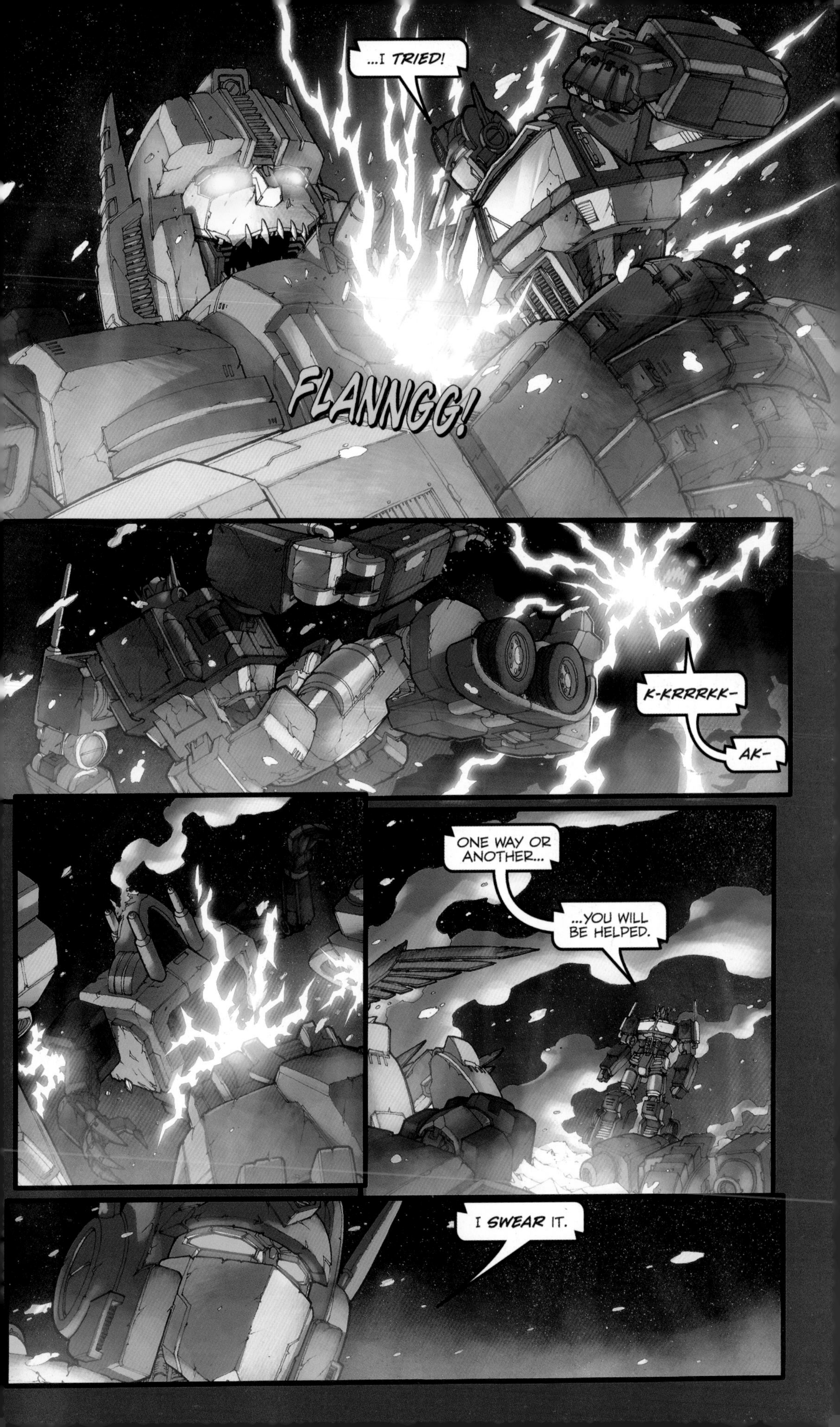
...I TRIED!
FLANNGG!
K-KRRRKK-
AK-
ONE WAY OR ANOTHER...
...YOU WILL BE HELPED.
I SWEAR IT.

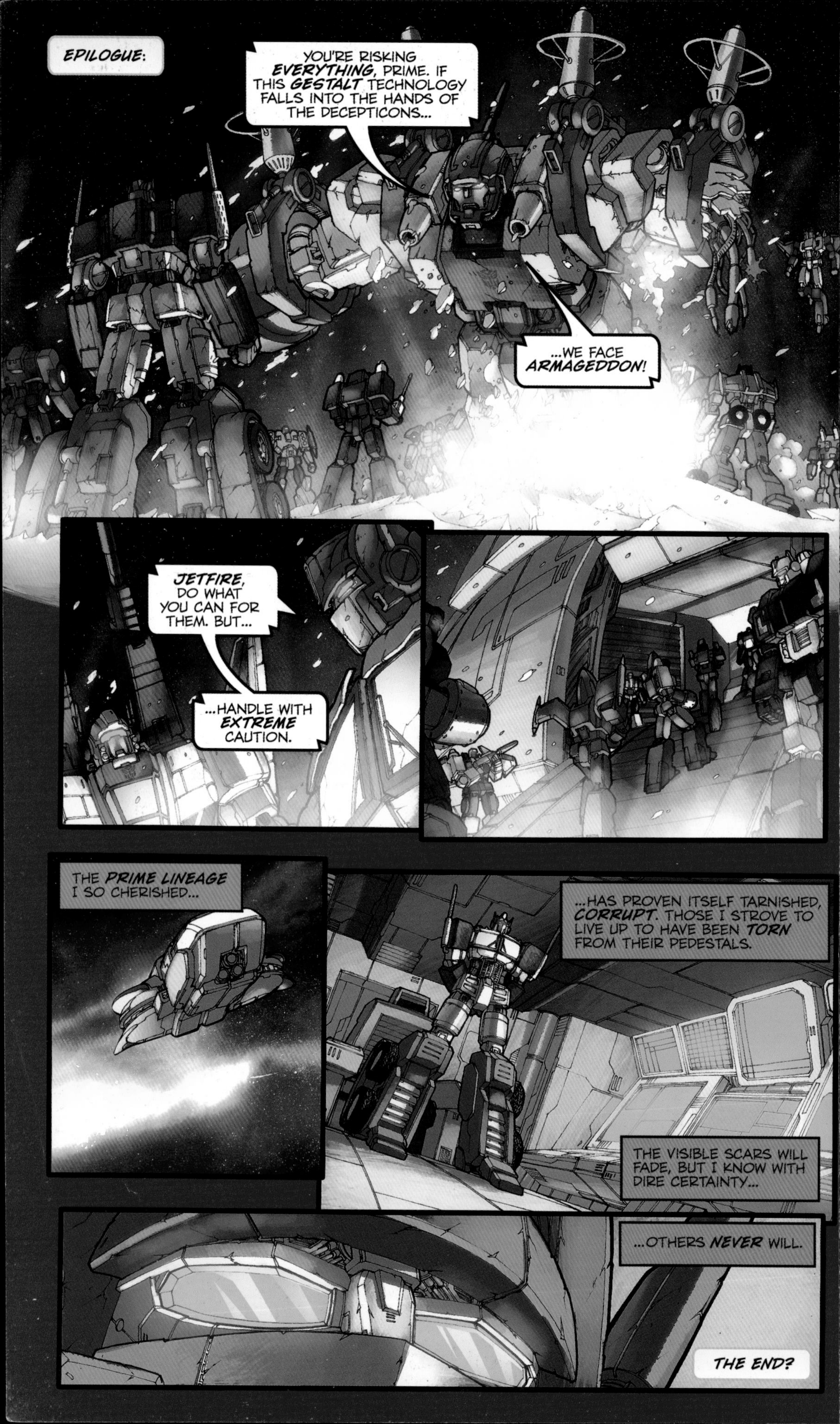
EPILOGUE:
YOU'RE RISKING EVERYTHING, PRIME. IF THIS GESTALT TECHNOLOGY FALLS INTO THE HANDS OF THE DECEPTICONS...
...WE FACE ARMAGEDDON!
JETFIRE, DO WHAT YOU CAN FOR THEM. BUT...
...HANDLE WITH EXTREME CAUTION.
THE PRIME LINEAGE I SO CHERISHED...
...HAS PROVEN ITSELF TARNISHED, CORRUPT. THOSE I STROVE TO LIVE UP TO HAVE BEEN TORN FROM THEIR PEDESTALS.
THE VISIBLE SCARS WILL FADE, BUT I KNOW WITH DIRE CERTAINTY...
...OTHERS NEVER WILL.
THE END?

THE TRANSFORMERS
THE BEST OF OPTIMUS PRIME

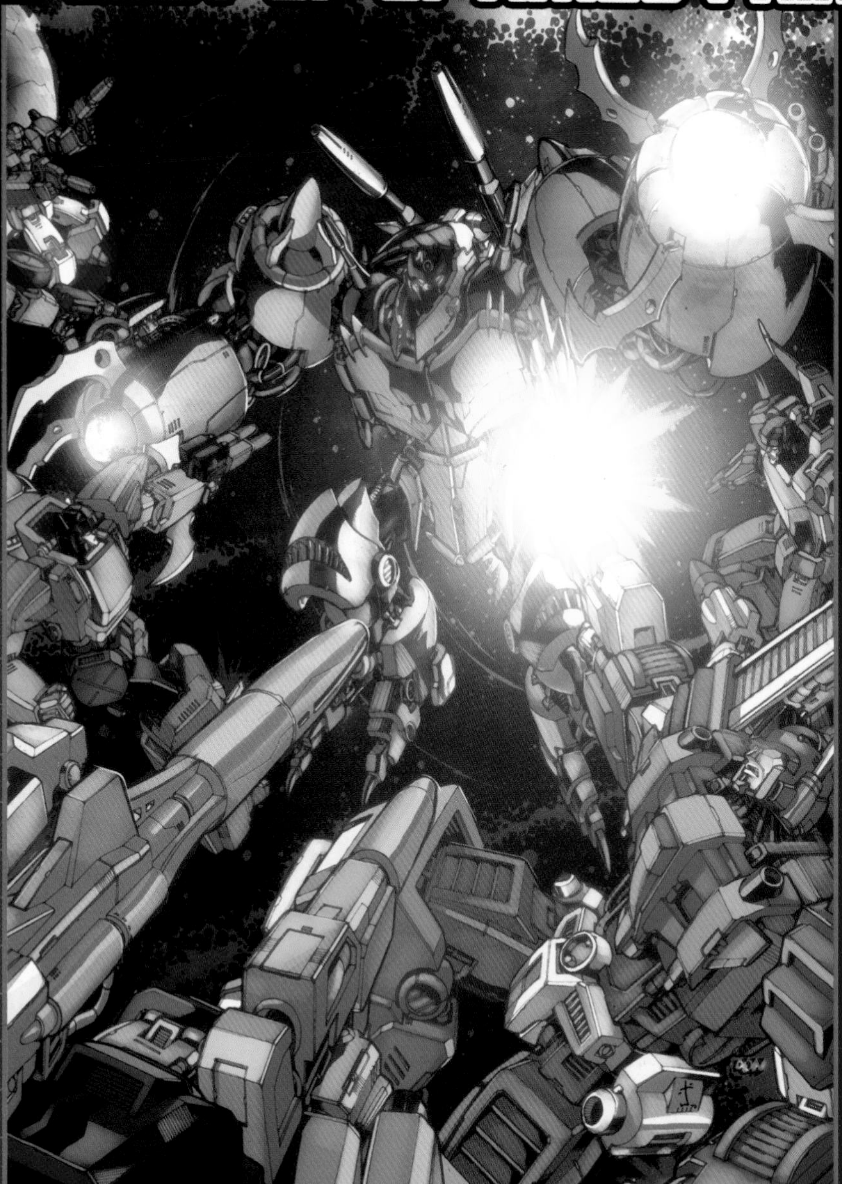

STORMBRINGER #4

Simon Furman delivered a great, pure robot action story arc with the STORMBRINGER series. In this concluding chapter to the series, OPTIMUS PRIME realizes that in order to save the fate of the TRANSFORMERS' planet CYBERTRON from THUNDERWING, it will take brains and brawn. Fully prepared to give his spark to prevent THUNDERWING from spreading destruction throughout the universe, PRIME is able to single-handedly save CYBERTRON from complete annihilation.

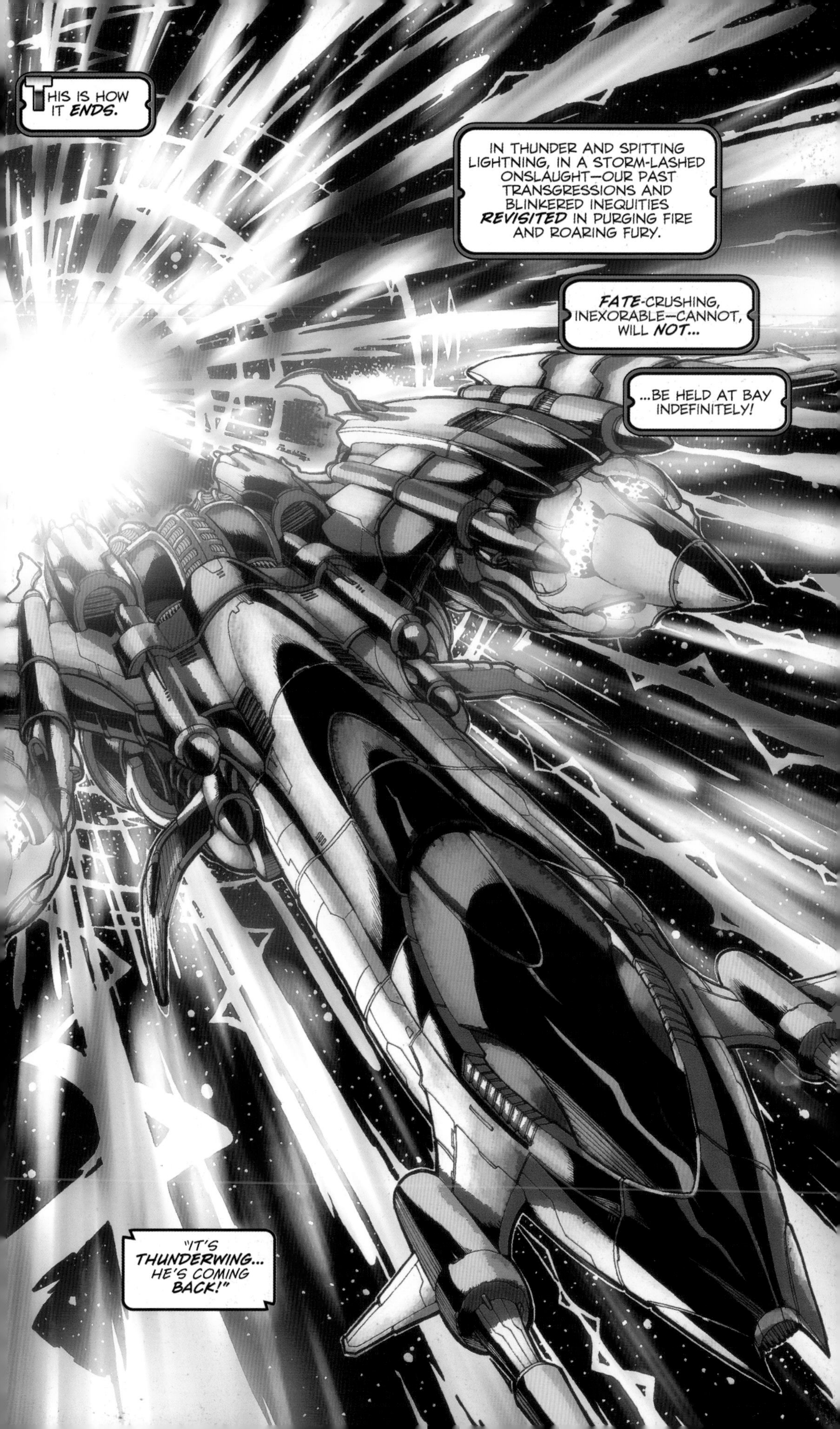
THIS IS HOW IT ENDS.
IN THUNDER AND SPITTING LIGHTNING, IN A STORM-LASHED ONSLAUGHT—OUR PAST TRANSGRESSIONS AND BLINKERED INEQUITIES REVISITED IN PURGING FIRE AND ROARING FURY.
FATE-CRUSHING, INEXORABLE—CANNOT, WILL NOT...
...BE HELD AT BAY INDEFINITELY!
"IT'S THUNDERWING... HE'S COMING BACK!"

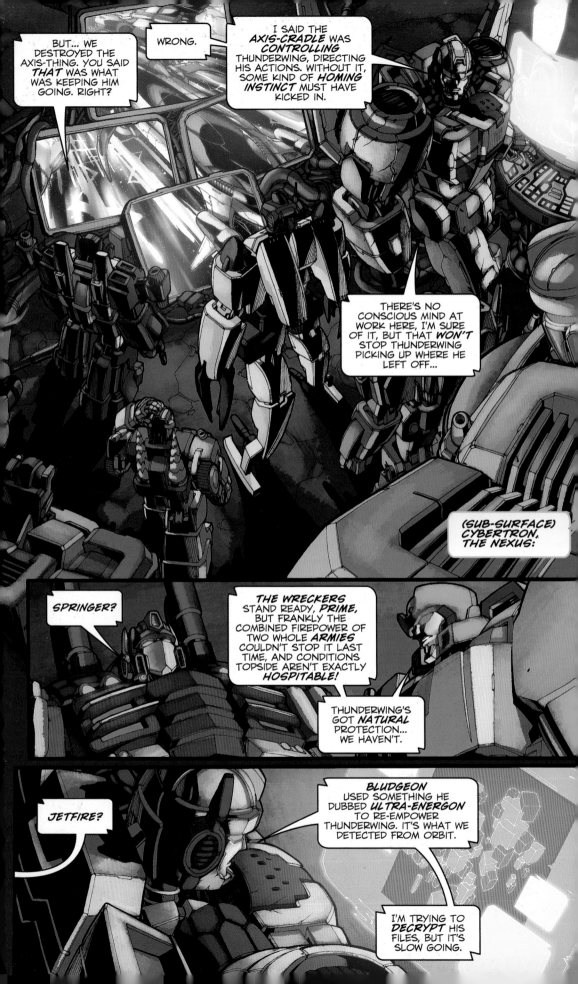

BUT... WE DESTROYED THE AXIS-THING. YOU SAID *THAT* WAS WHAT WAS KEEPING HIM GOING. RIGHT?

WRONG.

I SAID THE *AXIS-CRADLE* WAS *CONTROLLING* THUNDERWING, DIRECTING HIS ACTIONS. WITHOUT IT, SOME KIND OF *HOMING INSTINCT* MUST HAVE KICKED IN.

THERE'S NO CONSCIOUS MIND AT WORK HERE, I'M SURE OF IT, BUT THAT *WON'T* STOP THUNDERWING PICKING UP WHERE HE LEFT OFF...

(SUB-SURFACE) CYBERTRON, THE NEXUS:

SPRINGER?

THE WRECKERS STAND READY, *PRIME*, BUT FRANKLY THE COMBINED FIREPOWER OF TWO WHOLE *ARMIES* COULDN'T STOP IT LAST TIME, AND CONDITIONS TOPSIDE AREN'T EXACTLY *HOSPITABLE!*

THUNDERWING'S GOT *NATURAL* PROTECTION... WE HAVEN'T.

JETFIRE?

BLUDGEON USED SOMETHING HE DUBBED *ULTRA-ENERGON* TO RE-EMPOWER THUNDERWING. IT'S WHAT WE DETECTED FROM ORBIT.

I'M TRYING TO *DECRYPT* HIS FILES, BUT IT'S SLOW GOING.

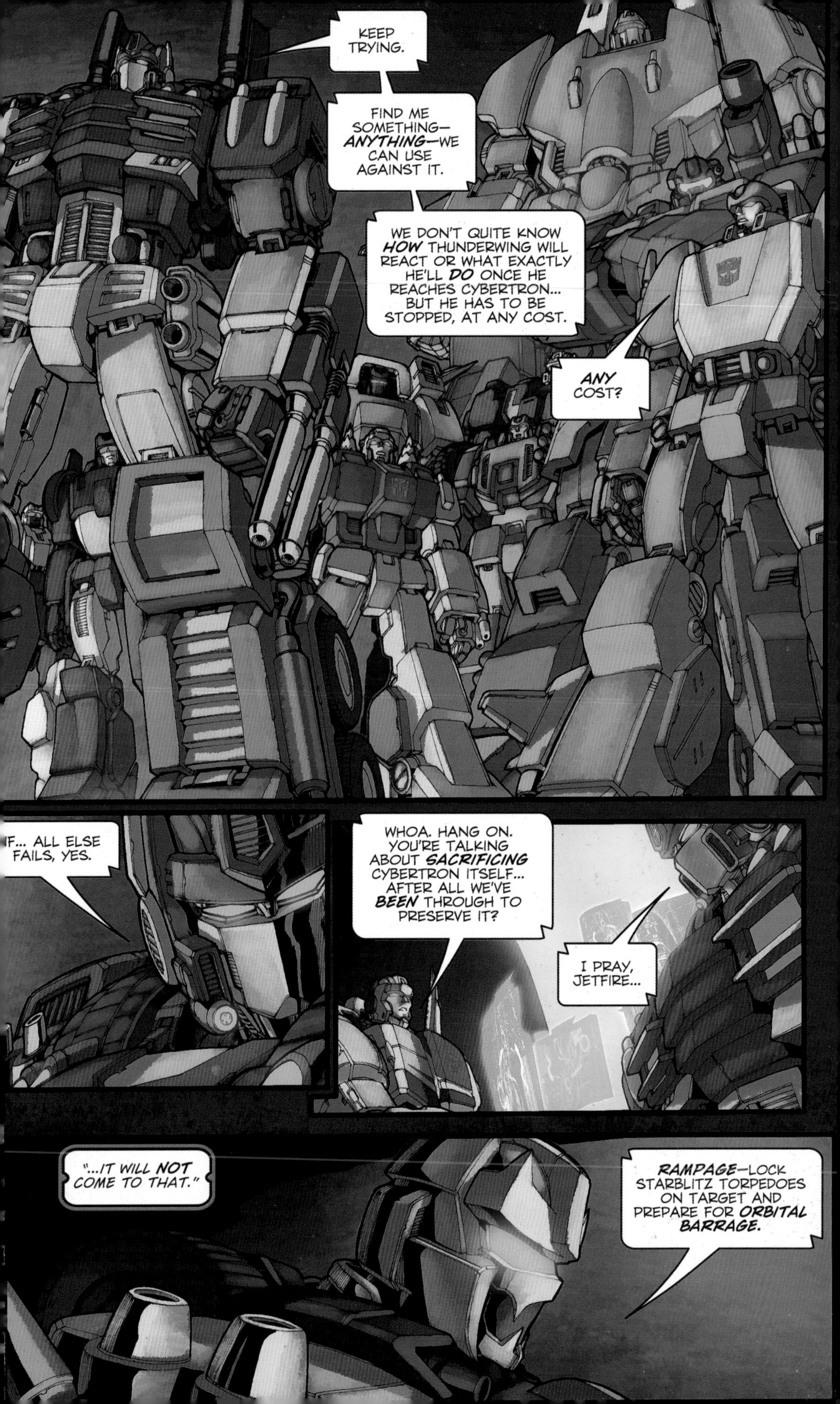
KEEP TRYING.
FIND ME SOMETHING—*ANYTHING*—WE CAN USE AGAINST IT.
WE DON'T QUITE KNOW *HOW* THUNDERWING WILL REACT OR WHAT EXACTLY HE'LL *DO* ONCE HE REACHES CYBERTRON... BUT HE HAS TO BE STOPPED, AT ANY COST.
ANY COST?
IF... ALL ELSE FAILS, YES.
WHOA. HANG ON. YOU'RE TALKING ABOUT *SACRIFICING* CYBERTRON ITSELF... AFTER ALL WE'VE *BEEN* THROUGH TO PRESERVE IT?
I PRAY, JETFIRE...
"...IT WILL *NOT* COME TO THAT."
RAMPAGE—LOCK STARBLITZ TORPEDOES ON TARGET AND PREPARE FOR *ORBITAL BARRAGE*.

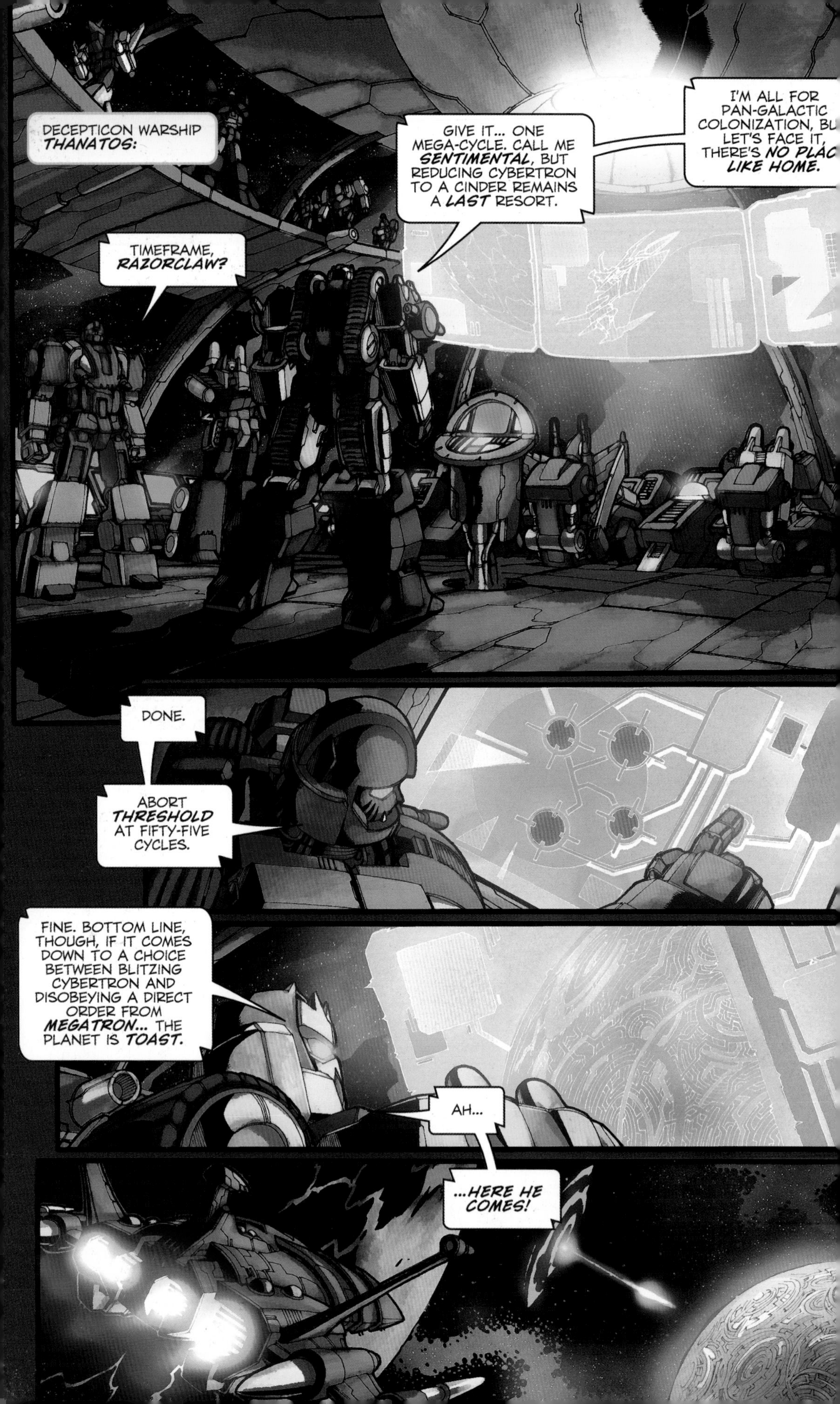

DECEPTICON WARSHIP THANATOS:
TIMEFRAME, RAZORCLAW?
GIVE IT... ONE MEGA-CYCLE. CALL ME SENTIMENTAL, BUT REDUCING CYBERTRON TO A CINDER REMAINS A LAST RESORT.
I'M ALL FOR PAN-GALACTIC COLONIZATION, BU LET'S FACE IT, THERE'S NO PLAC LIKE HOME.
DONE.
ABORT THRESHOLD AT FIFTY-FIVE CYCLES.
FINE. BOTTOM LINE, THOUGH, IF IT COMES DOWN TO A CHOICE BETWEEN BLITZING CYBERTRON AND DISOBEYING A DIRECT ORDER FROM MEGATRON... THE PLANET IS TOAST.
AH...
...HERE HE COMES!

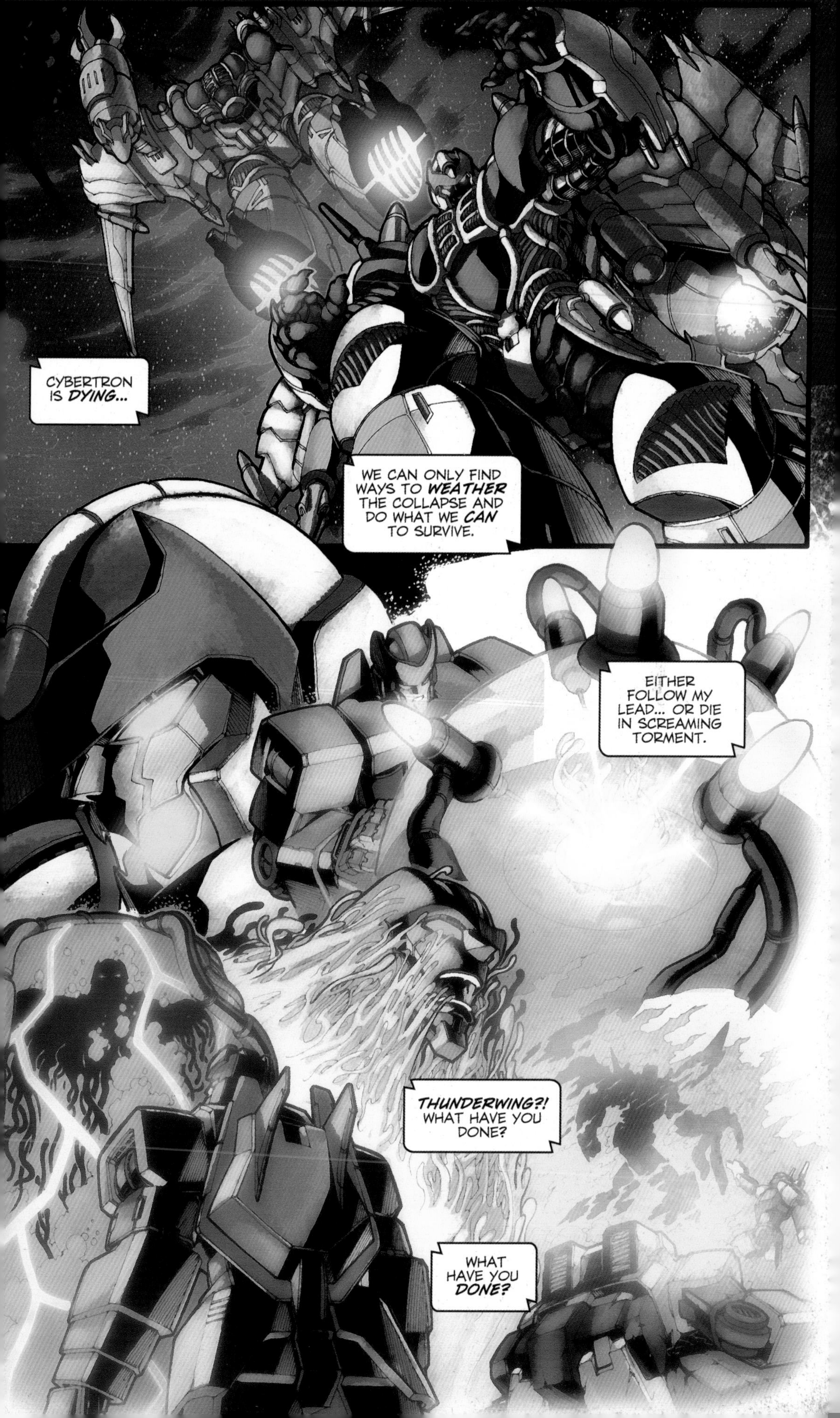
CYBERTRON IS DYING...
WE CAN ONLY FIND WAYS TO WEATHER THE COLLAPSE AND DO WHAT WE CAN TO SURVIVE.
EITHER FOLLOW MY LEAD... OR DIE IN SCREAMING TORMENT.
THUNDERWING?! WHAT HAVE YOU DONE?
WHAT HAVE YOU DONE?

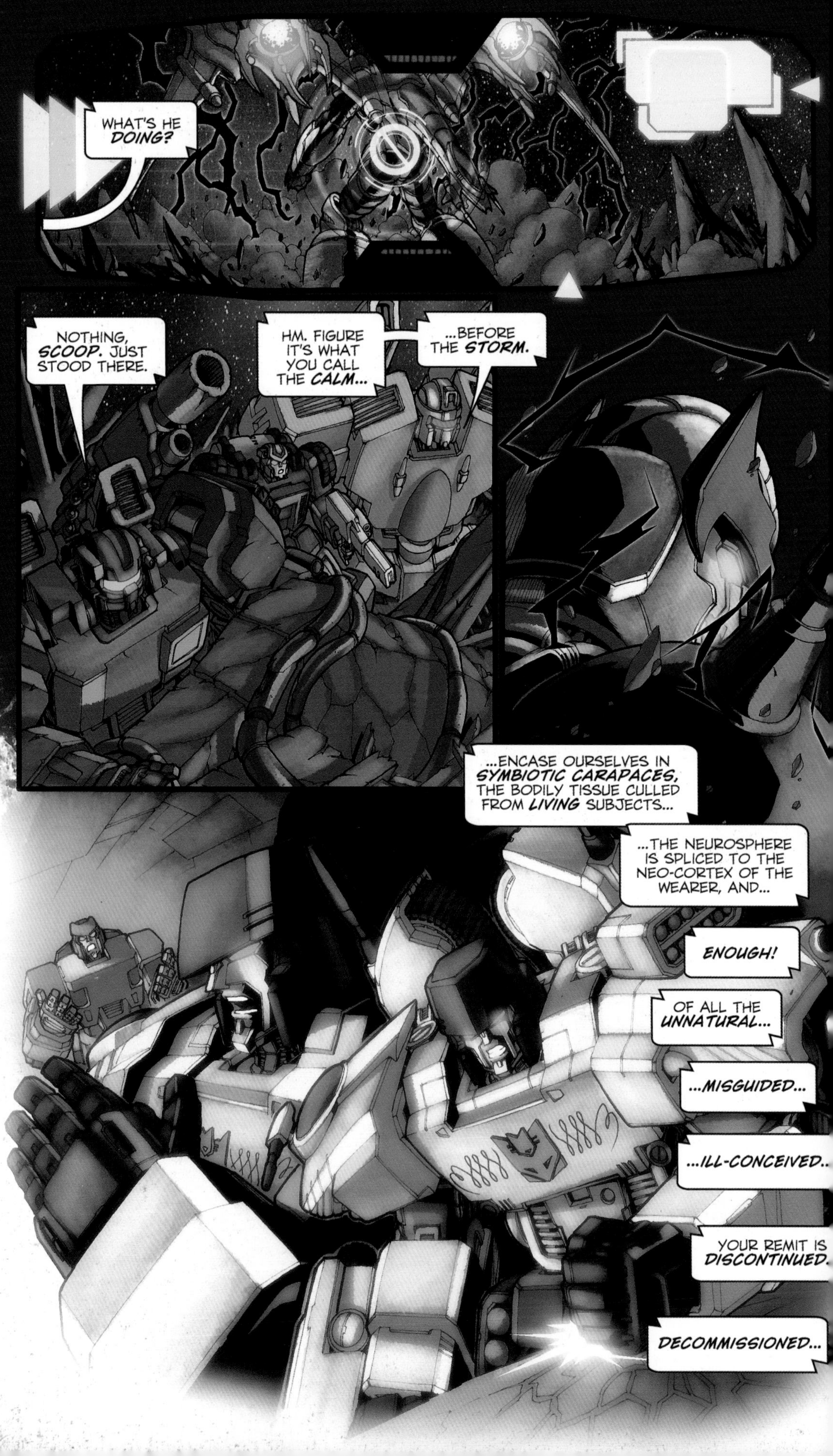

WHAT'S HE DOING?
NOTHING, SCOOP. JUST STOOD THERE.
HM. FIGURE IT'S WHAT YOU CALL THE CALM...
...BEFORE THE STORM.
...ENCASE OURSELVES IN SYMBIOTIC CARAPACES, THE BODILY TISSUE CULLED FROM LIVING SUBJECTS...
...THE NEUROSPHERE IS SPLICED TO THE NEO-CORTEX OF THE WEARER, AND...
ENOUGH!
OF ALL THE UNNATURAL...
...MISGUIDED...
...ILL-CONCEIVED...
YOUR REMIT IS DISCONTINUED.
DECOMMISSIONED...

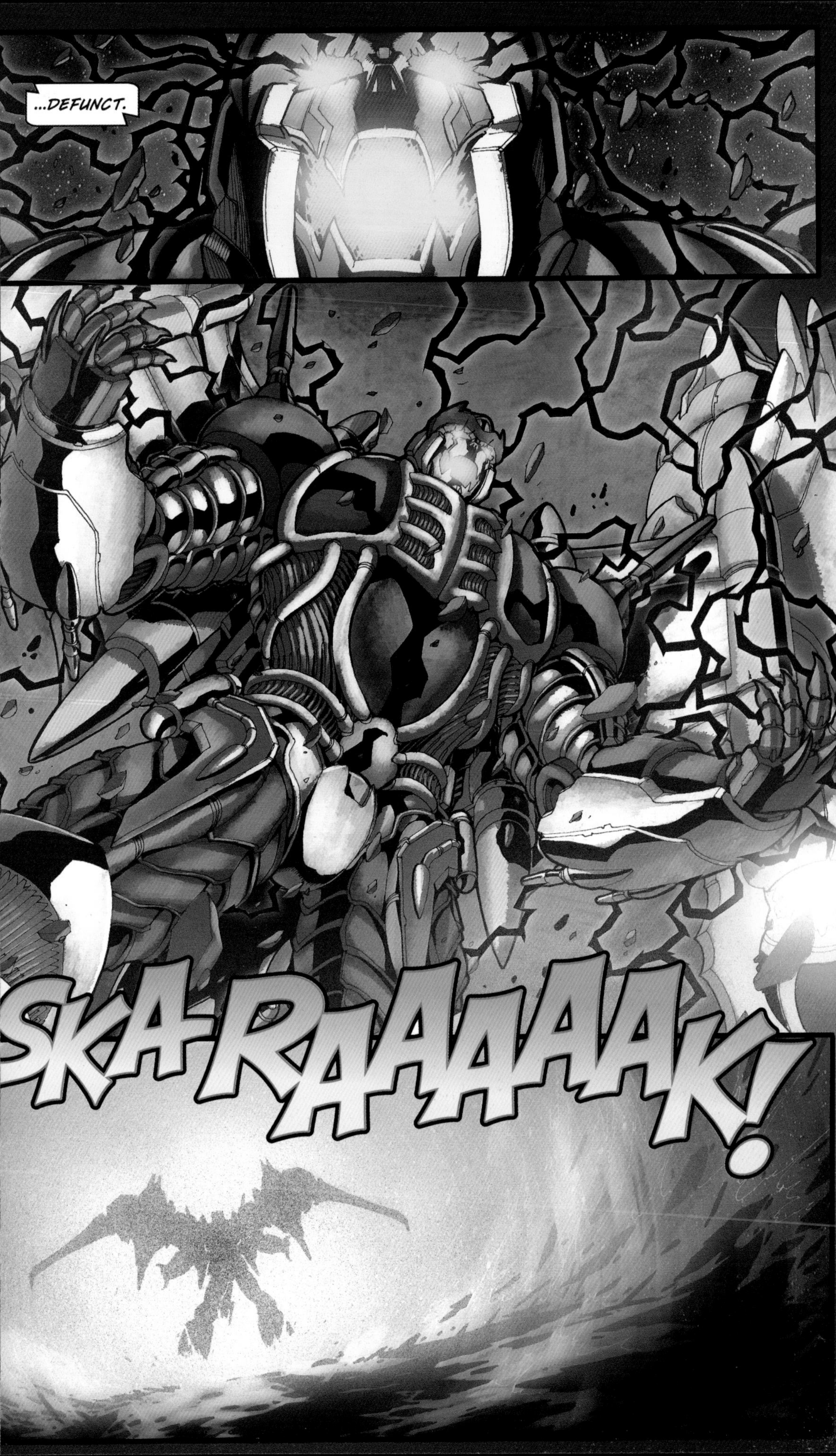
...DEFUNCT.
SKA-RAAAAAK!

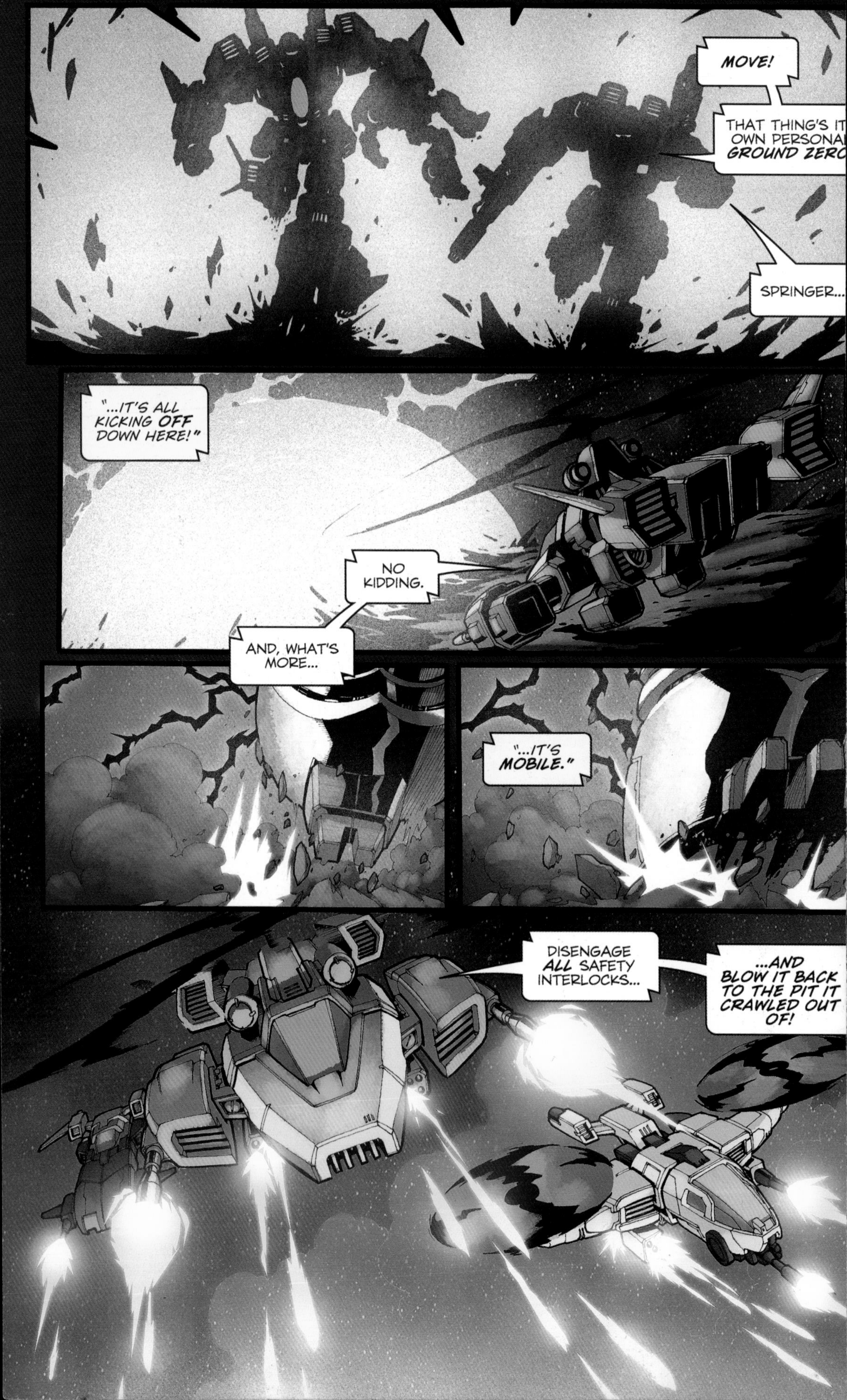
MOVE!
THAT THING'S IT OWN PERSONA GROUND ZERO
SPRINGER...
"...IT'S ALL KICKING OFF DOWN HERE!"
NO KIDDING.
AND, WHAT'S MORE...
"...IT'S MOBILE."
DISENGAGE ALL SAFETY INTERLOCKS...
...AND BLOW IT BACK TO THE PIT IT CRAWLED OUT OF!

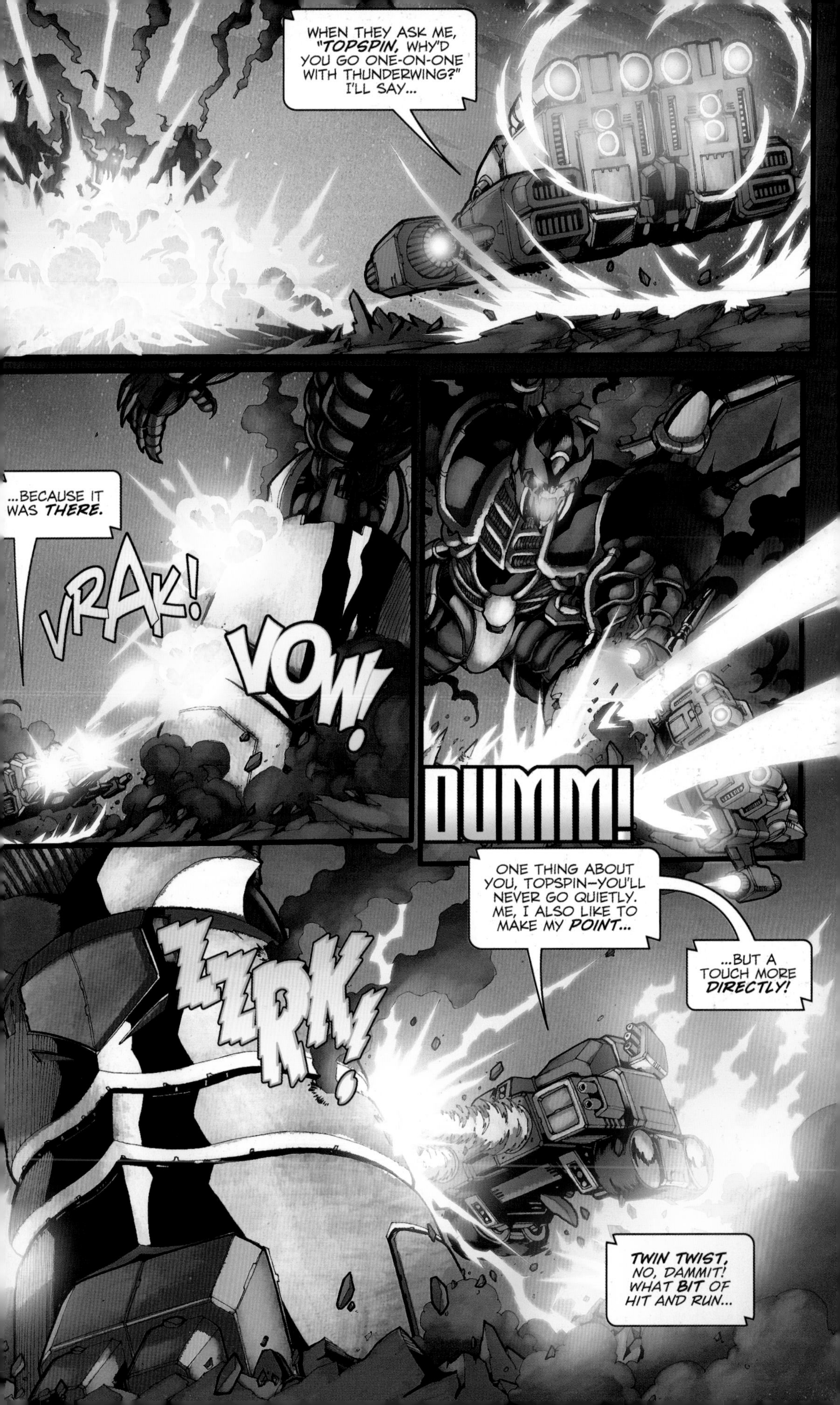
WHEN THEY ASK ME, "TOPSPIN, WHY'D YOU GO ONE-ON-ONE WITH THUNDERWING?" I'LL SAY...
...BECAUSE IT WAS THERE.
VRAK!
VOW!
DUMM!
ONE THING ABOUT YOU, TOPSPIN—YOU'LL NEVER GO QUIETLY. ME, I ALSO LIKE TO MAKE MY POINT...
...BUT A TOUCH MORE DIRECTLY!
ZZZRK!
TWIN TWIST, NO, DAMMIT! WHAT BIT OF HIT AND RUN...

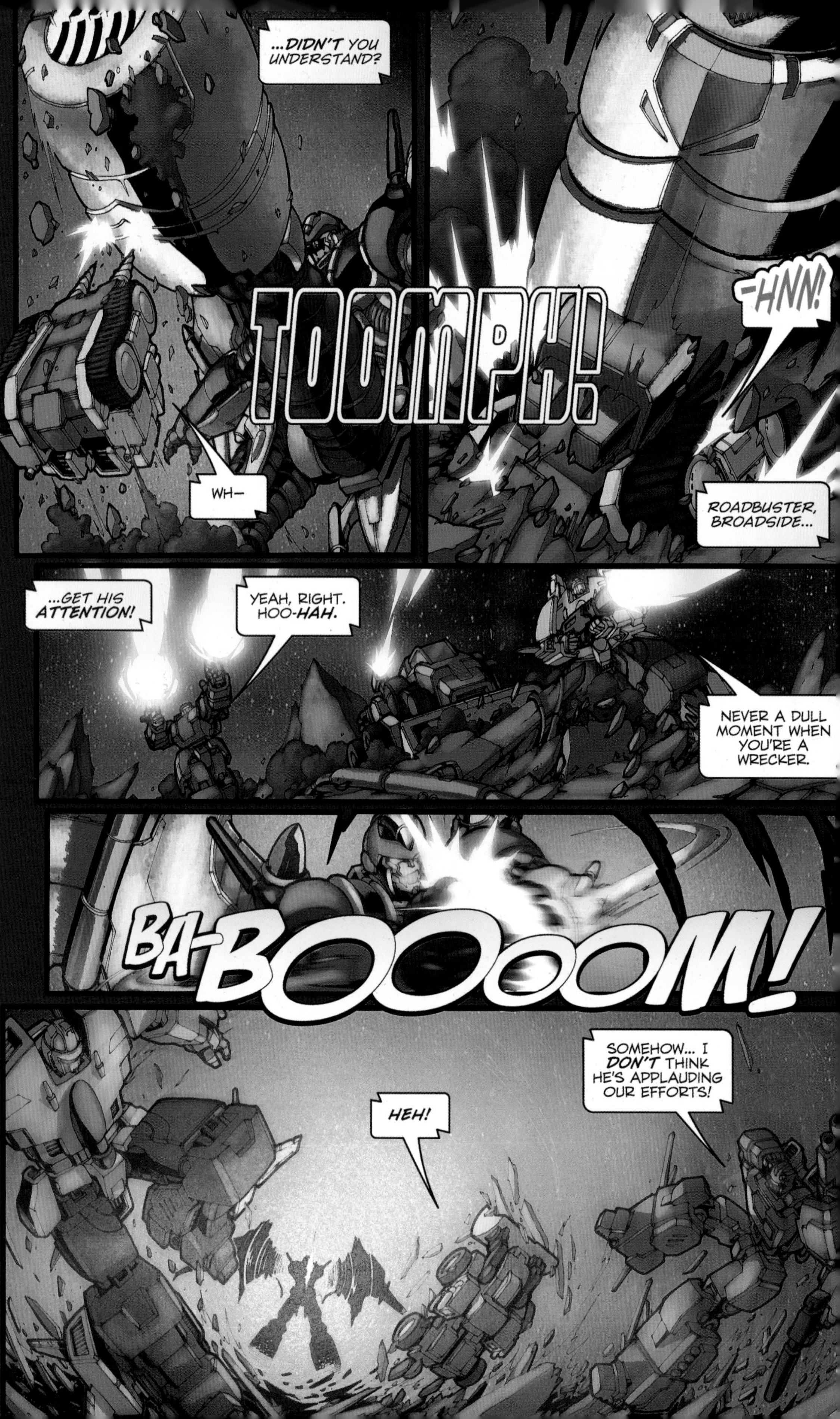
...DIDN'T YOU UNDERSTAND?
TOOMPH!
WH—
-HNN!
ROADBUSTER, BROADSIDE...
...GET HIS ATTENTION!
YEAH, RIGHT. HOO-HAH.
NEVER A DULL MOMENT WHEN YOU'RE A WRECKER.
BA-BOOOOOM!
SOMEHOW... I DON'T THINK HE'S APPLAUDING OUR EFFORTS!
HEH!

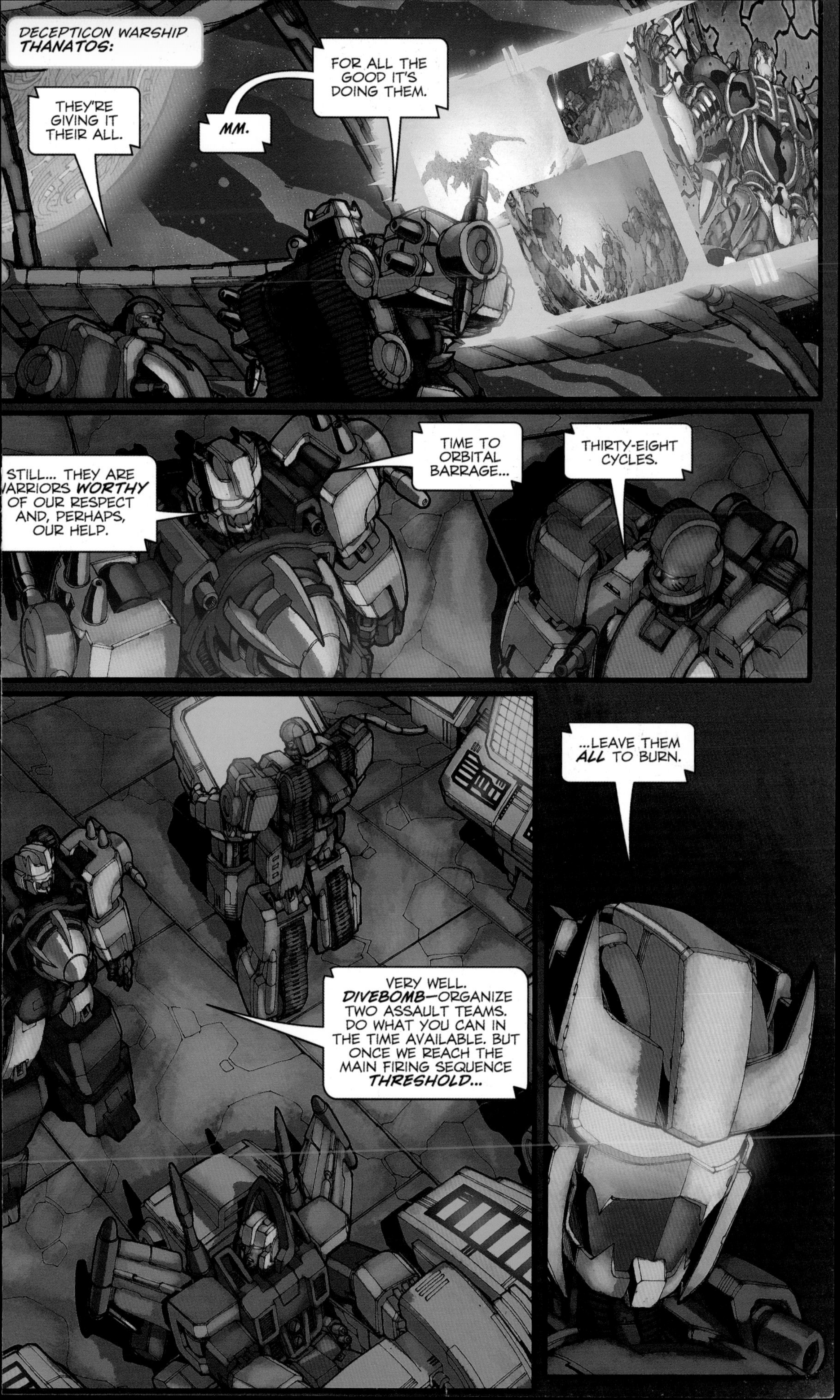

DECEPTICON WARSHIP THANATOS:
THEY'RE GIVING IT THEIR ALL.
MM.
FOR ALL THE GOOD IT'S DOING THEM.
STILL... THEY ARE WARRIORS WORTHY OF OUR RESPECT AND, PERHAPS, OUR HELP.
TIME TO ORBITAL BARRAGE...
THIRTY-EIGHT CYCLES.
VERY WELL. DIVEBOMB—ORGANIZE TWO ASSAULT TEAMS. DO WHAT YOU CAN IN THE TIME AVAILABLE. BUT ONCE WE REACH THE MAIN FIRING SEQUENCE THRESHOLD...
...LEAVE THEM ALL TO BURN.

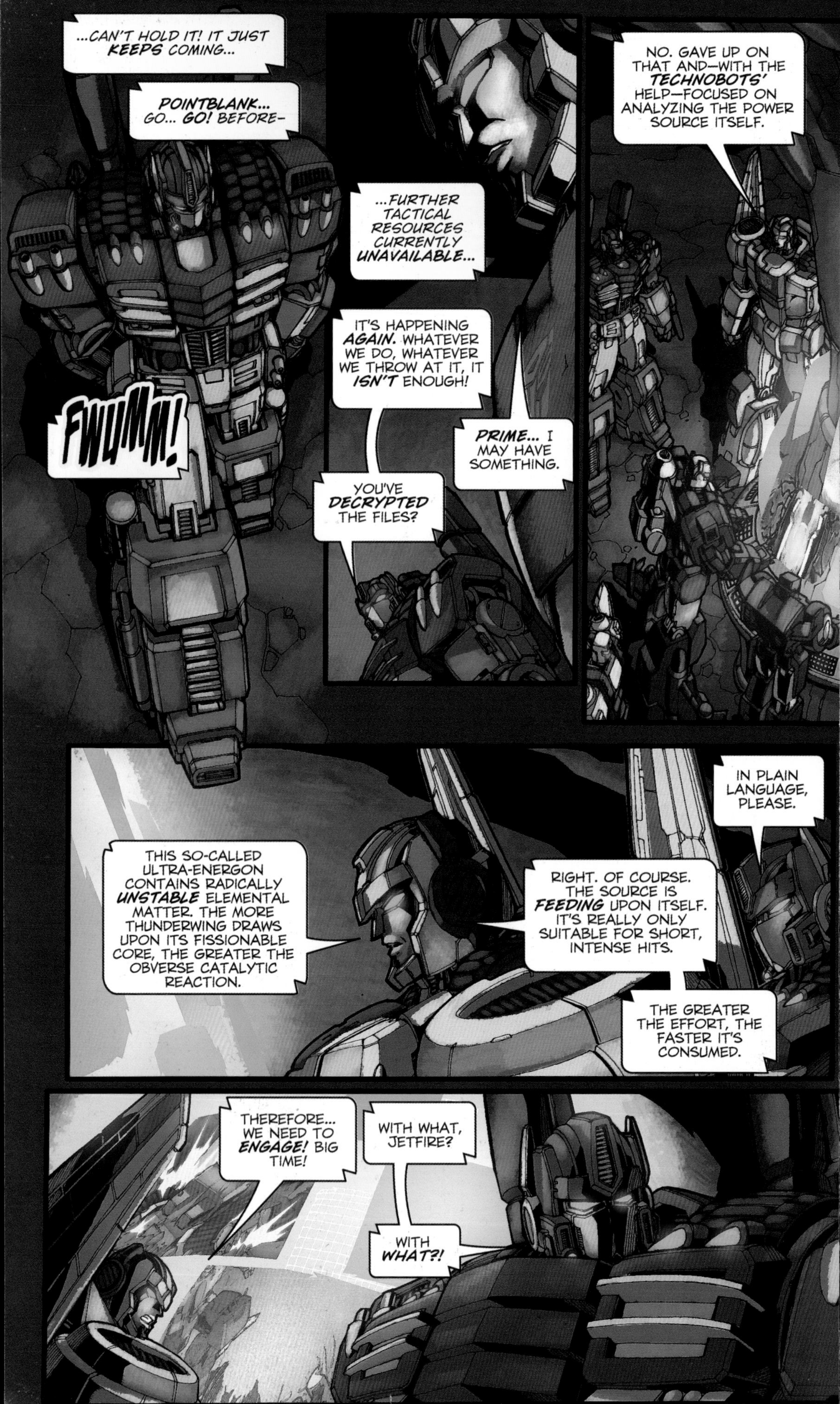
...CAN'T HOLD IT! IT JUST KEEPS COMING...
POINTBLANK... GO... GO! BEFORE-
FWUMM!
...FURTHER TACTICAL RESOURCES CURRENTLY UNAVAILABLE...
IT'S HAPPENING AGAIN. WHATEVER WE DO, WHATEVER WE THROW AT IT, IT ISN'T ENOUGH!
PRIME... I MAY HAVE SOMETHING.
YOU'VE DECRYPTED THE FILES?
NO. GAVE UP ON THAT AND—WITH THE TECHNOBOTS' HELP—FOCUSED ON ANALYZING THE POWER SOURCE ITSELF.
THIS SO-CALLED ULTRA-ENERGON CONTAINS RADICALLY UNSTABLE ELEMENTAL MATTER. THE MORE THUNDERWING DRAWS UPON ITS FISSIONABLE CORE, THE GREATER THE OBVERSE CATALYTIC REACTION.
IN PLAIN LANGUAGE, PLEASE.
RIGHT. OF COURSE. THE SOURCE IS FEEDING UPON ITSELF. IT'S REALLY ONLY SUITABLE FOR SHORT, INTENSE HITS.
THE GREATER THE EFFORT, THE FASTER IT'S CONSUMED.
THEREFORE... WE NEED TO ENGAGE! BIG TIME!
WITH WHAT, JETFIRE?
WITH WHAT?!

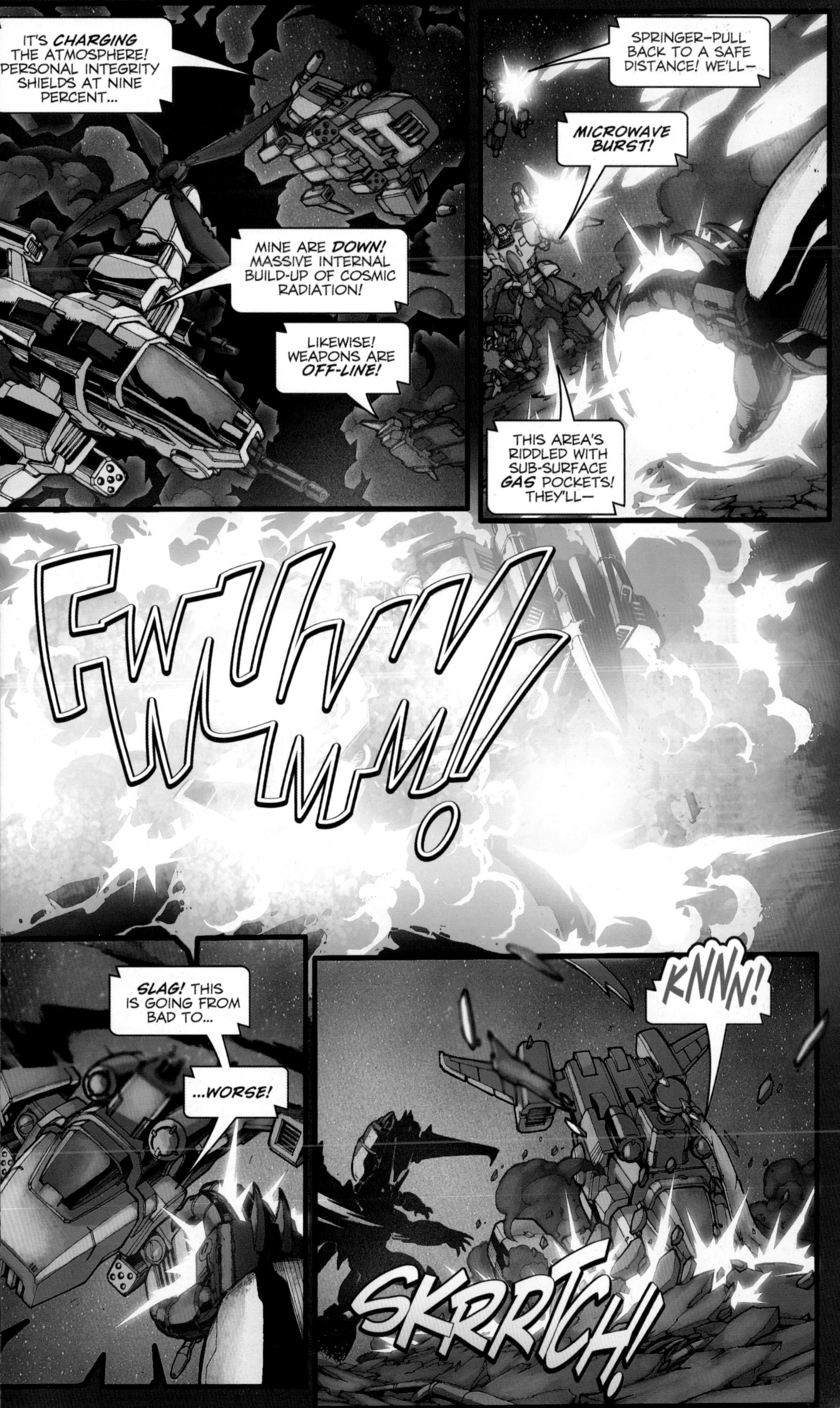
IT'S *CHARGING* THE ATMOSPHERE! PERSONAL INTEGRITY SHIELDS AT NINE PERCENT...
MINE ARE *DOWN!* MASSIVE INTERNAL BUILD-UP OF COSMIC RADIATION!
LIKEWISE! WEAPONS ARE *OFF-LINE!*
SPRINGER–PULL BACK TO A SAFE DISTANCE! WE'LL–
MICROWAVE BURST!
THIS AREA'S RIDDLED WITH SUB-SURFACE *GAS* POCKETS! THEY'LL–
FWHVVVVMM!
SLAG! THIS IS GOING FROM BAD TO...
...WORSE!
KNNN!
SKRRTCH!

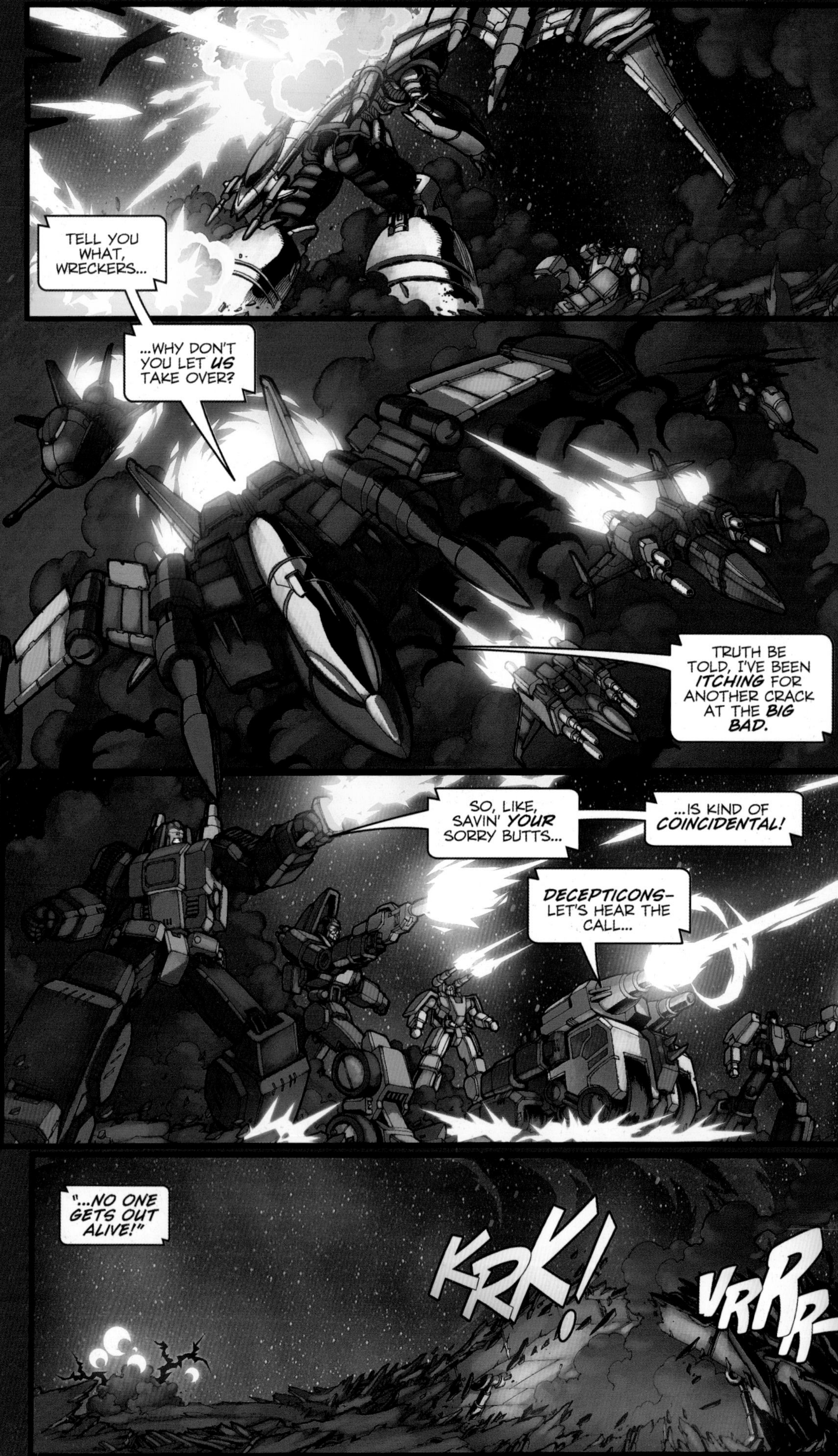
TELL YOU WHAT, WRECKERS...
...WHY DON'T YOU LET US TAKE OVER?
TRUTH BE TOLD, I'VE BEEN ITCHING FOR ANOTHER CRACK AT THE BIG BAD.
SO, LIKE, SAVIN' YOUR SORRY BUTTS...
...IS KIND OF COINCIDENTAL!
DECEPTICONS-- LET'S HEAR THE CALL...
"...NO ONE GETS OUT ALIVE!"
KRK!
VRRR

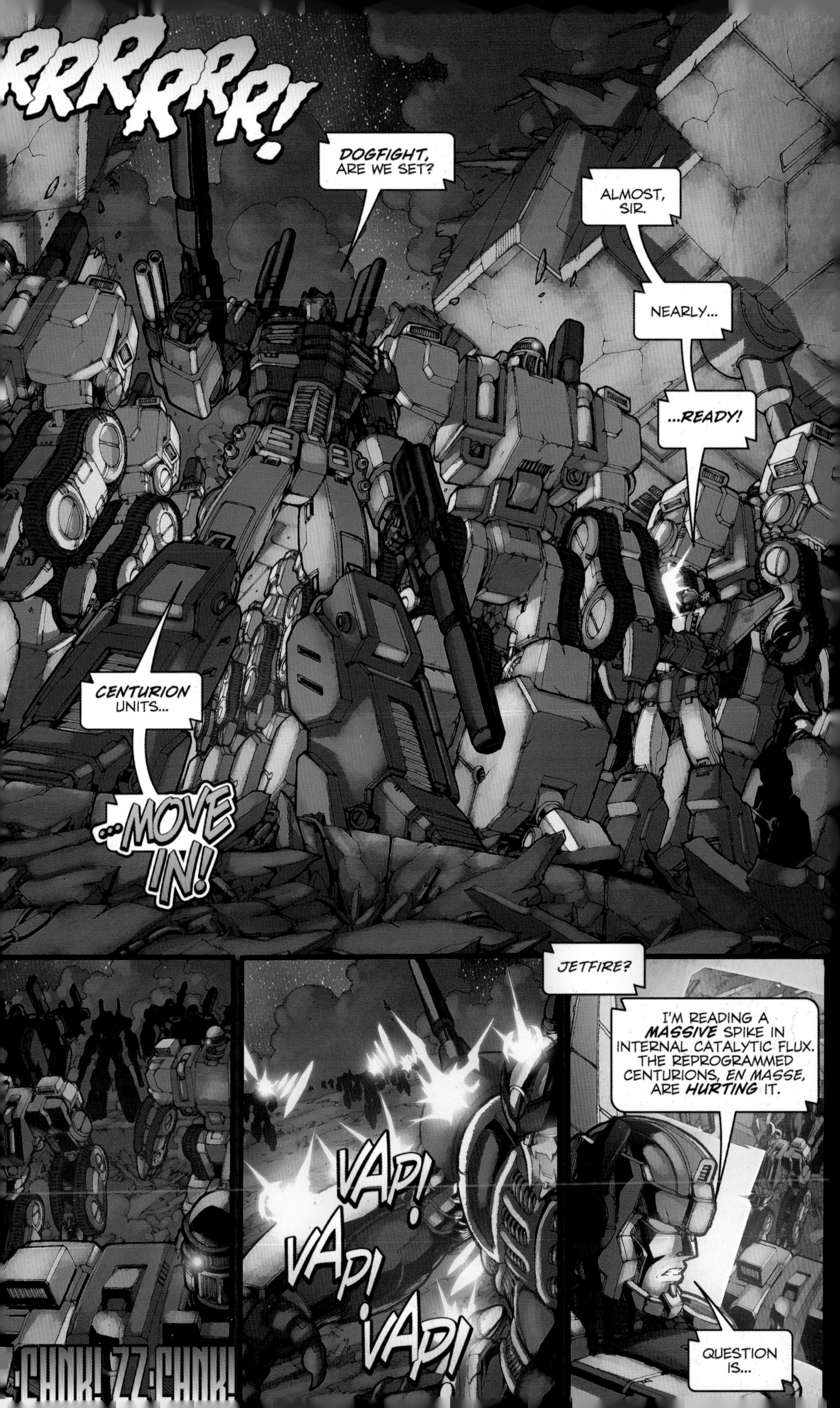
RRRRRR!
DOGFIGHT, ARE WE SET?
ALMOST, SIR.
NEARLY...
...READY!
CENTURION UNITS...
...MOVE IN!
CHNK! ZZ-CHNK!
VAP! VAP! VAP!
JETFIRE?
I'M READING A MASSIVE SPIKE IN INTERNAL CATALYTIC FLUX. THE REPROGRAMMED CENTURIONS, EN MASSE, ARE HURTING IT.
QUESTION IS...

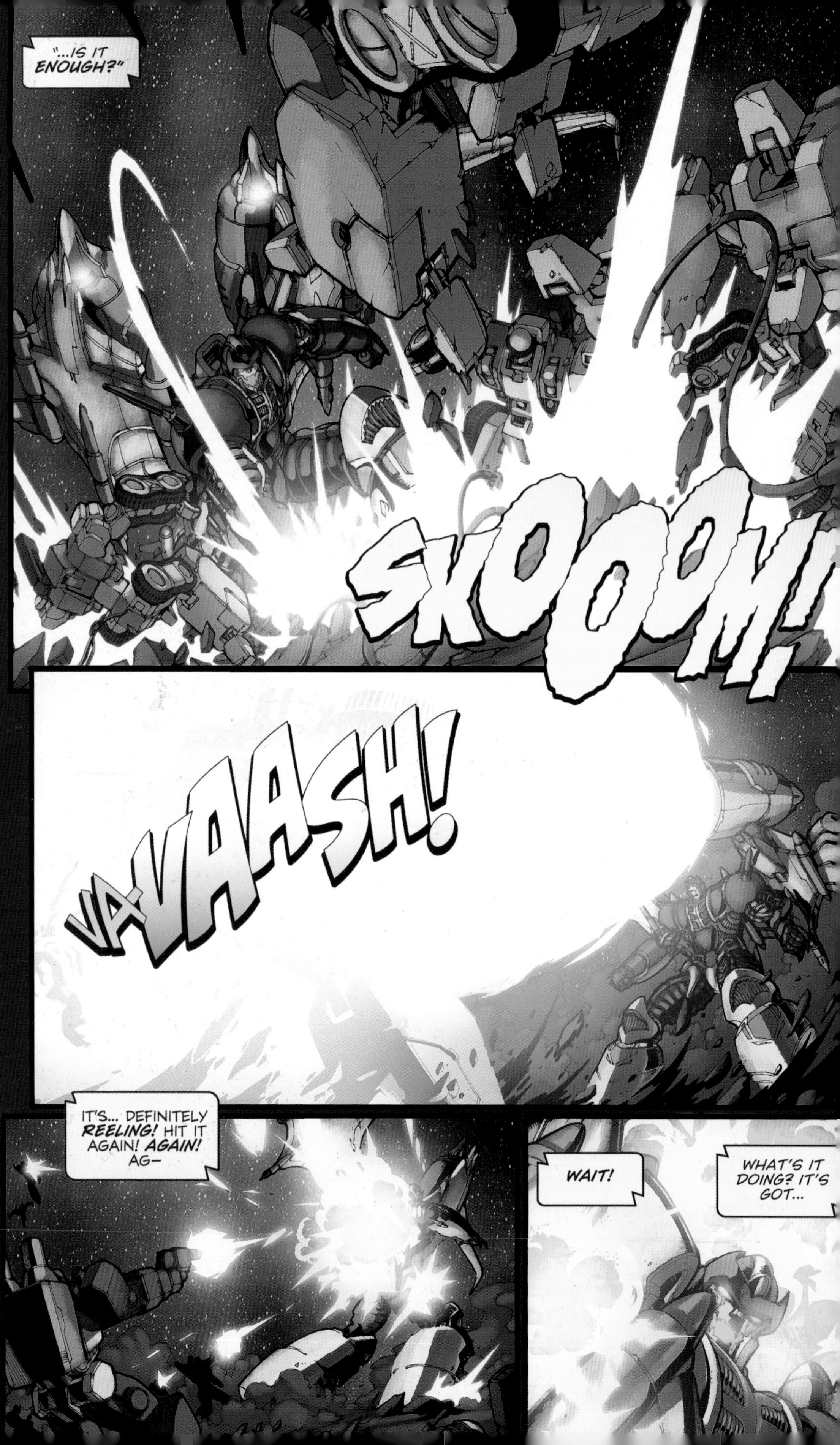
"...IS IT ENOUGH?"
SKOOOM!
VA-VAASH!
IT'S... DEFINITELY REELING! HIT IT AGAIN! AGAIN! AG—
WAIT!
WHAT'S IT DOING? IT'S GOT...

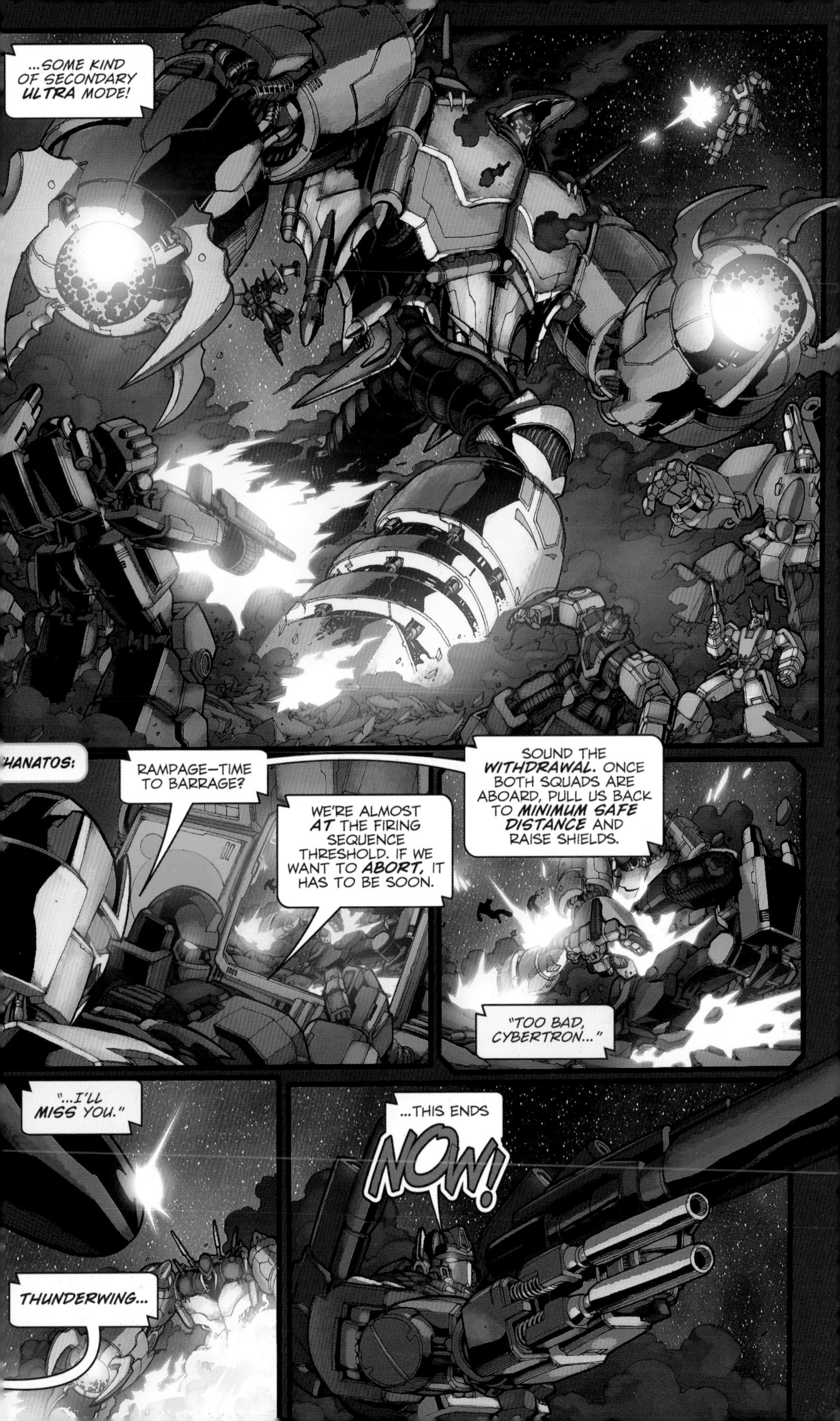
...SOME KIND OF SECONDARY ULTRA MODE!
THANATOS:
RAMPAGE—TIME TO BARRAGE?
WE'RE ALMOST AT THE FIRING SEQUENCE THRESHOLD. IF WE WANT TO ABORT, IT HAS TO BE SOON.
SOUND THE WITHDRAWAL. ONCE BOTH SQUADS ARE ABOARD, PULL US BACK TO MINIMUM SAFE DISTANCE AND RAISE SHIELDS.
"TOO BAD, CYBERTRON..."
"...I'LL MISS YOU."
THUNDERWING...
...THIS ENDS
NOW!

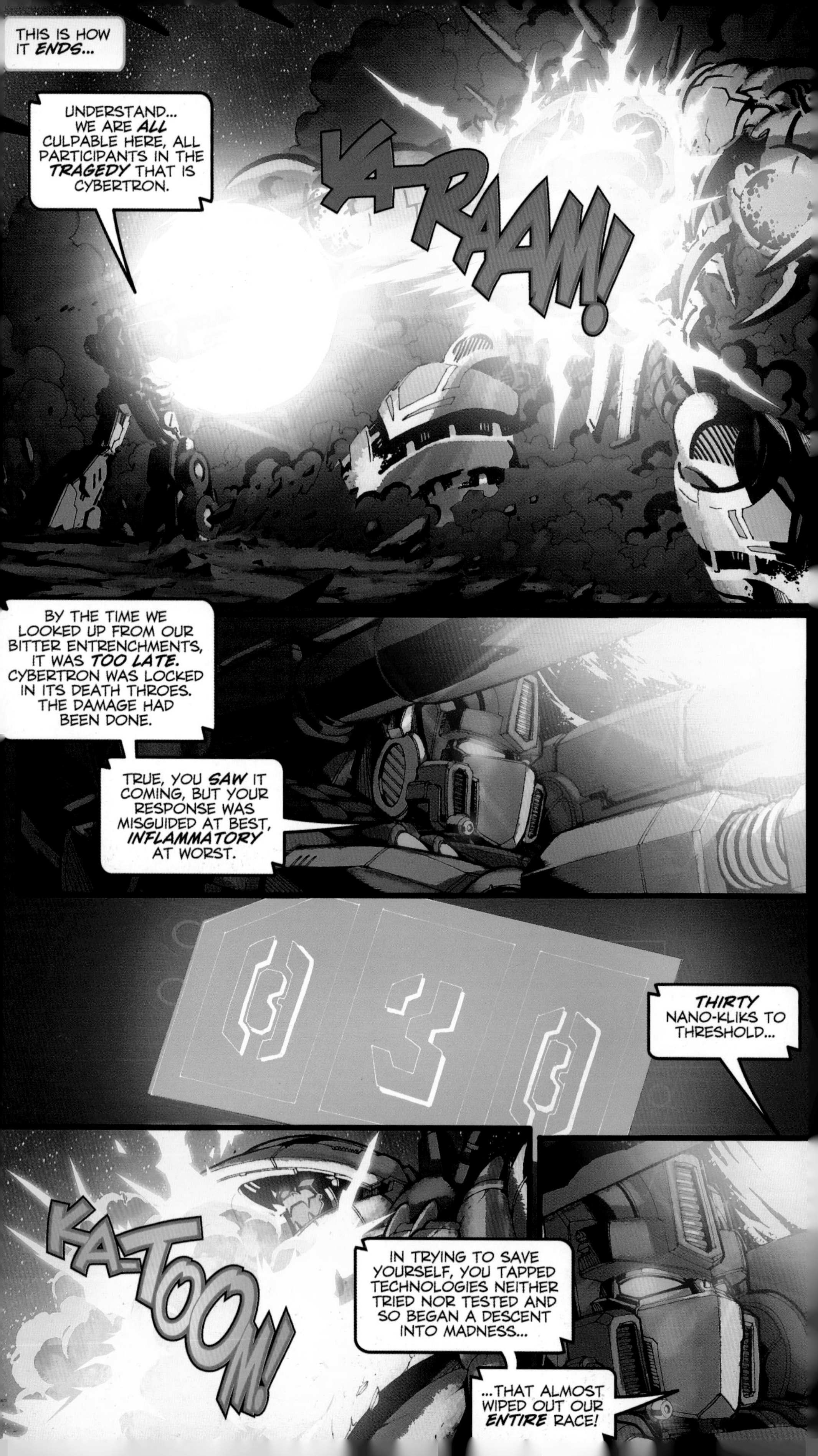
THIS IS HOW IT ENDS...
UNDERSTAND... WE ARE ALL CULPABLE HERE, ALL PARTICIPANTS IN THE TRAGEDY THAT IS CYBERTRON.
KA-RAAM!
BY THE TIME WE LOOKED UP FROM OUR BITTER ENTRENCHMENTS, IT WAS TOO LATE. CYBERTRON WAS LOCKED IN ITS DEATH THROES. THE DAMAGE HAD BEEN DONE.
TRUE, YOU SAW IT COMING, BUT YOUR RESPONSE WAS MISGUIDED AT BEST, INFLAMMATORY AT WORST.
030
THIRTY NANO-KLIKS TO THRESHOLD...
KA-TOOM!
IN TRYING TO SAVE YOURSELF, YOU TAPPED TECHNOLOGIES NEITHER TRIED NOR TESTED AND SO BEGAN A DESCENT INTO MADNESS...
...THAT ALMOST WIPED OUT OUR ENTIRE RACE!

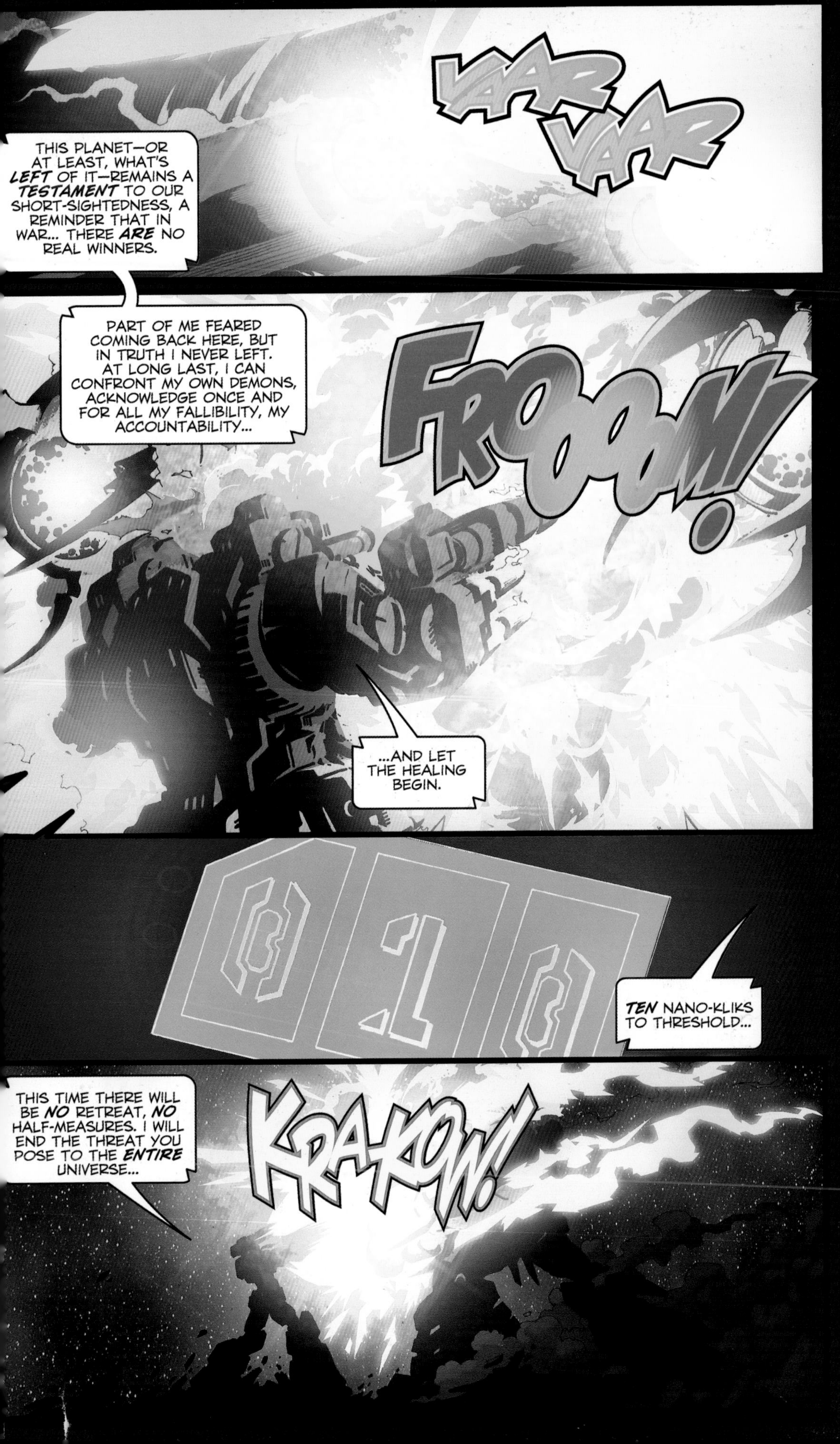
VAAR VAAR
THIS PLANET—OR AT LEAST, WHAT'S *LEFT* OF IT—REMAINS A *TESTAMENT* TO OUR SHORT-SIGHTEDNESS, A REMINDER THAT IN WAR... THERE *ARE* NO REAL WINNERS.
PART OF ME FEARED COMING BACK HERE, BUT IN TRUTH I NEVER LEFT. AT LONG LAST, I CAN CONFRONT MY OWN DEMONS, ACKNOWLEDGE ONCE AND FOR ALL MY FALLIBILITY, MY ACCOUNTABILITY...
FROOOOM!
...AND LET THE HEALING BEGIN.
010
TEN NANO-KLIKS TO THRESHOLD...
THIS TIME THERE WILL BE *NO* RETREAT, *NO* HALF-MEASURES. I WILL END THE THREAT YOU POSE TO THE *ENTIRE* UNIVERSE...
KRA-KOW!

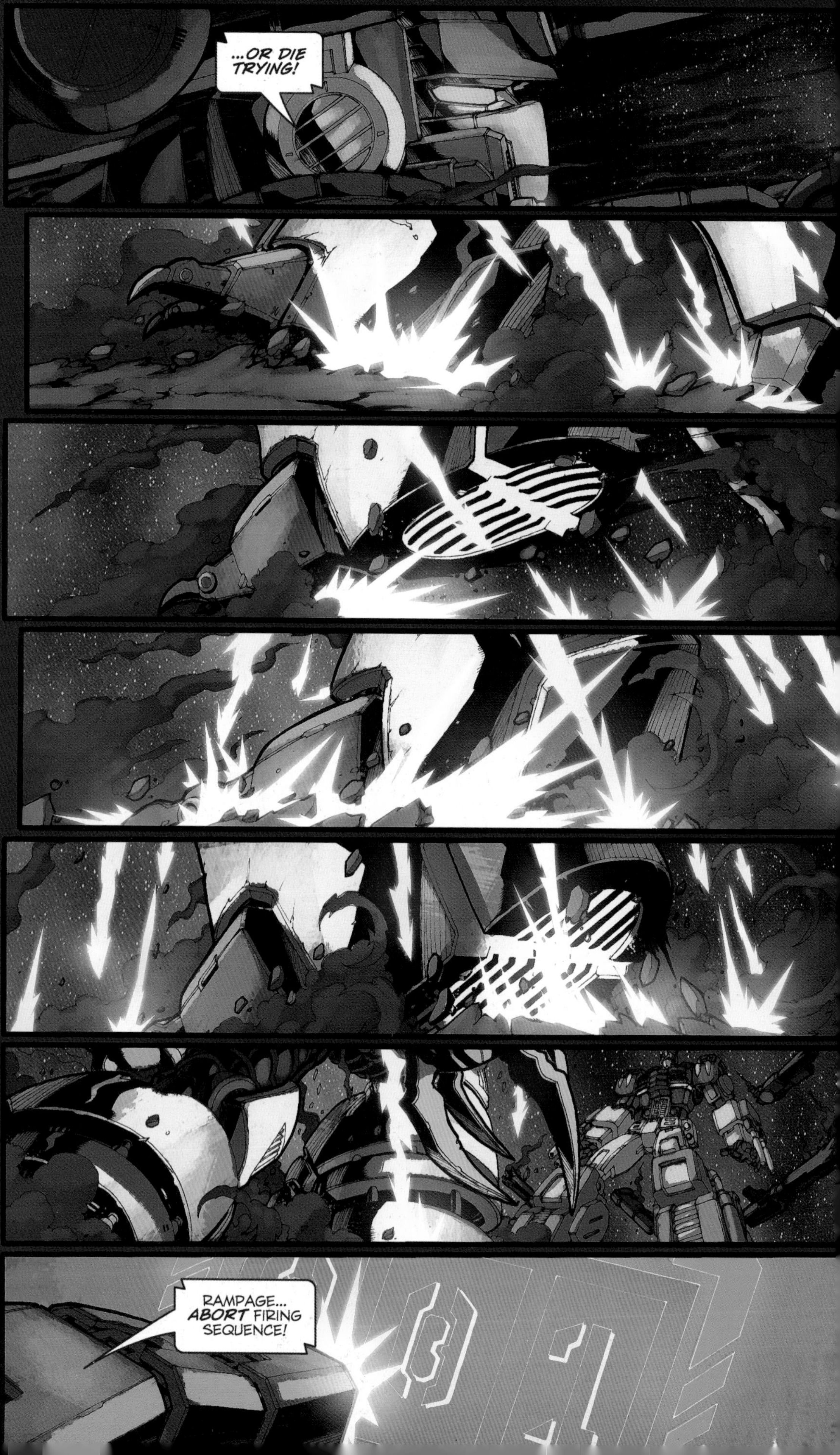
...OR DIE TRYING!
RAMPAGE... ABORT FIRING SEQUENCE!

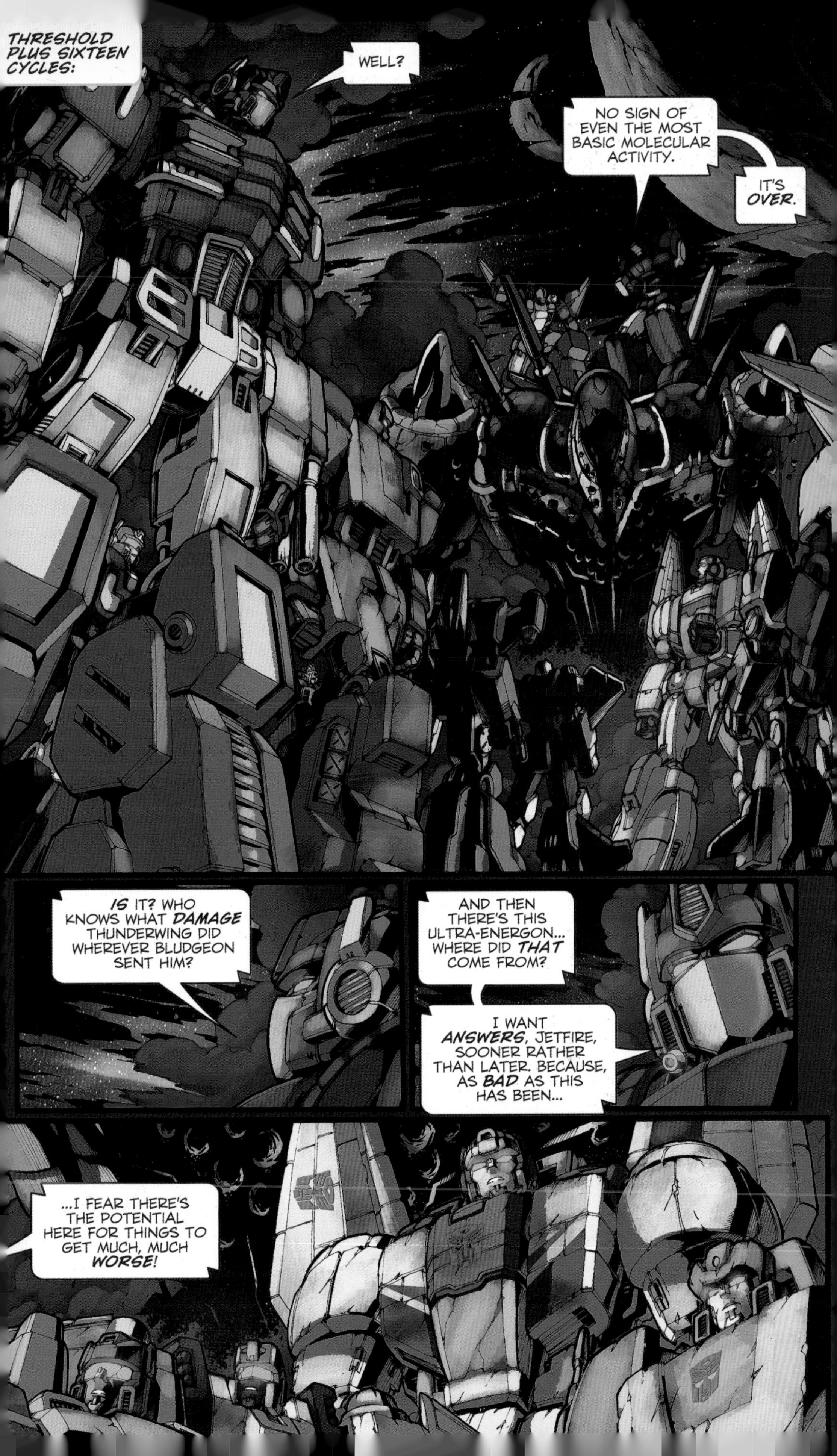
THRESHOLD PLUS SIXTEEN CYCLES:
WELL?
NO SIGN OF EVEN THE MOST BASIC MOLECULAR ACTIVITY.
IT'S OVER.
IS IT? WHO KNOWS WHAT DAMAGE THUNDERWING DID WHEREVER BLUDGEON SENT HIM?
AND THEN THERE'S THIS ULTRA-ENERGON... WHERE DID THAT COME FROM?
I WANT ANSWERS, JETFIRE, SOONER RATHER THAN LATER. BECAUSE, AS BAD AS THIS HAS BEEN...
...I FEAR THERE'S THE POTENTIAL HERE FOR THINGS TO GET MUCH, MUCH WORSE!

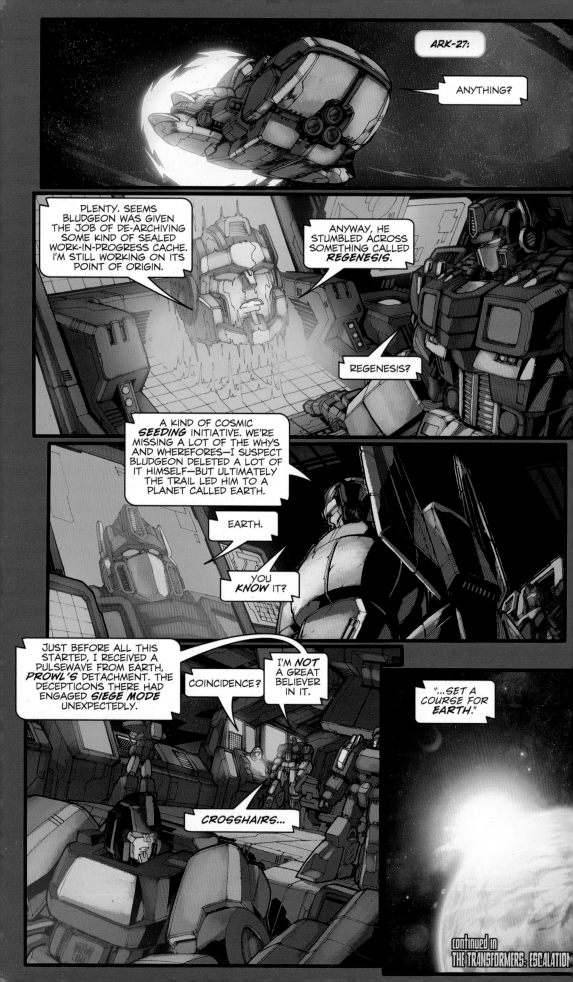

ANYTHING?

PLENTY. SEEMS BLUDGEON WAS GIVEN THE JOB OF DE-ARCHIVING SOME KIND OF SEALED WORK-IN-PROGRESS CACHE. I'M STILL WORKING ON ITS POINT OF ORIGIN.

ANYWAY, HE STUMBLED ACROSS SOMETHING CALLED *REGENESIS*.

REGENESIS?

A KIND OF COSMIC *SEEDING* INITIATIVE. WE'RE MISSING A LOT OF THE WHY'S AND WHEREFORES—I SUSPECT BLUDGEON DELETED A LOT OF IT HIMSELF—BUT ULTIMATELY THE TRAIL LED HIM TO A PLANET CALLED EARTH.

EARTH.

YOU *KNOW* IT?

JUST BEFORE ALL THIS STARTED, I RECEIVED A PULSEWAVE FROM EARTH, *PROWL'S* DETACHMENT. THE DECEPTICONS THERE HAD ENGAGED *SIEGE MODE* UNEXPECTEDLY.

COINCIDENCE?

I'M *NOT* A GREAT BELIEVER IN IT.

"...SET A COURSE FOR *EARTH*."

CROSSHAIRS...

CONTINUED IN THE TRANSFORMERS: ESCALATION

ART GALLERY

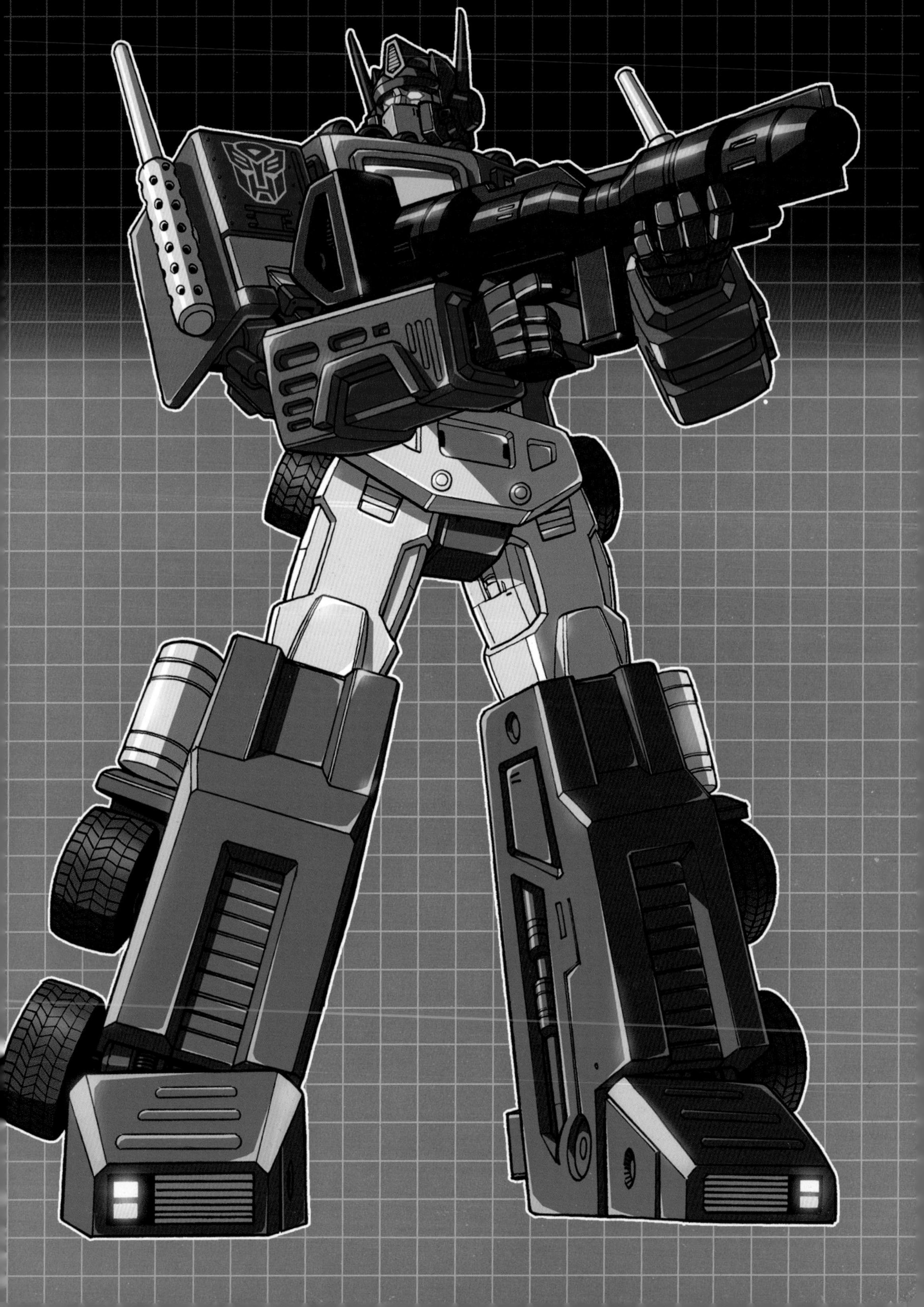

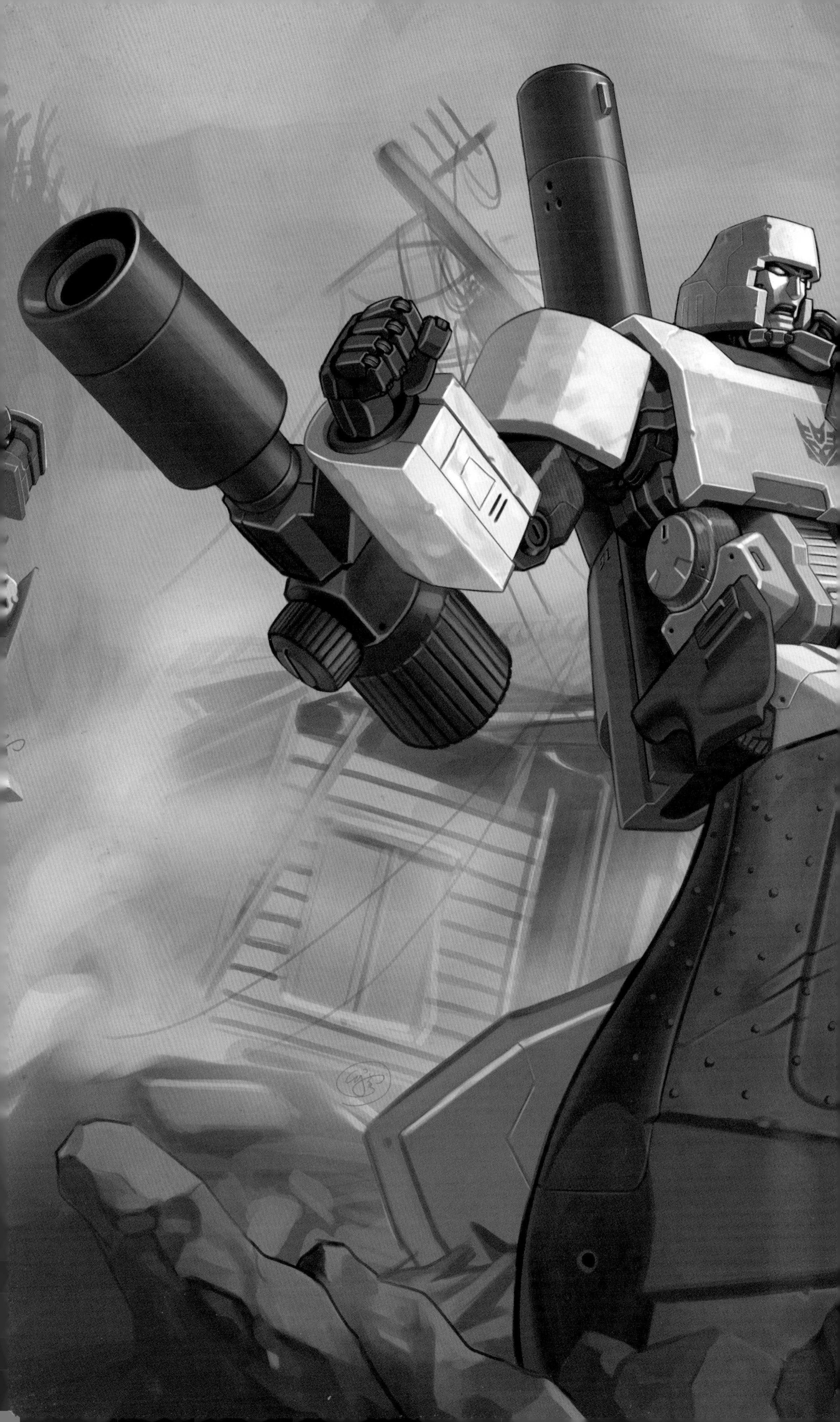

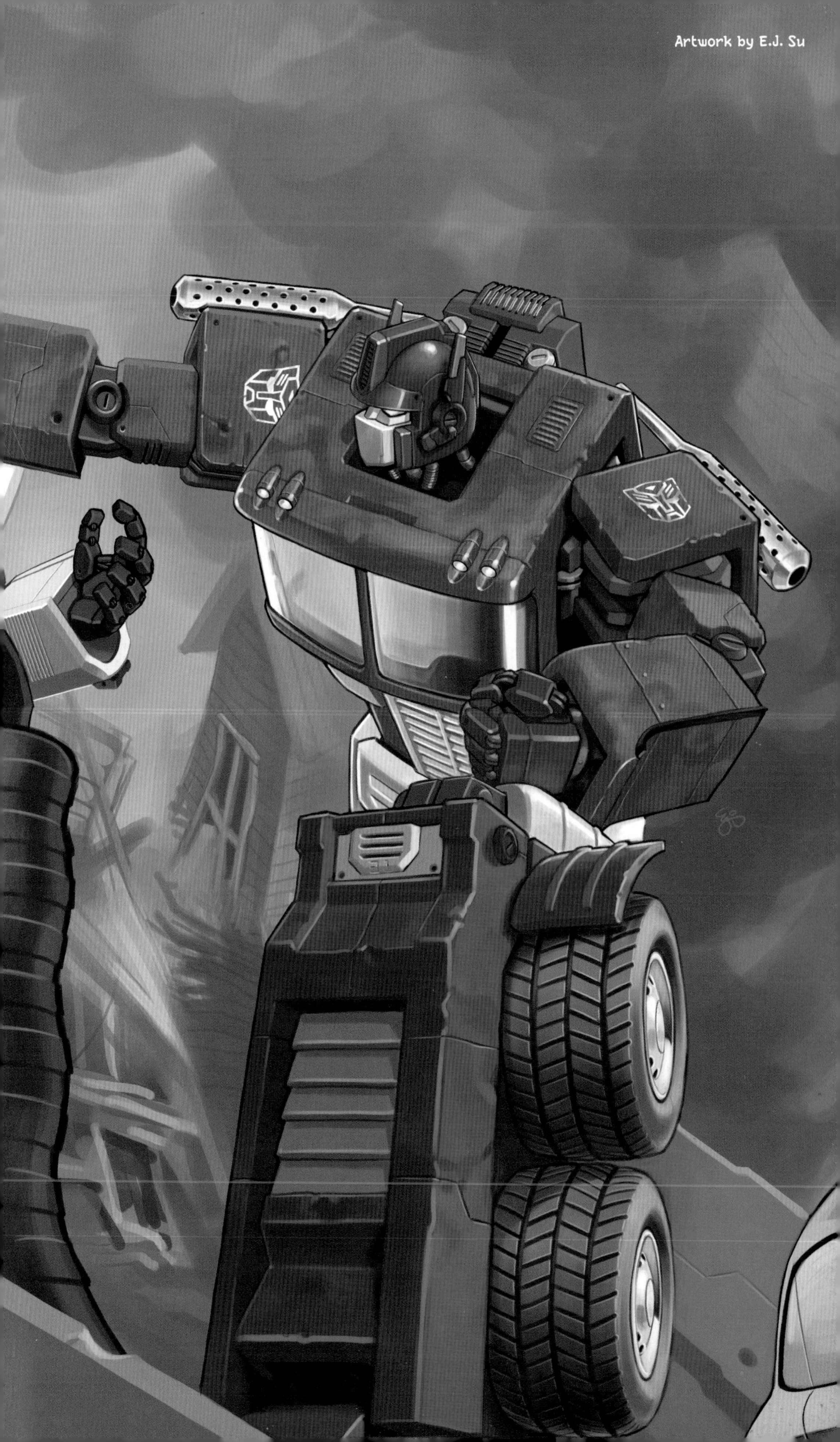

Artwork by E.J. Su

Art by Don Figueroa
Colors by Josh Burcham

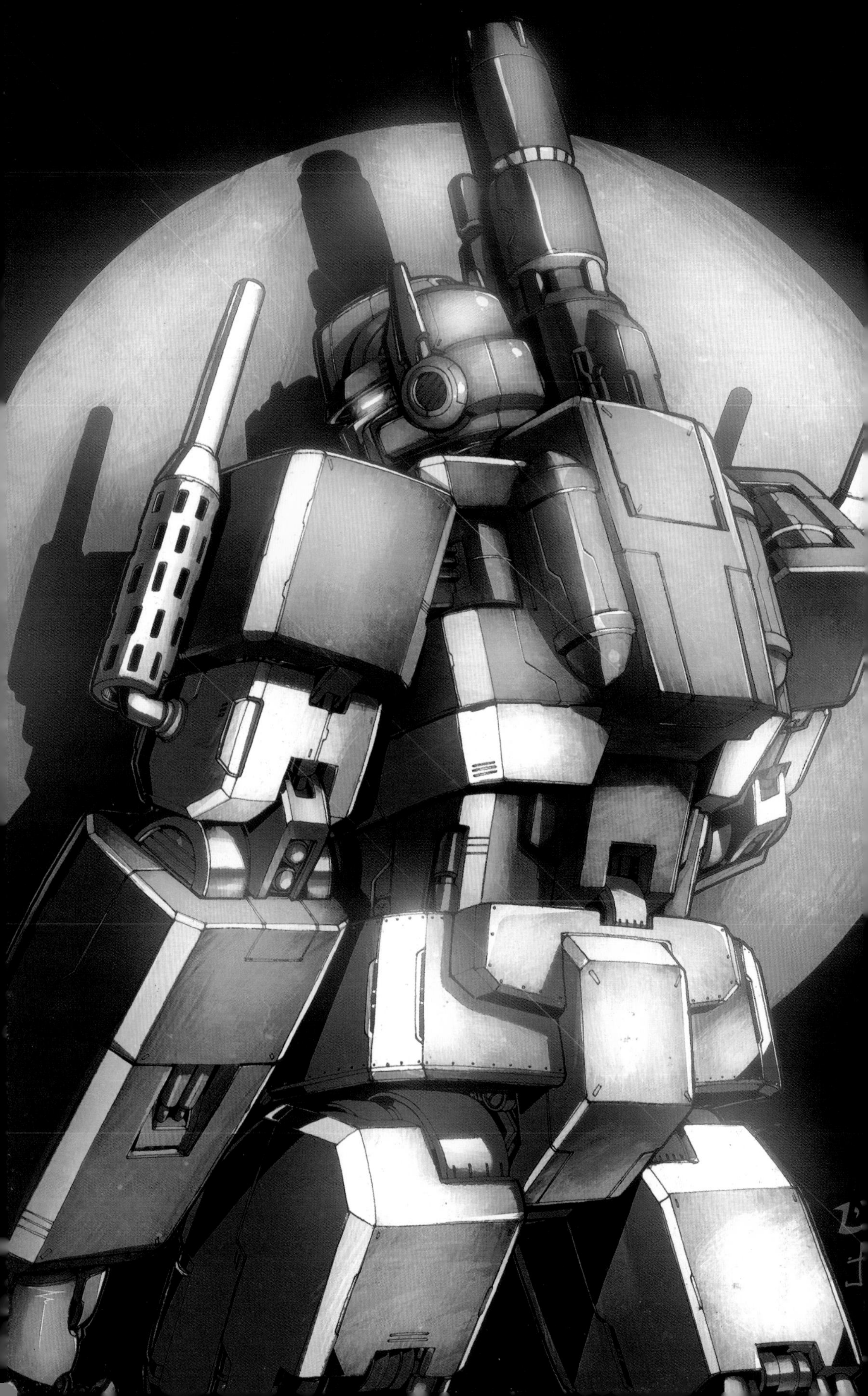

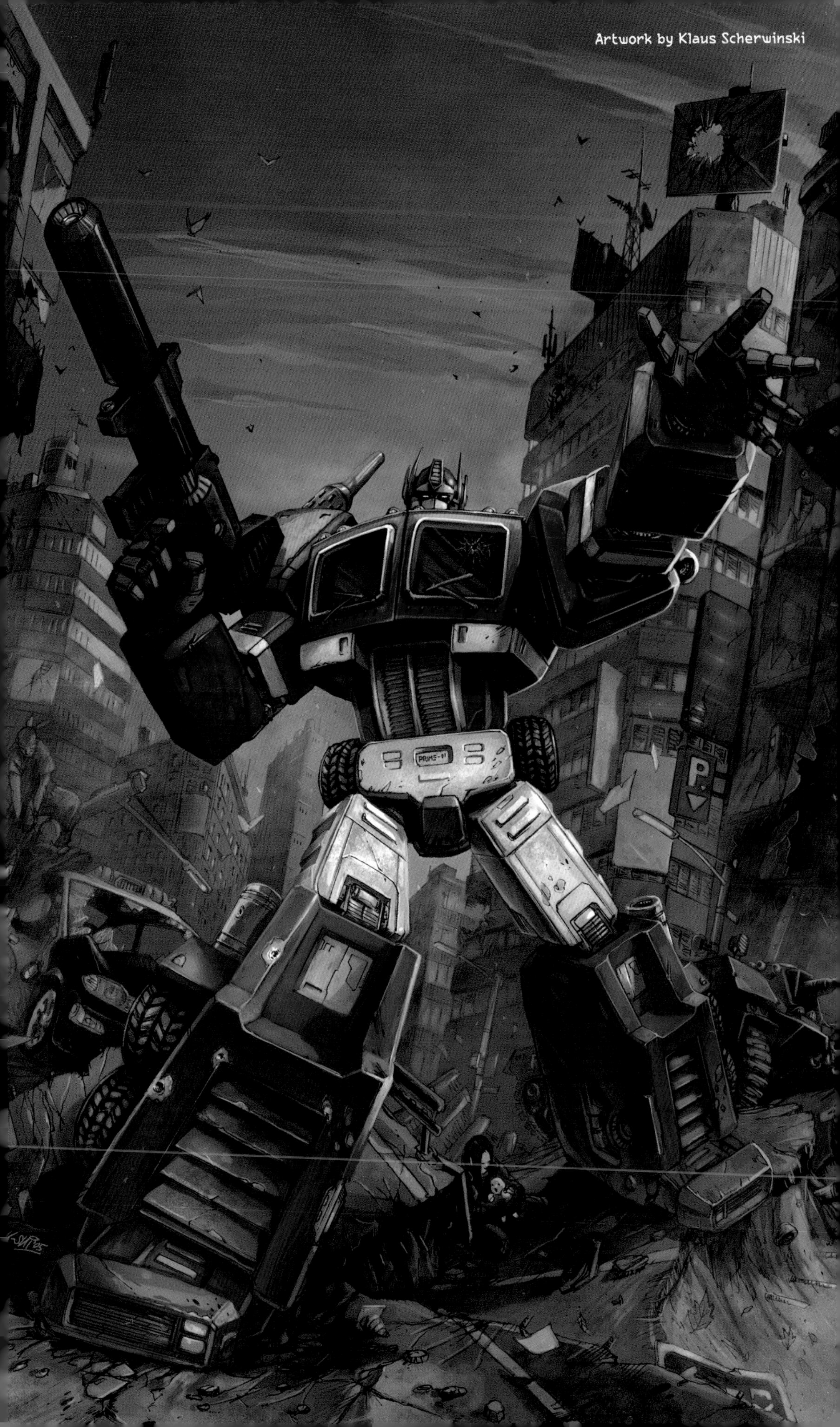
P
Artwork by Klaus Scherwinski

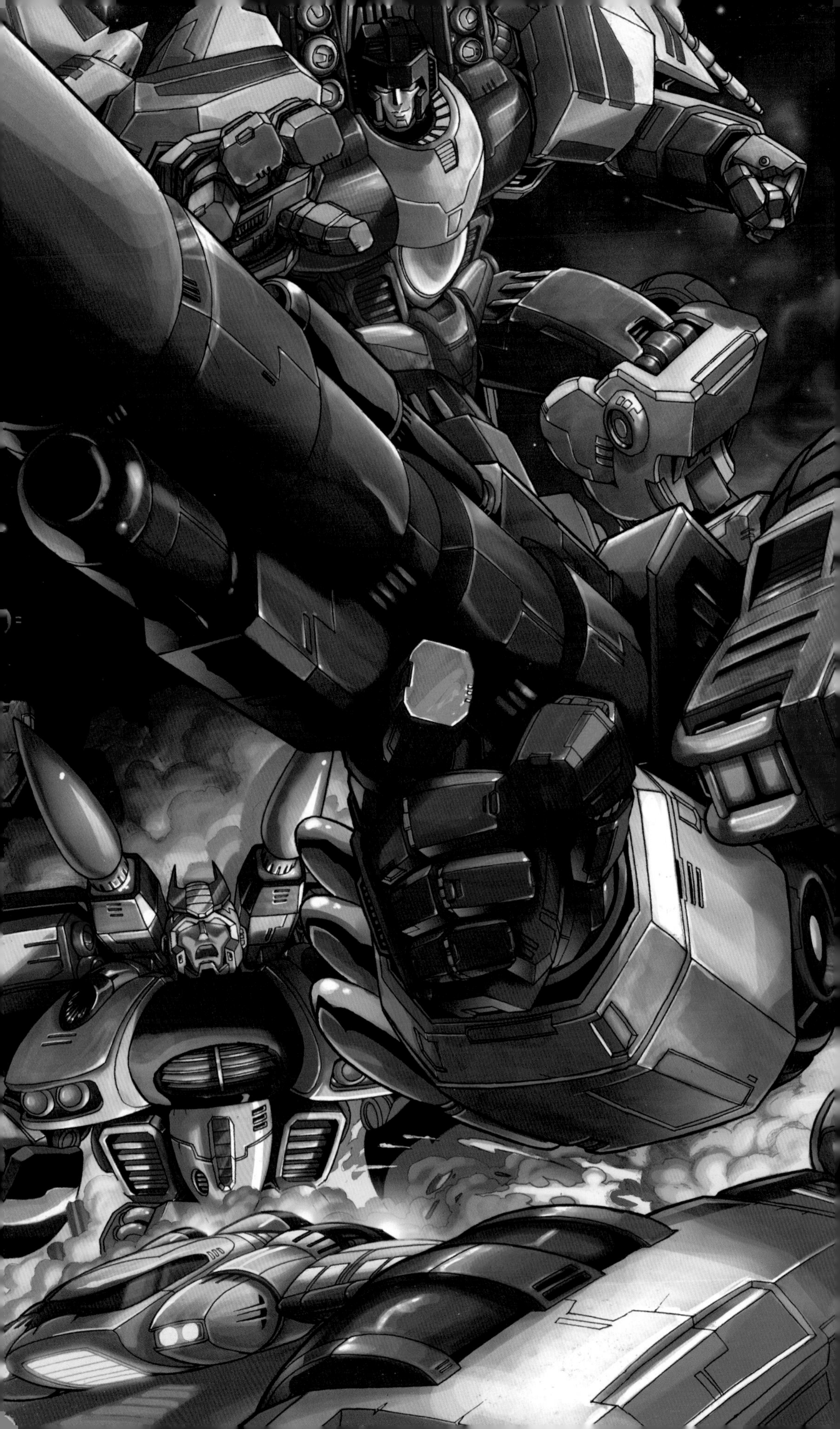

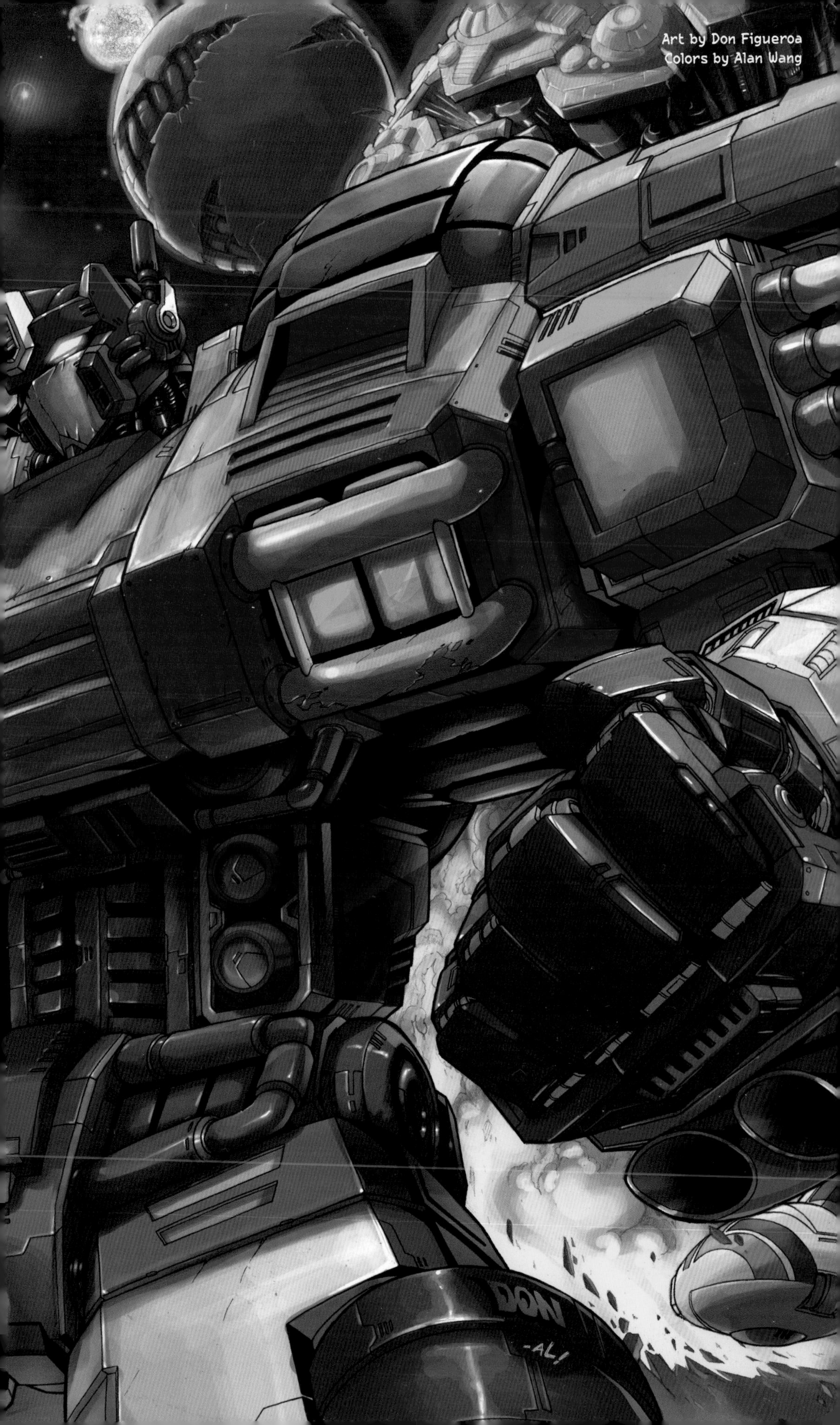
DON
-AL!

Art by Don Figueroa
Colors by Alan Wang

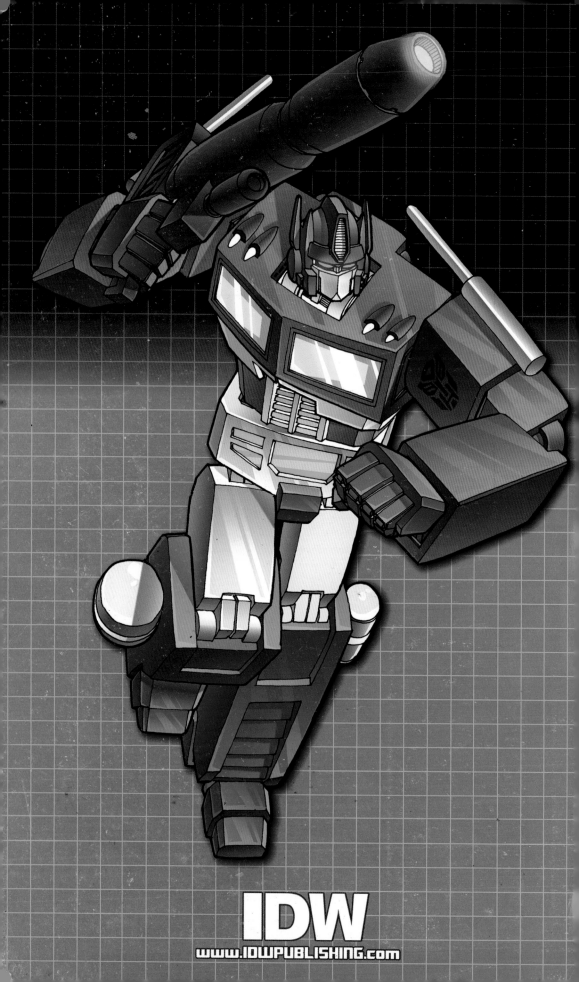